SINGA

MALAYSIA

To travel and experience the 'wonders of other worlds', must surely be one of life's great pleasures. To travel safely and return with tales to tell, is what dreams are made of.

At *Creative Tours*, we understand how important your dreams are, and we're very selective about the hotels and tours we recommend.

Getting the most out of your travel is important too! This excellent publication gives you important information about customs, currency, tips, local regulations and personal safety, plus a whole range of helpful ideas for touring and travelling around the countryside.

I wish you a most enjoyable journey, a safe return, and wonderful dreams. And I hope you travel with *Creative Tours* again soon.

Ian McNicol
Chief Executive
Creative Tours

SINGAPORE
&
MALAYSIA

Little Hills Press

© Text - **Little Hills Press, November 1995**
First published 1989
Revised and expanded, November, 1995
Editorial Board - Director: Fay Smith
Assistants: C. Ernest and C. Burfitt
© Photographs - Singapore Tourist Promotion Board
Tourism Malaysia

Cover by IIC Productions
Printed in Australia

Published by **Little Hills Press Pty Ltd,**
Regent House, 37 Alexander Street,
Crows Nest NSW 2065 Australia.

ISBN 1 86315 097 8

Published in the UK by:
Moorland Publishing Co Ltd
Moor Farm Road West,
Ashbourne, Derbyshire
DE6 1HD. England.

British Library Cataloguing in Publication Data.
A catalogue record for this book is available from the British Library.

DISCLAIMER

Whilst all care has been taken by the publisher and author to ensure
that the information is accurate and up to date, the publisher does not
take responsibility for the information published herein. The
recommendations are those of the author, and as things get better or
worse, places close and others open, some elements in this book may
be inaccurate when you get there. Please write and tell us about it so
we can update in subsequent editions.

CONTENTS

SINGAPORE

A small tropical island of only 617 sq km with 57 smaller islets, lying just one degree north of the Equator, Singapore is the world's busiest port. Hundreds of ships ride at anchor at this crucial junction of the Indian and Pacific Oceans, or glide in and out of her bustling container wharves. Giant oil refineries tower over the scattered islands of her harbour, making her the world's third biggest refining centre, after Rotterdam and Houston.

Singapore is the clearing house for the region's wealth. Her port trades in tin, rubber, coconut, oil, rice, timber, jute, spices and coffee. Her banking system is one of the world's key financial centres. Her shipyards and dry docks repair everything from island traders to vast tankers.

Changi International Airport is served by over 40 of the world's major airlines, with 10 million passengers passing through every year.

To the north, a one kilometre causeway links Singapore with Peninsular Malaysia at Johore Bahru. It is a vital artery for road traffic and a railway system that leads 1923km to Bangkok in Thailand.

HISTORY

In the 7th century AD Singapore was known as Temasek or "Sea Town", a trading centre of Sumatra's ancient Sri Vijayan Empire. By the 13th century she had become one of its three kingdoms. According to legend, the island was renamed Singa Pura or "Lion City" after a visiting prince, Sang Nila Utama, saw an animal he mistook for a lion, but which was more probably a native tiger.

The 14th century saw the empires of Java and Siam struggling for regional dominance with the Chinese Imperial Fleet under Admiral Cheng Ho. Within the next hundred years the great city of Singa Pura would be destroyed and reclaimed by the jungle.

Throughout the 16th century the Dutch, Portuguese and British sailed by. In 1811, a hundred Malays from Johore, led by the local chief, the Temenggong, settled at the mouth of the Singapore River.

Around this time Britain decided it needed a South-east Asian trading post for the British East India Company. The fishing village of

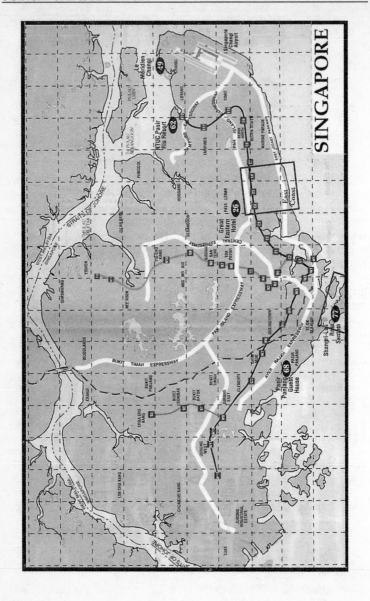

SINGAPORE

Singapore, with its natural harbour, sheltered anchorage and strategic location, was considered an ideal site, and on February 6, 1819, Sir Thomas Stamford Raffles signed a treaty with the locals. Although Raffles spent only nine months in Singapore, he laid the principles for the city's development as a free port, and by 1824, the population had risen from 150 to 10,000. By the time he died in 1827, the Sultan of Johore had ceded full sovereignty to Britain.

In 1832 Singapore became the centre of government for the Straits Settlements of Penang, Malacca and Singapore. The opening of the Suez Canal in 1869 and the advent of the telegraph and steamship increased Singapore's importance as a centre for expanding trade between East and West.

For many years, Singapore was considered to be Britain's strategic defence base in the Far East, but the myth of the island's impregnability was shattered in 1942 when it fell to the Japanese in a matter of weeks during the Second World War. The Japanese occupation lasted until September 1945.

Post-war Singapore became a Crown Colony, then the growth of a national identity led to self-government in 1959 with the Cambridge educated lawyer Lee Kuan Yew as the country's first Prime Minister.

In 1963, Singapore was part of a political and economic alliance formed between the Federation of Malaya, Sarawak and North Borneo (now Sabah), which had been proposed by the Malayan Prime Minister, Tunku Abdul Rahman. It was called Malaysia, but Singapore's involvement was short-lived, and in 1965 it became an independent republic.

Since then Singapore has relentlessly pursued the goal of becoming Asia's most important centre for tourism, trade and finance. To this end it has developed education and technical training programs, investment strategies, aviation and environmental policies.

With the world's busiest port, the third largest oil refining centre in the world, and its financial centre home to the world's major banks, not to mention the 12,000 visitors who arrive each day, it seems that Singapore is well on the way to achieving its goals.

POPULATION

The population of Singapore is around 2.7 million, made up of 78% Chinese, 14% Malays, 7% Indians and 1% others. Each racial group has retained its own cultural identity, but they are now first and foremost Singaporeans, and proud of it.

Singapore is, without doubt, one of the cleanest places in the world, with a fine of S$1000 for littering, and there are many places in the western world that could take a leaf out of their book. Part of the anti-litter law is the prohibition of chewing gum.

LANGUAGE

There are four official languages in Singapore - English, Malay, Mandarin and Tamil. English is the language of business and administration, and is widely spoken and understood. The Chinese Singaporèans have traditionally spoken their own dialects, but the government actively encourages the use of Mandarin.

RELIGION

With such a multi-racial population it is obvious that there would be several religions in Singapore, and the main ones are Buddhism, Christianity, Hinduism, Islam, Judaism, Sikhism and Taoism. There is freedom of worship, and it is not unusual to see a mosque next door to a church, with a temple a few doors down. The majority of the island's national monuments listed for preservation are houses of worship.

FESTIVALS

Because of the multi-cultural nature of the population, Singapore has a year-round calendar of festivals, in many of which visitors are welcome to participate. Most of the festivals are movable feasts, so we have given approximate months for them.

Thaiponggal (January)
Celebrated by the southern Indians, this is a time of thanksgiving. Rice, vegetables, sugar cane and spices are offered to the gods. Devotees then eat these offerings to cleanse themselves of their sins. One of the best places to witness this festival is the Sri Srinivasa Perumal Temple in Serangoon Road.

Thaipusam (January)
Hindu penitents pierce their bodies, foreheads, cheeks and even tongues with sharp skewers and weighted hooks, and walk in a trance-like state from the Sri Perumal Temple in Serangoon Road to the Chettiar Tank Road Temple.
  This festival always attracts large crowds.

Chinese New Year (January/February)
The origins of this festival come from a legend about a village where the mysterious disappearance of townsfolk at certain intervals became a cause for serious concern. A wise man was consulted and it was discovered that these disappearances were connected to a monster whose movements were dictated by planetary and lunar cycles.
  It was also shown that the monster was terrified of light, noise and the colour red. The wise man told the villagers to keep their homes well lit, make plenty of noise on the appointed evening, and paint

solid objects red. An extra safeguard would be to hand portraits of fierce-looking warriors on both sides of each doorway. Well, it worked, no-one disappeared, and the villagers celebrated.

Chinese New Year is now a time of prayer and parties, and several traditional happenings, such as paying bills and finishing tasks as it is bad luck to enter the new year with something hanging over from the old. Families gather for special meals, and children look forward to their annual *hong bao* - lucky red envelopes containing money, the colour signifying luck for both the giver and the receiver.

The holiday ends with the *Chingay* parade, when Orchard Road is closed to traffic and a spectacular parade of floats wends its way through the city. Two of the days are public holidays, but many businesses close down for a week or more.

Good Friday (March/April)
Christians commemorate the day Christ died to save mankind. Singapore's Catholics follow an effigy of Christ in a solemn candle-lit procession around the grounds of St Joseph's Church in Victoria Street. Good Friday is a public holiday.

Hari Raya Puasa (April)
This is the major Muslim festival and marks the end of the fasting month of Ramadan, when eating in daylight hours is forbidden. There are special prayers and, dressed in new clothing, Muslims celebrate with feasting and visiting friends and relatives.

Ramadan is the ninth month of the Islamic calendar, and is one of the best times of the year to try delicious Malay delicacies. Hari Raya Puasa is a public holiday.

Qing Ming (April)
The name translates as "pure and bright", and it is an important festival honouring a family's ancestors. Families visit the graves of their loved ones, ensuring the plots are tided and repaired. Food offerings are made, and incense papers and mock money are burned.

Vesak Day - Birthday of the Third Prince (May)
This is an important religious festival on the Buddhist calendar and commemorates the three great events in the life of Buddha. The first was his birth in 623BC, the second his enlightenment at the age of 35, and finally his death, when he attained ultimate peace, 45 years later. Devotees gather at the Buddhist temples. Vesak Day is a public holiday.

Dragon Boat Festival (June)
Traditionally celebrated on the fifth day of the fifth lunar month, the

Dragon Boat Festival in Singapore has become an international event with teams from all over the world competing in the World Invitational Dragon Boat Race. The festival honours Qu Yuan, an ancient Chinese poet, a loyal minister of state who became upset with the corruption associated with court intrigues. Deciding death was preferable to dishonour, he wrote to famous poems *Ai Ying* and *Huai Sha*, before walking to the river to drown himself. Nowadays, 12m boats with dragon's heads and tails are raced in honour of the patriotic poet. Traditionally one rower stands in the boat, looking for the poet's body, while a drummer on board tries to frighten away any evil creatures.

Hari Raya Haji (June)

This is a Muslim festival that commemorates the haj, or pilgrimage to Mecca, the birthplace of Muhammad. Muslims gather at Singapore's numerous mosques early in the morning for communal prayers, and later in the day animals are ritually slaughtered and the meat distributed to the poor. Hari Raya Haji is a public holiday.

Festival of the Hungry Ghosts (July/August)

The festival falls in the seventh lunar month when it is believed the souls of the dead, and especially those who have been ignored by relatives, roam the earth for the whole month.

As some of these spirits are likely to get up to a bit of mischief, special precautions are taken. Paper money and joss sticks are burned, food offered, and lavish performances of Chinese opera (*wayang*) are staged twice a day at market places or food centres.

National Day (August 9)

This is one celebration in which every ethnic group participates. Community and cultural groups, schools, bands, martial arts associations and military take part in the National Day Parade, which is held at the Padang, or the National Stadium. Admission is by ticket only. The National Day is a public holiday.

Mooncake Festival (September)

This festival is one of the most colourful as local children parade with ornate, jewel-like lanterns, many fashioned in animal shapes. Mooncakes, made from dough enfolding lotus nuts, sweet red bean paste or salted egg yolk, are exchanged as gifts to foster relationships between friends.

Birthday of the Monkey God (September)

The story of the Monkey God is told in the Chinese classic *Journey to the West*, and he is renowned for his bravery in protecting his master, a pilgrim monk sent by the Emperor during the Tang dynasty to collect the Buddhist Sutras from India.

The ceremony is performed at the Monkey God Temple in Eng Hoon Street, near Seng Poh Market. A sedan chair, carried shoulder high, rocks and jerks as if possessed by the spirit of the god. It heads a dramatic procession of mediums who, supposedly also possessed, slash themselves with sharp blades before distributing paper charms.

Festival of the Nine Emperor Gods (September/October)
It is believed that the nine emperor gods cure all ailments and grant longevity and good fortune when they visit earth during the nine days of this festival. There are many colourful *wayangs* (Chinese opera), and processions of flag bearers and decorated floats.

Pilgrimage to Kusu Island (September/October)
This month-long festival is observed by both the Malay and Chinese communities. It recalls a legend of salvation and harmony of a Malay and a Chinese fisherman.

Navarathiri (October)
The name means "nine nights", and the festival is celebrated at the Chettiar Temple in Tank Road, from 7-10pm for nine nights, when the consorts of the Hindu trinity of deities are revered through music.

Thimithi (October)
The Fire Walking Festival, or Thimithi, sees devotees gather at the Sri Mariamman Temple in South Bridge Road, where a four metre long pit glowing with burning coals awaits them. Protected by their prayers and total faith, they are able to walk the length of the red-hot pit barefoot, without injury, in front of hundreds of spectators.

Deepavali (October)
Known as the Festival of Lights, Deepavali has significance for the Indian community. The triumph of light over dark is shown in the lighting of oil lamps and coloured lights in Little India. The temples overflow with offerings of flowers, and the altars are piled with gifts. The congregation parades with statues of each temple's special deity. It is a public holiday.

Christmas Day (December 25)
During the Christmas period the main shopping area of Orchard Road is turned into a glittering fairyland of light, and all the stores and hotels compete to produce the most innovative decorations.

A public holiday, Christmas is celebrated by Christian and

non-Christians alike, with exchanges of gifts and feasting.

New Year's Day (January 1) is also a public holiday.

ENTRY REGULATIONS

Visitors to Singapore must have a valid passport or an internationally recognised travel document.

Citizens of Commonwealth countries and the United States of America do not need visas, but should have onward/return tickets and sufficient funds for their stay in Singapore.

There is no restriction on the amount of currency visitors may take into Singapore.

Travellers over the age of 18 arriving from countries other than Malaysia, can bring in the following duty-free: 1 litre of Spirits ,1 litre of Wine, 1 litre Beer, Stout, Ale or Port.

Note that there are no duty-free concessions on the import of cigarettes and other tobacco products. This means that if passengers buy duty-free cigarettes at their home airport, they will have to pay duty on them when arriving in Singapore.

A traveller who has prescribed medicines, especially sleeping tablets, must possess a prescription from a doctor confirming that the medicines are to be used for the traveller's well-being while travelling. The import of drugs is strictly prohibited and attracts heavy penalties.

EXIT REGULATIONS

There is no export duty on goods being taken out of Singapore. Export permits are required for arms, ammunition, explosives, animals, gold, platinum, precious stones and jewellery (except reasonable personal effects), poisons and drugs.

There is an Airport Tax of S$15 to all countries including Brunei and Malaysia. Airport tax coupons can be purchased in advance at most hotels, travel agencies and airline offices, and attached to the airline ticket.

EMBASSIES AND HIGH COMMISSIONS

Australia: 25 Napier Road, ph 737 9311 -
open Mon-Fri 8.30am-4.30pm.

Canada: 80 Anson Road, #14-00 IBM Towers, ph 225 6363 -
open Mon-Fri 8am-4.30pm.

New Zealand: 13 Nassim Road, ph 235 9966 -
open Mon-Fri 8.30am-4.30pm.

UK: Tanglin Road, ph 473 9333 - open Mon-Fri 8.30am-5pm.

USA: 30 Hill Street, ph 338 0251 - open Mon-Fri 8.30am-5.15pm.

MONEY

The monetary unit is the Singapore Dollar (S$) and 1S$ = 100 cents. Notes come in denominations of $2, $5, $10, $20, $50, $100, $500, $1000 and $10,000, and coins are 1c, 5c, 10c, 20c and 50c and $1.

Approximate exchange rates, which should be used as a guide only, are:

A$	=S$1.00
CAN$	=S$1.00
NZ$	= S$0.95
UK£	= S$2.20
US$	= S$1.40

Banking hours are Mon-Fri 10am-3pm, Sat 9.30am-1pm (some until 3pm). Some banks on Orchard Road are also open Sun 9.30am-3pm.

Most banks cash travellers cheques and change foreign currencies. A passport is required when cashing a travellers cheque, and a commission may be charged.

These services can also be obtained from money chargers, who are found in most shopping complexes. However, make sure that the sign says "Licensed Money Changer", to ensure that you get an honest exchange rate, which incidentally, will probably be better than that offered by a bank

COMMUNICATIONS

Telephones

International Direct Dialling is available, and the country code is 65. Calls can be made from any cardphone, credit card phone and, for an extra fee, from your hotel.

International Home Country Direct, which allows people overseas to be connected to their home operator for reverse charge (collect) calls, can be reached from any phone, and the numbers are:

Australia	-800 6100
Canada	-800 1000
New Zealand	-800 6400
UK	-800 4400
US	-800 0011 (AT&T)
	800 0012 (MCI)
	800 0877 (USPRINT)
HK	800 8520.

Emergency Phone Numbers -
Police - 999
Emergencies/Ambulance/Fire Brigade - 995.
Local calls made from pay phones cost 10c for every 3 minutes.

Post

Most hotel front desks will accept letters to be mailed.

The Changi Airport Post Office, and the post office at Orchard Point on Orchard Road are open Mon-Sat 8am-8pm. Stamps can be purchased at post offices, sub-post offices, postal agencies, stamp vendors and some hotels. For enquiries about any postal matter, ph 165 Mon-Fri 8am-10.30pm.

The cost of sending an Airmail Postcard to any country is 30c.

Radio

There is one station that broadcasts in English 24 hours, and another that broadcasts Sun-Thurs 6am-midnight, Fri-Sat and the eve of public holidays 6am-2am. Other stations broadcast in Mandarin or Tamil.

Television

Daily programs in the four official languages are transmitted by three channels - 5, 8 and 12. Times vary according to the day of the week. The local newspapers have full programs.

Newspapers

Singapore has three daily English-language newspapers: *Straits Times* and *Business Times* in the morning; *The New Paper* in the afternoon.

MISCELLANEOUS

Airport Facilities

Singapore Changi Airport was named the Best Airport in the World by *Business Traveller* for the third year running in 1994. It has two terminals capable of handling a total of 24 million passengers a year.

Together the terminals provide more than 100 shops, including a supermarket, business centres, fitness centres, hair salons, medical clinics, a swimming pool, gymnasium, facilities for the disabled and more than 100 day rooms with private bathrooms. There is even a karaoke lounge

Baggage storage services are available in the arrival hall and in both the east and west wings of the departure level.

on the 3rd level of the East Wing, where people can relax between flights. A Science Discovery Corner with hands-on displays, and Children's Play Areas, keep children amused during long waiting periods.

Other facilities include snack bars, restaurants, 24-hour banking service, post office, police station, pay phones, information, car hire counters, hotel reservation service and airfreight for unaccompanied baggage.

> Passengers can transfer between terminals via the Changi Skytrain which runs at one-and-a-half-minute intervals from 6am to midnight, and at other times at the press of a button.

Credit Cards

All major credit cards are accepted in shops, restaurants and hotels, although some of the small establishments try very hard to hit you with a surcharge of around 6% for the privilege. If this happens, contact the credit card company involved and corrective action will be taken. **Telephone numbers are:** American Express, ph 1800 732 2244; Diners, ph 1800 292 7566; Citibank Visa, ph 1800 225 5225; Mastercard, ph 530 1470; Visa, ph 223 7774.

Electricity

Singapore voltage is 220-240 volts AC, 50 cycles per second. Most hotels can provide visitors with a transformer that can reduce the voltage to 110-120 volts, 60 cycles per second.

Health

Singapore's medical facilities are very good, and doctors are listed under "Medical Practitioners" in the Yellow Pages of the Telephone Directory. Most large hotels have a doctor on-call twenty-four hours a day, and the staff can also advise the address of a nearby dentist.

Pharmaceuticals are available from numerous outlets, including supermarkets, department stores, hotels and shopping centres. Registered chemists work 9am-6pm.

The tap (faucet) water in Singapore is clean and safe to drink and there are no foods to avoid.

Local Laws

Jaywalking
Pedestrians crossing a road within 50m of a pedestrian crossing, an

overhead pedestrian bridge, or an underpass risk a fine of S$50.

Littering
Any person convicted of littering faces a fine of up to S$1000 for the offence, S$2000 for subsequent offences plus a stint of corrective work cleaning public places.

Smoking
Smoking in public service vehicles, museums, libraries, lifts, theatres, cinemas, air-conditioned restaurants, hair salons, supermarkets, department stores or government offices is an offence subject to a S$1000 fine. Note that smoking is permitted in air-conditioned pubs, discos, karaoke bars and nightspots.

Spitting
Spitting in public places is an offence subject to a fine of up to S$1000 for the first offence, S$2000 for subsequent offences.

Toilets
It is an offence not to flush public toilets after use. Those convicted face a fine of up to S$150 for a first offence, S$500 for a second offence, S$1000 for subsequent offences.

Tipping

Tipping is not a way of life in Singapore. It is prohibited at the airport and discouraged in hotels and restaurants that have a 10% service charge.

TRAVEL INFORMATION

HOW TO GET THERE

By Air

Changi International Airport is serviced by over 40 of the world's major airlines.

Singapore Airlines, the national flag carrier, has direct flights to Singapore from:

Adelaide	-	Mon, Tues.
Brisbane	-	Fri, Sat.
Christchurch	-	Wed.
Darwin	-	Sun.
Frankfurt	-	daily.
Hong Kong	-	daily.
Johannesburg	-	Wed, Fri, Sat.
London	-	daily.
Melbourne	-	Wed-Sun.
Paris	-	daily except Wed and Fri.
Perth	-	daily.
Sydney	-	daily.

Singapore Airlines phone number in Singapore is 223 8888.

Air New Zealand has direct flights to Singapore from:

Auckland	-	Tues, Wed, Fri, Sat, Sun.
Bangkok	-	Tues, Fri.

Air New Zealand phone number in Singapore is 535 8266.

British Airways has direct flights to Singapore from:

Brisbane	-	Sun.
London	-	daily.
Melbourne	-	Tues, Sat.
Perth	-	Mon, Wed-Fri.

British Airways phone number in Singapore is 253 8444.

Cathay Pacific has daily direct flights to Singapore from Hong Kong. Their phone number in Singapore is 533 1333.

Malaysia Airlines has daily direct flights to Singapore from Kuala Lumpur. Their phone number in Singapore is 336 6777.

Qantas has direct flights to Singapore from:

Adelaide	- Tues, Thurs, Sat-Sun.
Bangkok	- daily.
Brisbane	- daily.
Cairns	- Wed, Sat.
Darwin	- daily except Wed and Sat.
Hong Kong	- daily.
London	- daily.
Melbourne	- daily.
Perth	- daily.
Sydney	- daily.

Qantas phone number in Singapore is 737 3744.

United Airlines have daily direct flights to Singapore from Honolulu. Their phone number in Singapore is 220 0711.

By Sea

The Singapore Cruise Centre has an international passenger terminal with modern amenities, duty-free shops, banking facilities and restaurants. Cruise ships that call into Singapore include:

Andaman Princess - Siam Cruises Co Ltd, 33/10-11 Chaiyod Arcade, Sukhumvit Soi 11, Sukhumvit Road, Bangkok, 10110, Thailand, ph (662) 255 8950, fax (662) 255 8961.

Azerbaydzhan Belorussiya - CTC Lines, 1 Regent Street, London, SW1Y 4NN, UK, ph (071) 930 5833, fax (071) 839 2483.

Club Med 2, Club Mediterranee, 106/110 Brompton Road, London, SW3 1JJ, UK, ph (071) 581 1161, fax (071) 581 4769.

Coral Princess, Universal Boss Ltd, Worldwide House, 11th floor, 19 Des Voeux Road, Central, Hong Kong, ph (852) 868 1280, fax (852) 869 1337.

Fairstar, P & O Holidays, Level 10, 160 Sussex Street, Sydney, NSW, 2000, Australia, ph (02) 364 8880, fax (02) 364 8862.

Langkapuri Star Aquarius, Star Cruise Pte Ltd, 391B Orchard Road, #13-01 Ngee Ann City Tower B, Singapore, 0923, ph 733 6988. *Leisure World*, New Century Tours Corporation Pte Ltd, 100 Orchard Road, #02-03, Meridien Shopping Centre, Singapore, 0923, ph 732 8820, fax 732 8626.

Pacific Princess, Princess Cruises, 10100 Santa Monica Boulevard, Los Angeles, CA 90067-4189, USA, ph (310) 553 1770, fax (310) 277 6175.

Marco Polo, Orient Lines, 1510 SE 17th Street, Fort Lauderdale, FL 33316, USA, ph (305) 527 6660, fax (305) 527 6657.

Pearl, Pearl Cruises, 6301 NW 5th Way, Suite 4000, Fort Lauderdale, FL 33309, USA, ph (305) 772 8600, fax (305) 491 5099.

Renaissance VI, Renaissance Cruises, 1800 Eller Drive, Suite 300, PO

Box 350307, Fort Lauderdale, FL 33335-0307, USA, ph (305) 463 0982, fax (305) 463 8121.

Royal Odyssey, Royal Cruise Line, One Maritime Plaza, San Francisco, CA 94111, USA, ph (415) 956 7200, fax (415) 956 1656.

Royal Viking Queen, Royal Viking Line, 95 Merrick Way, Coral Gables, FL 33134, USA, ph (305) 460 4925, fax (350) 529 6358.

Sea Goddess II, Cunard Line, 555 Fifth Avenue, New York, NY 10017, USA, ph (212) 880 7500, fax (212) 949 0915.

Seabourn Spirit, Seabourn Cruise Line, 55 Francisco Street, San Francisco, CA 94133, USA, ph (415) 391 7444, fax (415) 391 8518.

Song of Flower, Seven Seas Cruise Line, 333 Market Street, Suite 2600, San Francisco, CA 94105-2102, USA, ph (415) 905 6000, fax (415) 905 6001.

By Bus from Malaysia

There are numerous bus services between Malaysia and Singapore. The most obvious is the SBS Bus service that leaves from Johor Bahru for Queen Street via Bukit Timah Road, Upper Bukit Timah Road and Woodlands Road. Passengers can board this service anywhere along the route and the maximum fare is S$0.90.

Other companies that operate bus services are:

PME: Pan Malaysia Express(S) Pte Ltd, ph 294 7034.
SSM: Syarikat Sri Maju Express, Sdn Bhd, ph 293 4160.
SJE: Singapore-Johor Express Pte Ltd, ph 292 8149.
KSE: Kuala Lumpur-Singapore Express Sdn Bhd, ph 292 8254.
MSE: Malacca-Singapore Express Sdn Bhd, ph 293 5915.

By Train from Malaysia

There is a train service from Bangkok in Thailand, through Butterworth and Kuala Lumpur in Malaysia, to Singapore.

The fares, in an air-conditioned express coach, are:

Butterworth to Singapore - RM127 First Class, RM60 Second Class, RM34 Third Class.

Kuala Lumpur to Singapore - RM68 First Class, RM34 Second Class, RM19 Third Class.

By Ferry from Malaysia

Regular services operate Singapore/the resort island of Tioman, and Singapore/Tanjong Belungkor in the eastern corner of Johor. Tanjong Belungkor is the gateway to Desaru, Mersing and other east coast Malaysia attractions.

Ferry companies are:

Ferrylink (S) Pte Ltd, 1 Shaw Road, #25-06, Shaw Centre, 0922.

Changi Ferry Terminal, 30 Changi Ferry Road, Singapore 1749, ph 545 3600, fax 545 5040.

Resort Cruises (S) Pte Ltd, 337 Telok Blangah Road, #01-03 Shing Loong Building, Singapore, 0409, ph 278 4677, fax 274 3819.

TOURIST INFORMATION

Tourist Information Centres are found at: Raffles Hotel Arcade #02-34, 328 North Bridge Road, ph 1800 334 1335 toll-free, open daily 8.30am-6pm; and Scotts Shopping Centre #02-03, Scotts Road, ph 1800 738 3778 toll-free, open daily 9.30am-9.30pm.

ACCOMMODATION

Singapore has many hotels, from international standard to budget, and here is a selection with prices for a standard double room per night in Singapore Dollars, which should be used as a guide only. The prices marked with an asterisk are subject to 10% service charge, plus 1% cess and 3% GST.

Orchard District

Hyatt Regency, 10-12 Scotts Road, ph 738 1234 - 748 rooms - restaurants, cocktail bars, coffee shop, swimming pool, tennis court, squash court, disco - $410-480*.

Goodwood Park Hotel, 22 Scotts Road, ph 737 7411 - 192 rooms,

Singapore City Skyline

restaurants, cocktail bars, coffee shops, swimming pool - $400-450*.

Sheraton Towers, 39 Scotts Road, ph 737 6888 - 404 rooms, restaurants, cocktail bars, coffee shops, swimming pool - $380-445*.

Shangri-La Hotel, 22 Orange Grove Road, ph 737 3644 - 750 rooms, restaurants, cocktail bars, coffee shop, swimming pool, tennis court, squash court - $345-580*.

Mandarin Singapore, 333 Orchard Road, ph 737 4411 - 1200 rooms, restaurants, cocktail bar, coffee shop, swimming pool, tennis court, squash court - $360-460*.

Regent, Singapore, 1 Cuscaden Road, ph 733 8888 - 441 rooms, restaurants, cocktail bar, coffee shop, swimming pool - $345-360*.

Hilton International Singapore, 581 Orchard Road, ph 737 2233 - 406 rooms - restaurants, cocktail bar, coffee shop, swimming pool - $320-420*.

Omni Marco Polo Hotel, 247 Tanglin Road, ph 474 7141 - 603 rooms, restaurants, cocktail lounge, coffee shop, swimming pool - $300-430*.

Royal Holiday Inn Crowne Plaza, 25 Scotts Road, ph 737 7966 - 493 rooms, restaurant, cocktail bar, coffee shop, swimming pool - $310*.

Le Meridien Singapore, 100 Orchard Road, ph 733 8855 - 413 rooms - restaurants, cocktail bar, coffee shop, swimming pool - $300-390*.

ANA Hotel Singapore, 16 Nassim Hill, ph 732 1222 - 456 rooms, restaurants, cocktail bar, coffee shop, swimming pool - $300-390*.

Holiday Inn Park View, 11 Cavenagh Road, ph 733 8333 - 320 rooms, restaurant, cocktail bar, coffee shop, swimming pool - $300-330*.

Orchard Hotel, 442 Orchard Road, ph 734 7766 - 350 rooms, restaurant, cocktail lounge, coffee shop, pool - $290-380*.

Crown Prince Hotel, 270 Orchard Road, ph 732 1111 - 288 rooms, restaurants, cocktail bar, coffee shop, swimming pool - $290-320*.

Boulevard Hotel, 200 Orchard Boulevard, ph 737 2911 - 500 rooms, restaurants, cocktail bar, coffee shop, swimming pool, squash court - $270-300*.

York Hotel, 21 Mount Elizabeth, ph 737 0511 - 324 rooms, restaurant, cocktail bar, coffee shop, swimming pool - $255-390*.

Orchard Parade Hotel, 1 Tanglin Road, ph 737 1133 - 271 rooms, restaurant, cocktail bar, coffee shop, swimming pool - $250*.

Hotel Phoenix, 277 Orchard Road/Somerset Road, ph 737 8666 - 300 rooms, restaurant, cocktail bar, coffee shop - $230-270*.

Cockpit Hotel, 6/7 Oxley Rise, ph 737 9111 - 176 rooms, restaurant, cocktail bar, coffee shop - $220-320*.

Cairnhill Hotel, 19 Cairnhill Circle, ph 734 6622 - 217 rooms, restaurant, cocktail bar, coffee shop, swimming pool - $220-240*.

Hotel Grand Central, 22 Cavenagh Road, ph 737 9944 - 344 rooms, restaurant, cocktail bar, coffee shop, swimming pool - $190-210*.

Ladyhill Hotel, 1 Ladyhill Road, ph 737 2111 - 174 rooms, restaurant, cocktail bar, coffee shop, swimming pool - $180-220*.

Hotel Royal, 36 Newton Road, ph 253 4411 - 299 rooms, restaurant, cocktail bar coffee shop, swimming pool - $170*.

Hotel Premier, 22 Nassim Hill, ph 733 9811 - 28 rooms, cocktail bar, coffee shop - S125.

Hotel Asia, 37 Scotts Road, ph 737 8388 - 146 rooms, restaurant, cocktail bar, coffee shop - $125-155*.

YMCA International House, 1 Orchard Road, ph 336 6000 - 111 rooms - McDonald's and coffee shop with Chinese and Western cuisine, swimming pool - $100*.

Hotel Supreme, 15 Kramat Road, ph 737 8333 - 86 rooms, coffee shop - $88 + 3% GST.

City Centre

Raffles Hotel, 1 Beach Road, ph 337 1886 - 104 suites, restaurants, cocktail bars, coffee shop, swimming pool - from $675*.

Oriental Singapore, 5 Raffles Avenue, Marina Square, ph 338 0066 - 518 rooms, restaurants, cocktail bars, coffee shop, swimming pool, squash court, tennis court - $375*.

Marina Mandarin Singa- pore, 6 Raffles Boule- vard, Marina Square, ph 338 3388 - 575 rooms, restaurant, cocktail bar, coffee shop, swimming pool, squash court, tennis court - $340-460*.

Pan Pacific Hotel, 7 Raffles Boulevard, Marina Square, ph 336 8111 - 800 rooms, restaurants, cocktail bars, coffee shop, swimming pool, tennis court - $300-480*.

The Westin Plaza, 2 Stamford Road, ph 338 8585 - 796 rooms, restaurant, cocktail bar, coffee shop, swimming pool, squash court, tennis court - $295-375*.

Carlton Hotel, 76 Bras Basah Road, ph 338 8333 - 420 rooms, restaurant, cocktail bar, coffee shop, swimming pool - $300-350*.

Allson Hotel, 101 Victoria Street, ph 336 0811 - 412 rooms, restaurant, cock- tail bar, coffee shop, swimming pool - $225-250*.

Golden Landmark Hotel, 390 Victoria Street, ph 297 2828 - 387 rooms, restaurant, cocktail bar, coffee shop, swimming pool - $190-230*.

Excelsior Hotel, 5 Coleman Street, ph 338 7733 - 274 rooms, restaurant, cocktail bar, coffee shop, swimming pool - $185-200*.

Singapore Peninsula, 3 Coleman Street, ph 337 2200 - 306 rooms, restaurant, cocktail bar, coffee shop, swimming pool - $175-190*.

Bayview Inn, 30 Bencoolen Street, ph 337 2882 - 117 rooms, restaurant, cocktail bar, coffee shop, swimming pool - $160-180*.

Metropole Hotel, 41 Seah Street, ph 336 3611 - 54 rooms, restaurant, coffee shop - $115-145*.

Strand Hotel, 25 Bencoolen Street, ph 338 1866 - 130 rooms, cocktail bar, coffee shop - $95.

Hotel Bencoolen, 47 Bencoolen Street, ph 336 0822 - 62 rooms, restaurant - $73-100*.

South East Asia Hotel, 190 Waterloo Street, ph 338 2394 - 51 rooms, restaurant, coffee shop - $79.

Mayfair City Hotel, 40/44 Armenian Street, ph 337 4542 - 27 rooms, cocktail bar - $74.

New 7th Storey Hotel, 229 Rochor Road, ph 337 0251 - 38 rooms, restaurant, cocktail bar - $59-75.

Chinatown/Havelock Districts

King's Hotel Clarion, 403 Havelock Road, ph 733 0011 - 316 rooms, restaurant, cocktail bar, coffee shop, swimming pool - $220-290*.

Furama Hotel Singapore, 60 Eu Tong Sen Street, ph 533 3888 - 355 rooms, restaurant, cocktail bar, coffee shop, swimming pool - $220-240*.

Apollo Hotel Singapore, 405 Havelock Road, ph 733 2081 - 323 rooms, restaurant, cocktail bar, coffee shop - $220-240*.

River View Hotel, 382 Havelock Road, ph 732 9922 - 472 rooms, restaurant, cocktail bar, coffee shop, swimming pool - $200-240*.

Concorde Hotel Singapore, 317 Outram Road, ph 733 0188 - 497 rooms, restaurant, cocktail bar, coffee shop, swimming pool, tennis court - $170-270*.

Majestic Hotel, 31-37 Bukit Pasoh Road, ph 222 3377 - 24 rooms (some with private facilities), restaurant - $55-69.

Serangoon District

New Park Hotel, 181 Kitchener Road, ph 291 5533 - 508 rooms, restaurant, cocktail bar, coffee shop, swimming pool - $140-180*.

Great Eastern Hotel, 401 Macpherson Road, ph 284 8244 - 151 rooms, restaurant, cocktail bar, coffee shop - $125-135*.

Broadway Hotel, 195 Serangoon Road, ph 292 4661 - 63 rooms, restaurant, coffee shop - $96-106 +3% GST.

Bukit Timah/Dunearn Road/Stevens Road/Balmoral Road Districts

Novotel Orchid Singapore, 214 Dunearn Road, ph 250 3322 - 412 rooms, restaurant, cocktail bar, coffee shop, swimming pool - $220-260*.

Hotel Equatorial, 429 Bukit Timah Road, ph 732 0431 - 195 rooms, restaurant, cocktail bar, coffee shop, swimming pool - $218*.

Garden Hotel, 14 Balmoral Road, ph 235 3344 - 209 rooms, restaurant, cocktail bar, coffee shop, swimming pool - $190*.

Sloane Court Hotel, 17 Balmoral Road, ph 235 3311 - 32 rooms, restaurant, cocktail bar, coffee shop - $88-120*.

East Coast District

Le Meridien Changi, 1 Netheravon Road, ph 542 7700 - 272 rooms, restaurant, cocktail bar, coffee shop, swimming pool, squash court, tennis court - $230-290*.

Sea View Hotel, 26 Amber Close, ph 345 2222 - 435 rooms, restaurant, coffee shop, swimming pool - $200-240*.

Singapore Paramount, 25 Marine Parade Road, ph 344 5577 - 250 rooms, restaurant, cocktail bar, coffee shop, swimming pool - $175-205*.

Lion City Hotel, 15 Tanjong Katong Road, ph 744 8111 - 159 rooms, restaurant, cocktail bar - $140-160*.

Metropolitan YMCA, 60 Stevens Road, ph 737 7755 - 87 rooms, restaurant, swimming pool - $65-90*.

West Coast District

Pasir Panjang Guest House, 404 Pasir Panjang Road, ph 778 8511 - 54 rooms, coffee shop - $75-100*.

Sentosa Island

Shangri-La's Rasa Sentosa Resort, 101 Siloso Road, ph 275 0100 - restaurant, cocktail bar, coffee shop, disco, swimming pool - $200-550*.

The Beaufort Singapore, Bukit Manis Road, ph 275 0331 - 167 rooms, restaurant, cocktail bar, coffee shop, disco, swimming pool, squash court - $270-300*.

LOCAL TRANSPORT

Singapore has one of the worlds most modern and efficient Mass Rapid Transit (MRT) systems, complemented by excellent bus services. Metered taxis are also plentiful and air-conditioned.

Singapore Mass Rapid Transit (SMRT)

Trains operate at intervals of between three and eight minutes from 6am until midnight, and there are stations all over the city. Fares range from S$0.60 to S$1.50, and there is a TransitLink S$10 farecard available at most MRT stations. It is valid on the MRT and bus services operated by the Singapore Bus Service (SBS) and the Trans Island Bus Service (TIBS). There is also a S$6 tourist souvenir ticket (ticket value S$5.50) available at MRT stations in the city where MRT guide maps can also be obtained. The TransitLink Hotline is 776 0100.

Bus

SBS and TIBS both operate regular and inexpensive services. A Singapore Explorer ticket is available from leading hotels, and costs are S$5 for a one-day pass, and S$12 for a three day pass. Bus guides are available from bookshops and the SBS head office at 205 Braddell Road. The Hotline number is 287 2727.

The *Singapore Trolley* is a bus service that runs between the Orchard Road area, Tanjong Pagar and the World Trade Centre, daily 9am-9pm. The ares are S$9 for adults, S$7 for children, and include discounts at shops and nightspots. Get tickets on board.

Taxi

There are more than 10,000 registered, air-conditioned taxis for hire in Singapore, operated by five different companies. The taxis can be hailed in the street, or hired at taxi stands conveniently located around the city and adjacent to many major shopping centres.

All taxis are metered and the initial flag-down meter fare is $2.40, which covers the first 1.5km. The fare then rises 10 cents for every 240m travelled.

If a taxi has a red destination label on its windscreen it means that the driver is finishing his shift and is only interested in heading in that direction.

There are some extra charges that are not shown on the meter, but are legitimate -

A 50% surcharge for travel between midnight and 6am.
A S$2.20 surcharge for bookings by phone, and a S$1 surcharge for every hour booked in advance.

A S$1 surcharge for trips originating from the CBD 4pm-7pm Mon-Fri, and noon-3pm Sat.

A S$3 surcharge for travel from Changi Airport. This does not apply to travel to the airport.

A S$3 surcharge for an Area Licence, which is needed to enter the CBD between 7.30am and 10.15am, and 4.30pm-6.30pm Mon-Fri, and 7.30am-10.15am Sat. Between 10.15am-4.30pm Mon-Fri and 10.15am-3pm Sat, the surcharge is S$2, and there is no surcharge on Sundays and public holidays. If the taxi is already displaying an Area Licence there is no surcharge.

A S$3 surcharge is levied for all trips in London cabs booked by telephone, and a S$4 surcharge if the booking is made 30 minutes in advance.

Car Hire

Cars can be hired by the day or by the week, and a current driver's licence from your country of residence will suffice, although an International Driving Licence is probably preferred. Traffic drives on the left, and if you are intending to enter the CBD during times mentioned in the Taxi section, you will have to purchase an Area Licence.

Nevertheless, here are some rental companies:

> With the low costs of public transport and the availability of taxis, a car is useful only for trips further afield.

AA Toyota Rental, 24 Leng Kee Road, ph 475 3855.

Ace Tours & Car Rentals, 37 Scotts Road (Asia Hotel), ph 235 3755.

A1 Car Rental, 401 MacPherson Road, #02-05 Great Eastern Hotel, ph 282 4057.

Budget Enterprise, Blk 30, Outram Park #01-479, ph 222 2355.

City Car Rentals & Tours, 401 Havelock Road, #02-20 Hotel Miramar, ph 733 2145.

Hertz Rent A Car, 125 Tanglin Road, Tudor Court Shopping Gallery, ph 734 4646.

Ken-Air Rent A Car, 277 Orchard Road, #01-41 Specialist Shopping Centre, ph 737 8282.

Ferry
From the domestic ferry terminal at the Cruise Centre ferries leave at 15-minute intervals for Sentosa, and the return fare is S$1.20. There are also daily services to Kusu and St John's, islands close to Singapore with quiet beaches and lagoons, and the return fare for both trips is S$6.

The regional ferry terminal has daily services at 30 minute intervals to the Indonesian island of Batam (S$26 return) and at 10.10am and 3pm to Indonesia's Bintan (S$68 return).

Trishaw
This is a fascinating way to explore the city, especially the back-lands and side-streets of Chinatown, but it is best to have your hotel, or a registered travel agent, organise one for you. There is no standard fare structure, so it is best to have some local advice about getting a good deal, otherwise it can be an expensive experience.

EATING OUT

The eating places in Singapore fall into several different categories. In the hotels there are specialty restaurants offering anything from fine European cuisine to food from all over Asia. The hotels also have coffee shops, known in Singapore as "coffee houses", which usually offer both international fare and Singaporean specialties.

Singapore's **Coffee Shops** serve coffee, tea and cold drinks, and have a number of stalls serving different types of cuisine. Sometimes coffee shops have a fully fledged restaurant inside, although a menu is not always available; diners look at all the basic ingredients on display and ask the chef to suggest a dish that contains the items they fancy.

The name **Eating House** refers to something that is somewhere between a coffee shop and a restaurant, and implies casual surroundings.

Hawker Centres, or Food Centres as they are sometimes known, are usually open-air, and have stalls serving meals from all the diverse ethnic groups for a very reasonable price.

Upmarket air-conditioned food centres have only come into being in Singapore in recent years.

The majority of Restaurants in Singapore are air-conditioned, while simple coffee shops and eating houses are normally cooled by ceiling fans only. Casual dress is OK, except in formal, elegant restaurants, and in the evenings, shorts and thongs are only worn in the most simple hawker centres.

Remember that smoking is completely banned in all air-conditioned restaurants.

A 10% service charge and a 3% government tax are levied on bills in restaurants classified as "tourist class", which includes all hotels. Suburban restaurants and simple eating places where no service charge is levied do not normally expect a tip, and tips are never offered or expected in hawker centres.

Cantonese

The Chinese people believe that this cuisine, from the Guandong province, is the best that China produces. The chefs prepare food by stir-frying, steaming and roasting. The food is characterised by

> Here we have listed restaurants under type of cuisine, and have classified them according to the price of a complete meal for one person (without drinks) as follows:
> Budget = up to S$15, Moderate = S$15-40, Expensive = over S$40.

lightness and delicacy, and by subtle seasoning, usually with soy sauce and oyster sauce.

Cantonese *dim sum*, known in other places as *yun char*, is very popular for breakfast or lunch. It consists of a range of steamed or deep-fried tidbits, which diners choose from trolleys wheeled around the restaurant.

Fook Yuen Seafood Restaurant, #03-05 Paragon Shopping Centre, 290 Orchard Road, ph 235 2211 - open 11am-3pm, 6-11pm - **Moderate** - air-conditioned - credit cards accepted.

Grand City Chinese Restaurant, #07-04 Cathay Building, 11 Dhoby Ghaut, ph 338 3622 - open 11.30am-2.30pm, 6.30-10.30pm - **Moderate** - air-conditioned - credit cards accepted.

Kirin Court Seafood & Shark's Fin Restaurant, 20 Devonshire Road, ph 732 1188 - open 11.30am-3pm, 6.30-11.30pm - **Moderate** - air-conditioned - credit cards accepted.

Tai Tong Hoi Kee, 3 Mosque Street, ph 223 3484 - open 10am-2pm - **Budget** - no credit cards.

Tsui Hang Village Restaurant, #02-142/145 Marina Square, 6 Raffles Boulevard, ph 338 6668 - open 11.30am-3pm (Sundays open 10am) 6-11pm - **Moderate** - air-conditioned - credit cards accepted.

Tung Lok Shark's Fin Restaurant, #04-07/09 Liang Court Complex, 177 River Valley Road, ph 336 6022 - open 11.30am-2.30pm, 6.30-10.30pm - **Expensive** - air-conditioned - credit cards accepted.

Yick Sang Restaurant, 7 Ann Siang Hill, ph 221 4187 - open 10am-6.30pm - **Budget** - no credit cards.

Hainanese

The best known dish of the Hainanese is Chicken Rice, a deceptively simple but flavourful combination of slow-cooked chicken, and rice simmered in chicken stock with chilli-garlic sauce as a condiment. In Singapore, the Hainanese became the chefs in Western and Peranakan (Nonya) restaurants and households. Over the years they created a great many adaptations of Western food with Hainanese-Singaporean overtones.

5 Star Hainanese Chicken Rice Restaurant, 224 East Coast Road, ph 440 2901 - open 5pm-1am - **Budget** - no credit cards.

Mooi Chin Palace Restaurant, #01-05, 109 North Bridge Road, ph 339 7766 - open 11am-10.30pm - **Budget** - air-conditioned - credit cards accepted.

Swee Kee Chicken Rice Restaurant, 51/53 Middle Road, ph 338 6986 -

open 11am-9.30am - **Budget** - no credit cards.

Yet Con Chicken Rice Restaurant, 25 Purvis Street, ph 337 6819 - open 10.30am-9.30pm - **Budget** - air-conditioned - no credit cards.

Hakka

The Hakka were a nomadic people, and their cooking reflects their frugal lifestyle. Beancurd is used more than meat, and preserved vegetables are a common ingredient. One of the tastiest dishes is *Yong Tau Fu*, a fish-ball paste stuffed into various types of beancurd and vegetables.

Moi Kong Restaurant, 22 Murray Street (Food Alley, off Maxwell Road), ph 221 7758 - open 11.30am-2.30pm, 5.30-9.30pm - **Budget** - air-conditioned - credit cards accepted.

Plum Village Restaurant, 16 Jalan Leban (off Upper Thomson Road), ph 458 9005 - open 11am-3pm, 6-10.30pm - **Budget** - air-conditioned - credit cards accepted.

Hokkien

This cuisine is not as sophisticated as that from its neighbour, Guandong, and uses a lot of garlic, soy sauce and soya bean pastes. Singapore's favourite noodle dish is Hokkien Prawn *Mee*, also known as Hokkien Fried *Mee*, and it is found at food stalls in hawker centres and coffee shops all over the island.

Bee Heong Palace Restaurant, #04-00 PIL Building, 140 Cecil Street, ph 222 9074 - open 10am-2.30pm - **Moderate** - air-conditioned - credit cards accepted.

Beng Hiang, 112-116 Amoy Street - open 11.30am-2pm, 6-9pm - **Moderate** - air-conditioned - credit cards accepted.

Beng Thin Hoon Kee Restaurant, #05-02 OCBC Centre, 65 Chulia Street, ph 533 2818 - open 11am-3pm, 6-10pm - **Moderate** - air-conditioned - credit cards accepted.

Hunanese

Hunan province was the home of Mao Tse Tung, and the food is spicy, similar to that of its neighbour Sichuan. The best known Hunanese dishes are Minced Pigeon steamed in a bamboo tube, Deep-fried Beancurd Skin and Honey-glazed Ham.

Charming Garden Restaurant, Novotel Orchid Inn, Dunearn Road, ph 251 8149 - open 11.30am-3pm, 6.30-11pm (Sundays and public holidays, *dim sum* served 7.30-11.30am) - **Moderate** - air-conditioned - credit cards accepted.

Cherry Garden, The Oriental Singapore, 6 Raffles Boulevard, ph 338 0066 - open noon-2.30pm, 6.30-10.30pm - **Expensive** - air-conditioned - credit cards accepted.

Peking

The Mongols and Manchus who invaded this city were Muslim, making Peking the only region where mutton is more highly regarded than pork. There is no doubt that the region's most famous dish is Peking Duck.

Pine Court, Mandarin Hotel, 33 Orchard Road, ph 737 4411 - open noon-3pm, 7-11pm - **Expensive** - air-conditioned - credit cards accepted.

Prima Tower Revolving Restaurant, 201 Keppel Road, ph 272 8822 - **Moderate** - air-conditioned - credit cards accepted.

Shanghainese

The cuisine of the city of Shanghai reflects its proximity to the coast and rivers. Favourite dishes include Shanghainese Braised Eel, and Braised Fish Tail in soy-based sauce.

Chang Jiang Shanghai Restaurant, Goodwood Park Hotel, 22 Scotts Road, ph 734 7188 - open 11am-3pm, 6.30-11pm - **Expensive** - air-conditioned - credit cards accepted.

Shanghai Palace, Excelsior Hotel, 5 Coleman Street, ph 339 3428 - open 12.30-2.30pm, 6.30-10pm - **Moderate** - air-conditioned - credit cards accepted.

Sichuan

Sichuan is a far western province of China, and its cuisine has become internationally known in recent years for its strong flavours and hot chillies, used either in paste or as whole dried chilies fried together with the main ingredient. Some of the most popular dishes include Duck Smoked over Tea Leaves and Camphor, Chicken or Prawns Stir-Fried with Whole Dried Chillies, and Hot Sour Soup.

China Palace, #02-00 Wellington Building, 20 Bideford Road, ph 235 1378 - open 10.30am-2.30pm, 6.30-10.30pm - **Moderate** - air-conditioned - credit cards accepted.

Golden Phoenix Sichuan Restaurant, Hotel Equatorial, 429 Bukit Timah Road, ph 732 0431 - open 11.30am-3pm, 6.30-11pm - **Moderate** - air-conditioned - credit cards accepted.

Long Jiang Sichuan Restaurant, Crown Prince Hotel, 270 Orchard Road, ph 732 1111 - open noon-2.30pm, 7-11pm - **Moderate** - air-conditioned - credit cards accepted.

Omei Restaurant, Hotel Grand Central, 22 Cavenagh Road, ph 737 2735 - open 11.30am-2.30pm, 6-10.30pm - **Moderate** - air-conditioned - credit cards accepted.

Teochew

The second biggest group of Chinese in Singapore, the Teochews produce light, delicately flavoured food. Teochew dishes are often steamed, with salted preserved vegetables or sour plums, and served with a range of interesting sauces. The best known dishes include Braised Goose or Duck, Steamed Fish or Crayfish, Pork & Liver Rolls.

Ban Seng Restaurant, 79 New Bridge Road, ph 533 1471 - open noon-2.30pm, 6-9.30pm - **Budget** - air-conditioned - credit cards accepted.

Delicious Kitchen, 30-38 Tanjong Pagar Road, ph 226 0607 - open 11am-3.20pm, 6-10pm - **Moderate** - air-conditioned - credit cards accepted.

Ellenborough Market Food Stalls, 3rd level, Ellenborough Market, cnr New Bridge Road & Tew Chew Street - open 7am-2.30pm - **Budget** - no credit cards.

Hung Kang Restaurant, 38 North Bridge Road, ph 533 5300 - open 11.30am-2.30pm, 6.30-10.30pm - **Moderate** - air-conditioned - credit cards accepted.

Liang Heng Teochew Eating House, 48 Mosque Street, ph 223 1652 - open 9am-10pm - **Budget** no credit cards.

Swatow Teochew Restaurant, #01-03 Plaza By The Park, 51 Bras Basah Road, ph 339 2544 - open noon-2.30pm, 6-11pm - **Moderate** - air-conditioned - credit cards accepted.

Teochew City Restaurant, #05-16 Centrepoint, 176 Orchard Road, ph 733 3338 - open 11.30am-2.30pm, 6.30-10pm - **Moderate** - air-conditioned - credit cards accepted.

Chinese Herbal

The Chinese invented the saying "a man is what he eats", and they believe that certain foods should be eaten to retain a health balance in the body. Food cooked with medicinal herbs has always played an important part in the Chinese diet. Turtle soup, for example, is thought to build up the body and be good for the heart. This cuisine has some delicious dishes.

Hua Tuo Guan, 22 Tanjong Pagar Road, ph 222 4854 - open 10am-10.30pm - **Budget** - no credit cards.

Imperial Herbal Restaurant, Metropole Hotel, 41 Seah Street, ph 337 0491 - open 11.30am-2.30pm, 6.30-11pm - **Moderate** - air-conditioned - credit cards accepted.

Chinese Vegetarian

Very few Chinese are strict vegetarians, but many believe that it is good for the body to abstain from meat on occasion. Originally the chefs tried to make vegetarian meals that tasted like meat, but now they concentrate on techniques that bring out the natural flavour of the ingredients.

Fut Sai Kai Vegetarian Restaurant, 143 Kitchener Road, ph 298 0336 - open 10.30am-9pm - **Budget** - air-conditioned - no credit cards.

Kingsland Vegetarian Restaurant, #03-43/46 People's Park Complex, ph 534 1846 - open 11am-10pm - **Budget** - air-conditioned - credit cards accepted.

Happy Realm Vegetarian Food, #03-16 Pearl Centre, Eu Tong Sen Street, ph 222 6141 - open 11am-8.30pm - **Budget** - air-conditioned - no credit cards.

Pine Tree Vegetaran Restaurant, 51 Robinson Road, ph 222 0067 - open 11.30am-10.30pm - **Moderate** - air-conditioned - credit cards accepted.

Northern Indian

The cuisine of the north is more sophisticated and less spicy than that of the south. A favourite at restaurants that have a tandoor oven is the unleavened bread, naan, often spiced with garlic, herbs or dried fruits.

Mayarani Restaurant, #01-09/13 Amara Hotel Shopping Centre, 165 Tanjong Pagar Road, ph 225 6244 - open noon-3pm, 6.30-11pm - **Moderate** - air-conditioned - credit cards accepted.

Orchard Maharajah, Cuppage Terrace, 25 Cuppage Rd, ph 732 6331 - open 11.30am-3pm, 6.30-11pm - **Moderate** - credit cards accepted.

Ujagar Singh, 7 St Gregory's Place, ph 336 1586 - open 11am -4.30pm, 6.30-10pm (Sundays noon-4pm) - **Budget** - no credit cards.

Southern Indian

Rice predominates in the south, and the butter and cream of the northern cuisine are replaced by oil and yoghurt. Southern Indian food is usually laced with chillies and highly seasoned.

Banana Leaf Apollo, 56 Racecourse Road, ph 293 8682 - open 10.30am-10pm - **Budget** - air-conditioned - credit cards accepted.

Muthu's Curry, 76/78 Racecourse Road, ph 293 2389 - open 10.30am-10pm (Sundays and public holidays 10am-10.30pm - **Budget** - air-conditioned - credit cards accepted.

Included in the wide range of curry dishes is a very popular Singapore version of a Kerala dish, Fish Head Curry. It comes recommended, but I must confess that I have never been game enough to try it.

Indian Vegetarian

A large percentage of Indians are vegetarians, so all kinds of savouries, breads, rice dishes, lentils (dals), soups, vegetable combinations, salads, desserts and sweetmeats have been created over the years. **Most meals are accompanied by crisp** *Pappadams* **(lentil wafers).**

Annalakshmi, #02-10 Excelsior Hotel & Shopping Complex, 5 Coleman Street, ph 339 3007 - open noon-3pm, 7-10pm (Thurs 11.30am-3pm) - **Moderate** - air-conditioned - credit cards accepted.

Bombay Woodlands Restaurant, #B1-06 Forum Galleria, 583 Orchard Road, ph 235 2712 - open noon-3pm, 6-10.30pm - **Moderate** - air-conditioned - credit cards accepted.

Komala Vilas Restaurant, 76/78 Serangoon Road, ph 293 6980 - open 7am-10pm - **Budget** - no credit cards.

Malay

Malay meals are based around rice, with an assortment of spiced dishes including fish, poultry, meat and vegetables, plus a condiment, or *sambal* of chillies. Fish predominates, and pork is never eaten as Malays are Muslim.

Aziza's Restaurant, 36 Emerald Hill Road, ph 235 1130 - open 11.30am-3pm, 6.30-11pm (closed for lunch Sun) - **Moderate** - air-conditioned - credit cards accepted.

Bintang Timur, #02-08/13 Far East Plaza, Scotts Road, ph 235 4539 - open 11am-9.45pm - **Moderate** - air-conditioned - credit cards accepted.

Sabar Menanti, 62 Kandahar Street - **Budget** - no credit cards.

Seafood

Garden Seafood Restaurant, Goodwood Park Hotel, 22 Scotts Road, ph 737 7411 - open 11am-2.15pm, 6.30-10.15pm - **Expensive** - air-conditioned - credit cards accepted.

Long Beach Seafood Restaurant, 610 Bedok Road, ph 445 8833 - open 5pm-12.30am - **Moderate** - credit cards accepted.

Ocean Spray, 31 Marins Park, ph 225 3055 - open 6pm-midnight (closed on Wed) - **Expensive** - credit cards accepted.

Singa Inn Seafood Restaurant, 920 East Coast Parkway, ph 345 1111 - open noon-2.30pm, 6-11pm - **Expensive** - credit cards accepted.

UDMC Seafood Centre, East Coast Parkway - open 6-11pm - **Moderate** - credit cards accepted.

Whee Heng Seafood Restaurant, 893 Ponggol Road, ph 288 9127 - open 11am-11pm - **Budget** - air-conditioned - credit cards accepted.

Hawker Centres

Every visitor to Singapore has to have at least one meal at a Hawker Centre. They may look a little tacky at first

Singapore is blessed with an abundance of seafood from nearby waters - silver and red fish, prawns of all sizes, lobsters, crabs, mussels, tiny sweet oysters, cockles and moon-white squid.

sight, but in fact they are very clean, and the range of different cuisines is astounding. You can sample dishes from different stalls, or order a whole meal from one.

Upon entering the centre, find a spare table, make a note of its number, and have one member of your party stay there and mind it while the rest check out the different stalls. The tables and chairs belong to the whole centre, not to any individual kitchen. You can then order food from any of the stalls and ask them to bring it to your table. When the dish arrives, you pay for it.

The prices are very reasonable, with many dishes, such as noodles or soups costing as little as S$3, and the bill for a whole meal ranging from S$10 per person, unless you order expensive seafood. One thing that might make you wonder is the sign at some stalls saying "Cooked Food". This actually means that the meals are not partially prepared

Clarke Quay, Food Spread by Tenants

beforehand, but made from scratch when you order.

Hawker Centres are open for extended hours, from breakfast to late suppers.

Bugis Square, Foch Road, off Lavender Street - busiest at night.

High Street Centre, 1 North Bridge Road - busiest at lunch time.

Hill Street Centre, 64 Hill Street - popular with office workers for lunch.

Newton Circus - although many of the stalls are open for breakfast, this is at its best during the evening. Newton Circus is the centre that, in days gone by, was a car park during the day and a hawker centre at night. It is the biggest centre, and you can get just about anything you can think of in the way of Asian, Indian, Malay, etc.

Rasa Marina, 2nd level Marina Square, 6 Raffles Boulevard - best for lunch or an early dinner.

Satay Club, Connaught Drive - best for satay and other Malay dishes at night.

Taman Serasi, off Cluny Road, opposite the Botanical Gardens - open at breakfast right through to supper.

Telok Blangah, World Trade Centre - has Malay, Indian Muslim and Chinese dishes.

Air-conditioned Food Centres

Esplanade Food Park, 2nd level, Marina Square, 6 Raffles Boulevard - open 10am-10pm - local specialties plus Japanese and Thai food, and Danish(!) ice-cream.

Fountain Food Court, 51 Neil Road, Tanjong Pagar - open 11am-11pm - Thai, Vegetarian, Eurasian and Chinese food.

Lucky Plaza Food Centre, 5th level, Lucky Plaza, 304 Orchard Road - open 10am-9.30pm - local specialties - lunch crowds really test the air-conditioning.

Orchard Emerald Food Court, basement Orchard Emerald, 218 Orchard Road, open Mon-Fri & Sun 11am-10pm, Sat 11am-11pm - local specialties, fruit salads, frozen yoghurt.

Scotts Picnic Food Court, basement Scotts Shopping Centre, 6 Scotts Road - open 10.30am-11pm - excellent selection of food - crowded for each meal.

Yaohan Supermarket, basement 1, Plaza Singapura, 68 Orchard Road - the food centre is at the entrance of the supermarket - open 10am-10pm - no proper seating, but usually crowded on weekends.

ENTERTAINMENT

There is absolutely no reason to stay in your hotel room after dark in Singapore. There is plenty of nightlife to suit even the most jaded palate.

CINEMAS

The daily newspaper *The Straits Times* has programs for the 50+ cinemas.

Golden Village Bishan Junction 8 Shopping Centre, 9 Bishan Place, ph 353 8885.

Golden Village Yishun 10, 51 Yishun Central, ph 257 4266.

Jade Classics, 100 Beach Road, Shaw Towers, ph 293 2581.

Jurong 4 Cineplex, Ground Floor, Jurong Entertainment Centre, Jurong East Street 13 (opposite Jurong East MRT), ph 569 3463

Lido 5 Cineplex, Shaw Centre, 13th Floor, 1 Scotts Road, ph 732 4124.

Pavilion Cineplex, 10 Tampines Central 1, #01-01, ph 787 9277.

Picturehouse, 11 Dhoby Ghaut, ph 338 3400.

PUBS, BARS, DISCOS

Singapore's pub scene was originally along Orchard Road, but it has now spread to old shophouses and warehouses in interesting corners of the city. Most pubs have Happy Hours when drinks are sold at reduced prices, or two for the price of one. At other times a glass of Tiger Beer (the local brand) sells for around S$9.

Smaller venues do not usually have a cover charge, but those with live bands and dancing may charge anything between S$15 and S$25, which generally includes at least one drink, sometimes more. Also, the cover charge may be less during the week, and sometimes women do not have to pay as much as men.

All prices at nightspots include a 10% service charge, plus the 4% government tax (1% cess and 3% GST) so tipping is not necessary.

Boat Quay District

Harry's Quayside Cafe, 28 Boat Quay, ph 538 3029 - American pub and cafe featuring western cuisine and live jazz. Open Mon-Fri 11.30am-2pm, Tues-Sat 7.30-10.30pm - happy hours noon-8pm Tues-Sat. Harry's is a short walk from Raffles Place MRT station (C1).

Taps Pub & Entertainment, 54 Boat Quay, ph 532 2685 - karaoke pub with a disc jockey during singing breaks. Open Mon-Fri 4pm-1am, Sat 4pm-2am, Sun 6pm-12am - happy hours 4-8pm daily. Also a short walk from Raffles Place MRT station (C1).

City District

Bar and Billiard Room, Raffles Hotel Arcade, 1 Beach Road, ph 337 1886 - live jazz nightly Mon-Sat, two billiard tables all the time and a very relaxed atmosphere. Open for cocktails daily 11.30am-1am; lunch daily 11.30am-2pm; high tea Sat-Sun and public holidays 3.30-5pm. Raffles is a short walk from City Hall MRT station (C2).

Boom Boom Room, Bugis Village, ph 339 8187 - beautifully decorated nightclub with cabaret style shows. Open Sun-Thurs 8.30pm-1am, Fri-Sat and eve of public holidays 8.30pm-2am. Showtimes are Sun-Thurs 10-45pm-12.45am, Fri-Sat and eve of public holidays 11pm-1.45am.

Boom Boom Bar, Bugis Village, ph 339 1026 - similar in decor to Boom Boom Room but with live jazz bands every night except Sunday, when amateur bands have jam sessions. Open Sun, Tues-Thurs 8.30pm-1am, Fri-Sat and eve of public holidays 8.30pm-2am.

Bugis Village is a short walk from Bugis MRT station (E1).

Champions Singapore, Level 1, Marina Mandarin Singapore, 6 Raffles Boulevard, Marina Square, ph 331 8567 - a sports bar and nightclub with a disc jockey and seven sports-themed karaoke rooms. Open Mon-Thurs 5pm-2am, Fri-Sun and public holidays 5pm-3am. Close to City Hall MRT station (C2).

Elvis Place, 298 Beach Road, The Concourse, Basement 1 #01-13, ph 299 8403 - the name says it all. Open Mon-Thurs 4pm-midnight, Fri-Sat 4pm-1am; happy hours 4pm-8.30pm Mon-Sat. Walk towards Beach Road from the Bugis MRT station (E1).

Scandals, Westin Plaza Hotel, 2 Stamford Road, ph 338 8585 - a disco for 21s and over that hosts different theme parties each week, such as Arabian Night. Open daily 8pm-3am; happy hours 8-10.30pm daily. Scandals is near the City Hall MRT station (C2).

Singsation, Plaza Hotel, 7500 Beach Road, ph 298 0011 - a karaoke pub with 19 theme rooms

Long Bar, Levels 2 & 3, Raffles Hotel Arcade, 1 Beach Road, ph 337 1886 - a legendary bar with ceiling fans, cane furniture, peanut shells scattered on the floor, and the famous Singapore Sling. Open Sun-Thurs 11am-1am, Fri-Sat and eve of public holidays 11am-2am; happy hours Mon-Fri 6-9pm. Raffles is a short walk from City Hall MRT station (C2).

Bugis Street

and a main hall. Open Sun-Thurs 7pm-2am, Fri-Sat and eve of public holidays 7pm-3am; happy hours 7-9pm Sun-Thurs. The Plaza is a short walk from City Hall MRT station (C2).

Somerset's Bar, Westin Plaza Hotel, 2 Stamford Road, ph 338 8585 - a very popular jazz venue. Open daily 5pm-2am; happy hours 5-830pm daily. City Hall MRT station (C2).

The Warehouse, River View Hotel, 382 Havelock Road, ph 732 9922 - Singapore's first warehouse disco, where a disc jockey and a live band alternate. There is also a total of 18 karaoke rooms. Open Sun-Thurs 5pm-2am, Fri-Sat and eve of public holidays; happy hours 6-8pm daily. Take SBS bus nos 64, 123, 139 or 143 from Orchard Road.

Boon Tat Street, adjacent to the Lau Pa Sat Festival Market, is closed nightly to become the only street in Singapore where people can dine al fresco on local foods.

Clarke Quay

The Quay is divided into five areas - Merchants' Court, The Cannery, Shophouse Row, Traders' Market and The Foundry - and houses various eateries and nightspots.

Stationary *Tongkangs* along the river serve cool drinks and light snacks, adding to the atmosphere.

Bugsy Malone, Traders Market, 3E Clarke Quay, River Valley Road, #02-01, ph 339 8717 - a nightspot for lovers of karaoke, pool, live entertainment and, on Sunday, a jazz band. Open Sun-Thurs 3pm-1am, Fri-Sat and eve of public holidays 3pm-2am; happy hours 3-8pm daily.

Party Doll, Shophouse Row, 3D River Valley Road, #03-01/02, ph 339 3139 - the restaurant serves Japanese and Western food, and patrons jive to the music from the 50s and 60s. There are karaokerooms, and a live band starts playing at 9pm. Open Mon-Sat 4pm-2am; Japanese restaurant daily noon-3pm; KTV Lounge daily 2pm-2am; happy hours 2-7pm.

Suzie Wong's, Merchants' Court, 3A River Valley Road, #01-26, ph 433 0174 - an intimate bar with dancing, and live French, English, Shanghainese, Cantonese and Mandarin music. Open Sun-Thurs 5pm-2ama, Fri-Sat, eve of public holidays and public holidays 5pm-3am; happy hours 5-8pm daily.

Holland Village

Holland Village is a quiet suburb about 15 minutes by taxi from Orchard Road. It has only recently become a nightlife centre.

After 5 Beer, Wine & Cafe, 27A Lorong Liput, ph 467 8600 - a friendly atmosphere with good food, but the only entertainment is piped music and TV. Open Mon-Fri 2pm-midnight, Sat noon-midnight, Sun 3-11pm; happy hours Mon-Fri 2-7pm, Sat noon-7pm, Sun 3-7pm. From Orchard Road take SBS bus no 7, 105 or 106.

Wine Lovers, 18 Lorong Mambong, ph 462 4510 - a bar and brasserie with Spanish music and food. Lunch is served from noon and light snacks are available throughout the day. Open Sun-Thurs noon-midnight, Fri-Sat and eve of public holidays noon-1am; happy hours 3-7pm daily. Take SBS bus nos. 7, 105 or 106 from Orchard Road.

Orchard Road

Many visitors still consider this area to be the centre of Singapore nightlife.

Anywhere, 19 Tanglin Road, #04-08/09 Tanglin Shopping Centre, ph 734 8233 - the resident band Tania is well known throughout Singapore. Open Mon-Thurs 6pm-2am, Fri 6pm-3am, Sat 8pm-3am; happy hours 6-8.30pm Mon-Sat. Anywhere is a short walk from Orchard MRT station (N3).

Brannigans, Hyatt Regency Singapore, 10-12 Scotts Road, ph 733 1188 - a well-known pub with a disc jockey and live bands that attract a mostly young crowd. Open Sun-Thurs 5pm-1am, Fri-Sat and eve of public holidays 5pm-2am; happy hours 5-8pm. The Hyatt is a short walk from Orchard MRT station (N3).

Caesar's, 400 Orchard Road, #02-46 Orchard Towers, ph 737 7665 - A disco with early Roman decor and live bands that alternate with a disc jockey. Open daily 9pm-3am; happy hour 9pm-midnight. Caesar's is a short walk from Orchard MRT station (N3).

5 Emerald Hill Bar & Restaurant, 5 Emerald Hill Road, ph 732 0818 - a two-storey pub and restaurant behind Peranakan Place has piped music ranging from Brazilian to Motown. Open Mon-Thurs noon-2am, Fri-Sat and eve of public holidays noon-3am, Sun 5pm-2am; happy hours 6-9pm daily. Take the MTR to Somerset station (N2).

Fabrice's World Music Bar, Basement, Dynasty Hotel, 320 Orchard Road, ph 738 8887 - music and decor from all over the world, and a disc jockey and a live band alternating. Open Mon-Fri 5pm-3am, Sat-Sun and eve of public holidays 7pm-3am; happy hours 5-8pm Mon-Fri, 7-8pm Sat-Sun and eve of public holidays. the Dynasty is a short walk from Orchard MRT station (N3).

Fire Discotheque, 150 Orchard Road, #04-19 Orchard Plaza, ph 235 0155 - a two-level entertainment centre featuring a disco, pub and karaoke. A live band performs nightly, and Tea Dances are held for the 12 to 21s. Open daily 8pm-3am; **tea dance Sat-Sun and public holidays 2-6pm;** happy hours 5-8pm Mon-Fri.
Somerset MRT station (N2) is the closest.

Hard Rock Cafe, 50 Cuscaden Road, ph 235 5232 - another in the world-wide chain of look-alikes. Open Sun-Thurs 11am-2am, Fri-Sat and eve of public holidays 11am-3am; meals 11am-10.30pm daily; happy hours 4-7pm Mon-Fri, 3-5pm Sat-Sun; dance hours are after 11pm daily. The cafe is a short walk from Orchard MRT station (N3).

J.D.'s Pub & Bistrotheque, 180 Orchard Road, Peranakan Place, ph 732 6966 - night-time entertainment includes karaoke and dancing to live bands (after 9pm), or you can pop in for a delicious lunch. Open Mon-Thurs 11am-1am, Fri-Sat and eve of public holidays 11am-3am; lunch 11am-3pm Mon-Sat; happy hours 11am-8pm Mon-Sat. MRT Somerset station (N2).

Sparks, Level 8 Ngee Ann City, 391 Orchard Road, ph 735 6133 - South-east Asia's newest and largest nightspot with a jazz club, a Canton-pop club, a disco, 20 karaoke rooms and a pub. Sparks has a minimum age limt of 23 years for men and 18 for women. Open Mon-Thurs 5pm-2am, Fri 5pm-3am, Sat 7pm-3am, Sun 7pm-2am; happy hours 5-8pm Mon-Fri. Take the MRT to Orchard station (N3).

Saxophone Bar & Restaurant, 23 Cuppage Road, Cuppage Terrace, ph 235 8385 - fine continental dining and jazz music, inside and outdoors. Open daily noon-3pm, 6pm-2am; lunch noon-3pm; dinner 7-11.15pm; happy hours 6-8pm. Somerset MRT station (N2).

Top Ten, 400 Orchard Road, #04-35 Orchard Towers, ph 732 3077 - originally a cinema, now a disco with a live band and a disk jockey. Open daily 5pm-3am; happy hours 5-9pm Mon-Sat. Near Orchard MRT station (N3).

Xanadu, Shangri-La Hotel, 22 Orange Grove Road, ph 737 3644 - a disco with spectacular lightshows and plenty of gadgetry, plus three karaoke rooms. Open Mon-Sat and eve of public holidays 8.30pm-3am. Take a taxi from Orchard MRT station (N3).

Tanjong Pagar

Duxton's Chicago Bar & Le Coq Restaurant, 6 & 9 Duxton Hill Road, ph 222 4096 - features reasonably priced French cuisine and jazz and blues music. Open Mon-Thurs 11am-2am, Fri-Sat 11am-1am, Sun 1pm-midnight; lunch daily noon-2pm; dinner daily 7-10pm; happy hours 11am-8.30pm. Duxton's is a short walk from Tanjong Pagar MRT station (W1).

Flag & Whistle, 10 Duxton Hill, ph 223 1126 - traditional English pub that serves traditional English food. Open Sun-Thurs 11am-midnight, Fri-Sat 11am-2am; happy hours daily 11am-8pm. A short walk from Tanjong Pagar MRT station (W1).

Nightshift, 38/39 Craig Road, ph 225 7010 - housed in a restored shophouse, Nightshift has a karaoke lounge on the first level and an Indian band playing Indian bangra music on the second. Open Mon-Thurs 5pm-1.45am, Sat-Sun 5pm-2.45am; happy hours 5-8.30pm daily. Close to Tanjong Pagar MRT station (W1).

The Europa Connection

There is a string of Europa pubs all over the island of Singapore, and they are one-stop night spots that range from a karaoke to a sushi bar.

Europa Changi, Block 5 Changi Village Road, #01-2001, ph 542 5617 - the first of the chain that has been operating for over 50 years and serves lunch and dinner outdoors. Open Sun-Thurs noon-1am, Fri-Sat and eve of public holiday noon-2am; happy hours 3-9pm daily. Take the MRT to Tanah Merah station (E9), then SBS bus 2.

Europa East Coast, 902 East Coast Parkway, ph 447 0869 - the largest in the chain offers food, live bands, a pub and karaoke, all under one roof. Open Sun-Thurs 6pm-2am, Fri-Sat and eve of public holidays 6pm-3am; happy hours 6-8.30pm daily. The only way to get there is to grab a cab, but it will be worth the fare.

Europa Ridley's, 16 Nassim Hill, ph 235 0135 - named after the first director of Singapore's Botanic Gardens, and the man who introduced the rubber plant into this part of the world, this member of the chain is a multi entertainment venue. Open Mon-Fri 6pm-3am, Sat-Sun and eve of public holidays 7.30pm-3am; happy hours 6-9pm daily. Take the MRT to Orchard station (N3), and a taxi from there.

Europa Serangoon Gardens Cafe Pub, 68 Serangoon Gardens Way, ph 382 4087 - a karaoke pub in a quiet residential district. Open daily 4pm-midnight; happy hours 4-8pm Mon-Fri. Take the MRT to Ang Mo Kio station (N9), then Sbs bus 136.

Other Districts

Cheers, Novotel Orchid, 214 Dunearn Rd, ph 250 3322 - a fun pub with a live band from 9pm until closing. Open Sun-Thurs 5pm- 1am, Fri-Sat and eve of public holidays 5pm-2am; happy hours 5-8pm daily. Take SBS bus 171 or TIBS bus 182 from Orchard Road.

Frontpage Pub, 9 Mohamed Sultan Road (off River Valley Road), ph 235 1884 - an informal pub that is a favourite for Singapore's media people. Open Mon-Thurs 3pm-1am, Fri-Sat 3pm-2am, Sun 3pm-midnight; happy hours 3-8pm daily. Take the MRT to Dhoby Ghaut station (N1) then walk along Penang Lane/Clemenceau Avenue towards River Valley Road.

Nextpage Pub, 15 Mohamed Sultan Road (off River Valley Road), ph 235 6967 - two levels of a shophouse with two pool tables and a disc jockey who spins jazz, blues, Brazilian, New World and 70s funk music. Open daily 3pm-2am; happy hours 3-8pm daily. Take the MRT to Dhoby Ghaut station (N1) and walk along Penang Lane/Clemenceau Avenue towards River Valley Road.

Zouk, 17-21 Jiak Kim Street (off Kim Seng Road), ph 738 2988 - three warehouses have been converted into one great party venue. Open: Zouk Disco Tues-Sun 10pm-3am; Music Video Bar Tues-Sun 8pm-3am; happy hours 8-10pm Tues-Sun. Zouk Restaurant Mon-Sat 7-11.30pm; Zouk Wine Bar daily 6pm-3am; happy hours 6-10pm daily. Take a taxi or the MRT to Outram station (W2), then SBS bus 75 or 195.

THEATRE RESTAURANTS AND NIGHTCLUBS

Dallas Theatre Lounge and Nite-Club, 165 Tanjong Pagar Road, #05-01 Amara Hotel, ph 221 3311 - open daily 4.30pm-2.45am. Tanjong Pagar MRT station (W1).

Golden Million Deluxe Nite-Club, 3 Coleman Street, #05-00 Peninsula Hotel, ph 336 6993 - open daily 9pm-3am. City Hall MRT station (C2).

Kabuki Deluxe Nite-Club, 1 Grange Road, #06-00 Orchard Building, ph 737 8922 - open daily 9.30pm-3am. Somerset MRT Station (N2).

Lido Palace Nite-Club, 317 Outram Road, #05-01 Concorde Hotel, ph 732 8855 - open daily 9pm-3am. SBS bus 123 from Orchard Rd, or taxi.

Neptune Theatre Restaurant, 50 Collyer Quay, #07-00 Overseas Union House, ph 224 3922 - open Mon-Sat 11.30am-2.30pm, Sun & public holidays 10.30am-2.30pm, daily 7-11pm. Raffles Place MRT station (C1).

Regent Night Club, 5 Koek Road, #05-03 Cuppage Plaza, ph 732 3288 - open daily 9pm-3am. Somerset MRT station (N2).

CHINESE STREET OPERA (WAYANG)

Spend your evening at the opera - in the streets. Chinese Opera is an unforgettable experienced. Performed during temple celebrations and the Festival of the Hungry Ghosts (August/September, wayang is actually meant for the gods and spirits; but less-than-divine eyes are also free to enjoy this spectacle of glittering costumes and painted faces. The operas are free to anyone who cares to stay and listen, but I must say that it takes an acquired taste to enjoy them.

Contact the STPB Tourist Information Centres for information on venues and times.

THEATRE

The following venues stage local plays, musicals and ballets as well as international productions. Current programs are advertised in the daily newspapers.

Harbour Pavilion, 1 Maritime Square, #09-72 World Trade Centre, ph 321 2783.

Kallang Theatre, Stadium Walk, ph 345 8488.

Singapore Indoor Stadium, No 2 Stadium Walk, Kallang, ph 344 2660.

TheatreWorks Singapore Ltd, The Black Box, Cox Terrace, Fort Canning Park, ph 338 4077.

The Drama Centre, Canning Rise, ph 336 0005.

The Substation, 45 Armenian Street, ph 337 7800.

CULTURAL SHOWS

Singapore's multi-ethnic heritage ensures that cultural presentations are varied and interesting.

The Merlion Ballroom, Cockpit Hotel, 67 Oxley Rise, ph 737 9111 - nightly. Admission, including dinner, is adult S$38 + taxes, child under 12 years S$26 + taxes. Dinner is at 7pm, showtime is 8pm. Take a short walk from Somerset MRT station (N2).

Mandarin Hotel, 333 Orchard Road, ph 737 4411 - poolside show features music, sons and dances from Singapore, Malaysia, Thailand, Indonesia and the Philippines. Admission, including dinner, is adults S$48 nett, child 5-10 years S$26.25. Show only prices are adult S$21 + tax, children 5-10 years S$14 + taxes. Dinner is at 7pm, show time is 8pm.

Singa Inn Seafood Restaurant, 920 East Coast Parkway, ph 345 1111 - Chinese, Malay and Indian dancers perform Mon-Fri at 8pm. Meals are at a la carte prices, and there is no surcharge for the floorshow. The only way to get there is to take a taxi.

SHOPPING

Singapore is a shopper's paradise, overflowing with all the exciting and exotic treasures of the East, and the fashionable luxuries of the West. Few countries in the world can match the variety of goods sold in Singapore, nor can they match the prices because just about everything is duty-free. In fact, many goods sell at a lower price than in their country of origin!

Shops are open seven days a week from around 10am till at least 9pm.

SHOPPING HINTS

Always compare prices before buying. It is best to get prices from at least three outlets and from advertisements in the local newspapers. Make sure, though, that you check the quality as well as the price, or it could be that you are really paying less for less. This applies particularly to fabric outlets and tailors.

When ordering articles from a tailor, make sure all specifications are in writing, and that a sample of the chosen material is attached to the deposit receipt. If ordering more than one item, have the invoice itemised, not simply showing a total figure.

Never make full payment before the final product is ready. A deposit of up to 20% is reasonable with the balance on delivery after you have inspected the garment. Always insist on a fitting, and do not expect a suit or dress tailored within 24 hours to be of good workmanship. Normally it takes two days for a suit or dress to be made-to-measure.

Visitors should look for shops that are members of the Good Retailers Scheme (GRS). These retailers have been approved by the Singapore Tourist Promotion Board (STPB) and the Consumers Association of Singapore (CASE). They display a red and white Merlion sticker on the door or window, and customers can be assured of quality goods that are not pirated or defective, and can expect fair pricing. CASE, ph 270 5433, will act on complaints regarding unethical business practices, and the Small Claims Tribunals have a fast-track procedure for visitors so that cases can be held within two days. Fees are minimal - only S$10 to have the case heard.

With regard to watches, cameras and all electrical and electronic items, ensure that you receive an International Warranty Card so that it is applicable in your home country.

Check the voltage and cycle for electrical and electronic goods. Countries such as Singapore, United Kingdom, Australia, New Zealand and Hong Kong use 220-240 volts, 50 cycles. Others, such as Canada, United States, Japan, Indonesia and the Philippines, use 110-120 volts, 60 cycles. Some equipment is universal and can be used in any country, otherwise a special adaptor or transformer may be necessary.

Haggling over the price of goods is still part of the fun of shopping, but it is mainly confined to the smaller outlets. When a sign tells you that the prices are fixed, it is pointless trying to bargain.

Don't listen to touts and unlicensed tourist guides. If approached, ask to see their official Singapore Tourist Promotion Board guide badge and licence.

GST Tourist Refund Scheme

A 3% Goods and Services Tax was introduced on April 1, 1994, and visitors may apply for a refund of the tax paid on goods worth S$500 or more. This amount must have been spent in the one shop (or shops belonging to the same retail chain) that has a TAX REFUND sticker displayed. The shop supplies the Claim forms, and visitors may be asked to show their passports, then the forms must be presented to Customs at the airport on departure. The Customs stamp the forms and return them to the shops, which mail the refund in a Singapore Dollar cheque to the visitor's home address. Refunds can also be made to a nominated credit card account.

All this hardly seems worth the trouble, unless you have spent thousands of dollars, but if you decide to make a claim remember that banks usually charge fees for depositing a foreign cheque to a bank account, so depositing to a credit card account is a better option.

BEST BUYS

Antiques

Asian antiques are available in shopping centres at Tanglin Road and Cuppage Road. They can also be found in shops in hotel arcades.

Chinese antiques are the most widely available, and include ceramics, jade, bronze items and scrolls. The range of ceramics is particularly good, and collectors can find pieces from the Tang and

Qing dynasties. Thai ceramics from the kilns of Sawankalok and Sukhothai are also available.

Indonesian antiques include wooden dance masks, figures of mythical beasts, silver daggers, gongs and puppets. Indian antiques include brass lamps, bronze statuettes and in-laid jewellery boxes.

Batik

The best place to buy batik is in Arab Street. It is sold in lengths, or already made into clothing, table-cloths, etc.

Camera Equipment

Available at stores in these areas: North Bridge Road, High Street, Middle Road, Bras Basah Road, Raffles Place, Orchard Road and Scotts Road. You can obtain price lists from the appropriate agent, then shop around for the best price.

Carpets

Orchard Road and Tanglin Road are the best places to shop for rugs from Iran, China, Afghanistan, Turkey and Pakistan. Handmade woollen carpets from India, with designs based on Hindu mythology, can be found at shops in Orchard Road.

Reproductions of Chinese Tai Ping carpets can be seen in the showroom of Singapore Carpet Manufacturers in Orchard Towers. It is possible to have a carpet made to your own design. To visit the factory and see how the carpets are produced, write in advance to Singapore Carpet Manufacturers Pte Ltd, 2 Tractor Road, ph 265 0822.

Electrical Goods

A large range, including calculators, shavers, fans, hair-dryers, audio-visual equipment, irons, kettles and other household appliances, can be found at duty-free prices at complexes and stores in Orchard Road, North Bridge Road, Raffles Place and Sim Lim Square.

Fabrics

Chinese silk stores are found in Tanglin Shopping Centre, Scotts Shopping Centre, Lucky Plaza and in Chinese emporiums. Many sell ready-made silk garments, and will make silk garments to measure from the lengths of fabric they sell.

Fashion Goods

Most department stores and shopping complexes have a wide range of women's clothing, from casual wear to after-five. European fashion boutiques tend to be in hotel arcades and in shopping complexes in Orchard and Scotts Roads.

Tailoring shops are in shopping complexes, hotel arcades and along Coleman Street, Selegie Road, North Bridge Road, Orchard Road and Tanglin Road.

Jewellery

Good outlets for gold, jade, pearls and diamonds are found along Orchard Road, South Bridge Road, New Bridge Road, Arab Street and People's Park Complex. Traditional Indian jewellery is available in Serangoon Road. The Pidemco Centre in South Bridge Road is home to Singapore's Jewellery Mart.

Optical Goods

Leading brands of sunglasses, contact lenses, frames and prescription glasses are available from qualified opticians at reasonable prices. Retail outlets are in the major shopping centres.

Reptile Skin Goods

Handbags, shoes, belts and other accessories made from crocodile, snake and lizard skins are sold in department stores and shopping complexes.

If you are intending to buy skin goods, check if you will be allowed to take them into your home country. They may be a prohibited import.

Sporting Equipment

Most major complexes have a sports store that will meet general needs. For scuba gear visit Plaza Singapura, and windsurfers should try East Coast Sailing Centre in East Coast Parkway. Waterskiing equipment is found in Marina Square, and golf clubs, etc. in Far East Plaza, Centrepoint and Orchard Towers.

Watches

As with electrical goods, watches are duty-free, and are readily available at all shopping complexes.

MAJOR SHOPPING AREAS

☐ Airport

Changi Airport has metropolis-style shopping in its two Terminals, with an extensive range of shops selling international brands of duty-free goods from cosmetics to sporting equipment. The range is particularly extensive in the transit and departure areas, but duty-free shopping is also available to arriving passengers.

The duty-free complex in Terminal Two is the largest in Asia with a selection of over 50 shops, and a one-minute Skytrain ride links the two terminals daily 7am-11pm.

☐ Arab Street

The best place to buy batik, ready-made Malay clothes, basketware, caneware, luggage, ethnic jewellery and perfumes.

☐ Beach Road

Shaw Leisure Gallery is a great place to shop for casual and sportswear, computers and electronic games.

Raffles Hotel Arcade has 70 shops on two levels of the Raffles Hotel, offering high fashion goods, exclusive jewellery, silk, leather, cloisonne ware, carpets and antiques. There are also shops that specialise in Raffles Hotel memorabilia.

☐ Bras Basah Road

Raffles City Shopping Centre is in the Raffles City Complex, which also houses two hotels, a convention centre, a Japanese department store, *Sogo*, and a variety of shops. The centre has many outlets for embroidered linen, handkerchiefs and scarves.

☐ Chinatown-Tanjong Pagar

The shophouses in Chinatown sell many things that Western visitors would not be interested in purchasing, but you can usually get bargain-priced porcelain dinnerware and jade.

The Tanjong Pagar area has been renovated, and is worth a visit for the traditional teashops even if you are not in the market for Asian handicrafts and artifacts. This is also where you can pick up wooden clogs, kites, painted masks, waxed paper umbrellas and lacquerware.

☐ Holland Village

This suburban village is more for the locals, but it has a good range of Asian and continental restaurants, and you may be able to pick up a bargain in antiques, etc.

☐ Little India

Everything Indian can be purchased in this part of the city, and the upper story of Zhujiao Centre with its bazaar-like atmosphere offers goods at unbeatable prices.

☐ Marina Square

The square is a huge mall with *Metro* department store, a supermarket, two mini-cinemas, two entertainment centres, two hawker centres (one indoor, one outdoor), and more than 200 specialty shops. This is a good centre for clothes, shoes, souvenirs, children's wear, sporting goods and leather products.

☐ North Bridge Road-High Street-Coleman Street

The *Capitol Building* on North Bridge Road has four-storeys of high fashion, as well as a sports centre, hair salon, music store and some good restaurants.

The *Funan Centre* in Coleman Street is home to *Tokyu Department Store*, as well as Singapore's largest collection of computers and related products.

Chinatown

☐ Orchard Road

The name is synonymous with shopping and first-time visitors will be amazed at the amount of shopping opportunities presented in this street.

Tudor Court was built in 1927 as a home for junior British officers. It now has designer boutiques,including the biggest *Kookai* boutique in Asia, Ken Done designs from Australia, and top Singapore designers such as Dick Lee, Project Shop, Perry Lim,Montage, Lam, Bods and Jeffrey Seah. Other shops stock leather accessories, children's wear, carpets and bicycles.

Tanglin Shopping Centre, on the tip of Orchard Road, has four levels and some of the tenants are *Antiques of the Orient*, *Hassan's Carpets*, *China Silk House* and *Design Thai*.

Delfi Orchard has six levels of quality shops selling, amongst other things, Royal Selangor pewterware, Waterford crystal, Wedgewood china and a large range of jewellery.

Orchard Towers offers jewellery, antiques, electronic goods, tailors and leathers stores in its five levels.

Palais Renaissance has four levels of designer boutiques such as Karl Lagerfield, Dunhill, Cartier, Christian Dior and Gucci.

Forum Galleria is a small centre, but its main attraction, *Toys 'R' Us* ensures that it has its share of customers.

Far East Shopping Centre has seven levels offering everything imaginable. *Kwok Gallery* on level 3 sells quality antiques.

Liat Towers is home to *Galeries Lafayette* of Paris with its large range of French designer goods.

Lane Crawford is an upmarket department store covering five floors and two sub-basements. The first of this chain in Singapore, it is known as "Hong Kong's answer to Harrods".

International Building is across the street from Liat Towers and has *Melwani's* for Bally shoes, Pancaldi bags and Van Laak fashions.

Shaw House has the Japanese department store *Isetan* that stocks everything. There is also a 5-cinema complex and specialty shops.

Shaw Centre offers fashion, jewellery, shoes and sporting goods.

Pacific Plaza has Studebakers, one of the largest restaurant/fun pubs in the world, and Tower Records, the largest record chain in the USA.

Far East Plaza has five levels with something for everyone from jewellery and tailoring shops to health equipment and computers, and is home to *Metro Department Store*.

Scotts Shopping Centre has two department stores - *Nex'is* and *St Michael's* - a food court, and 55 specialty shops.

C.K. Tang has five floors of goods ranging from household to fashion, books to electronics, shoes to fabrics. This emporium has been operating since 1932.

Lucky Plaza has a few fixed price shops, but the majority are not and bargaining is the way to go.

Wisma Atria is the bright blue centre with the *Isetan Department Store* on one side and a number of boutiques on the other. In the Basement is an aquarium where fish are hand-fed by divers.

Ngee Ann City is one of the largest shopping centres in South-East Asia, and dominates Orchard Road. It is home to *Takashimaya Shopping Centre* which has a department store, specialty shops, restaurants, a health club, a swimming pool and an events hall. Another tenant is world-famous *Tiffany's*.

The Promenade is a "walk-around" shopping centre that has

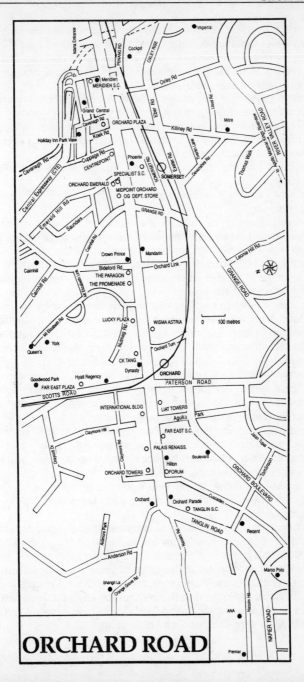

ORCHARD ROAD

Glamourette Boutique, *Allmilmo Mobel* and *Benjamin Electronic Supermart*. There are also fashion boutiques, home furnishings and food.

The Paragon has a *Metro* department store and designer boutiques such as *Gucci*, *Dunhill*, *Bruno Magli*, *Salvatore Ferragamo* and *Cerutti*. A *Sogo* supermarket is in the basement.

Orchard Building is just down from the Mandarin Hotel, and tenant *Halleys* offers one-stop shopping for all types of luxury goods.

OG Department Store is across from the Somerset MRT station, and a good range of clothing and footwear on its eight floors. **Larger sizes are catered for in this centre**.

Midpoint has music shops, art and signage shops and food and snack outlets.

Orchard Emerald is home to Swatch watches, Sony electronics and Fila sportswear.

Specialist Shopping Centre was one of the first in Orchard Road, and has four levels that include the *John Little's* department store. A good place to look for clothes for cooler weather.

Centrepoint contains the legendary *Robinson's Store*, which began trading in 1959. It still offers reasonably-priced home furnishings, clothing, shoes and accessories.

Orchard Point is a popular centre with five levels of shops and a good food court in the basement. Mostly fashion goods are featured.

Orchard Plaza has four levels selling mostly cameras and electronics, although you will find some custom-made shoes and souvenirs.

Meridien Shopping Centre has a huge store in the basement, DFS Collections, which specialises in duty-free goods. On the upper floors there are clothing and accessory boutiques, tailors and souvenir shops.

Plaza Singapura is more less arranged according to levels: 6th floor has musical instruments; 5th, household and sports goods; 4th, lighting, furniture and building supplies; 3rd, audio and video equipment; 2nd, fashion; 1st, electrical goods and appliances; basement, supermarket.

Park Mall is home to boutiques featuring Singapore's leading fashion designers. It also has a factory outlet - Stockmart.

Riverside

Liang Court is a favourite with Japanese visitors. It has *Daimaru*, *Mitsumine & Marusho*, *Kinokuniya* and *Paris Miki*.

Shenton Way

Clifford Centre and the Arcade has a good variety of shops from those selling souvenirs to those who will tailor an outfit in a couple of days.

OUB Shopping Centre is in the heart of the city's banking district. It has five levels of retail shops and food outlets, and a branch of *Galeries Lafayette*. Most shops in this centre close at 8pm.

SIGHTSEEING

CITY

Raffles Hotel

Originally built in 1886, Raffles is one of the last of the great 19th century hotels. It was the haunt of the social elite throughout the colonial era, and many famous writers, including Somerset Maugham, Rudyard Kipling and Joseph Conrad, stayed here. The hotel was given an extensive S$160 million face-lift in the early 1990s.

The Tiffin Room still specialises in the famous Curry Tiffin, and you can still get a Singapore Sling, originally created by a Raffles barman more than 60 years ago.

Raffles now has a shopping arcade with 70 shops, a museum featuring memorabilia from a bygone era, and a Victorian-style playhouse named Jubilee Hall.

The hotel is on Beach Road, a short walk from the MRT station City Hall (C2).

Lau Pa Sat Festival Market

Lau Pa Sat is the largest remaining Victorian filigree cast-iron structure in South-East Asia, and it is located in the heart of Singapore's business district. Built in 1894, it was a wet market, then a food centre, and it has now been restored into a festival market offering food, shopping and entertainment, ph 222 9930. Nearby is Boon Tat Street, Singapore's only street that is closed for evening al fresco dining. Open daily 7am-midnight, the market is a short walk from Raffles Place MRT station (C1).

Statues of Sir Stamford Raffles

A statue of Singapore's founder stands in front of Victoria Theatre, and a copy stands at North Boat Quay on the spot where he is believed to have first stepped ashore. It is obviously known as Raffles' Landing Site.

Civilian War Memorial

Located in Memorial Park, Beach Road, it is dedicated to civilians who died during the Japanese occupation. The simple structure has four tapering white columns that reach 70m into the sky, each representing a different ethnic group. The park is a short walk from City Hall MRT station (C2).

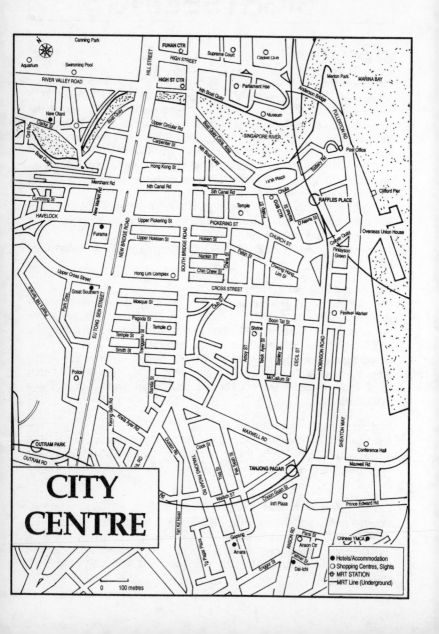

CITY CENTRE

Supreme Court & City Hall

The Supreme Court is in St Andrew's Road and was built in 1939. It is a stately building with Corinthian columns and spacious interiors that feature murals by Italian artist, Cavaliere Rodolfo.

Next door is City Hall, the site of the Japanese surrender to Lord Mountbatten in 1945. Visitors are allowed in the public gallery, but they must be suitably dressed, ie no shorts or thongs, and must not have pagers or portable telephones. The complex is open Mon-Fri 8am-5pm, and access is by MRT to City Hall (C2) and walk along St Andrew's Road towards the Padang.

National Museum

The museum, in Stamford Road, was originally called the Raffles Museum when it opened in 1887. Each of its two levels reflects a different order of classical Greek architecture. Its highlights include 20 dioramas, three-dimensional reconstructions of historical scenes and events from Singaporean history.

It has the Haw Par Jade Collection, various cultural exhibits and the Children's Discovery Gallery. It is open Tues-Sun 9am-5.30pm, and admission is S$2 adults, S$1 child (6-16 years). Note that special exhibitions may involve extra charges. Take the MRT to Dhoby Ghaut (N1) and walk towards Stamford Road.

National Art Gallery

The Gallery adjoins the Museum and has an excellent collection of Singaporean and ASEAN art built around 115 paintings donated by collector and benefactor, the late Dato Loke Wan Tho. It is open Tues-Sun 9am-5.30pm and admission is free.

National Museum

Peranakan Showhouse Museum

Situated at 180 Orchard Road, adjacent to Centrepoint, this small museum is the centre-piece of a neighbourhood steeped in the culture of the intermarriage of Straits-born Chinese with Malays. It has exhibits of the Peranakan lifestyle, with a typical home, and the special rituals associated with a Peranakan wedding. It is open Mon-Fri 10.30am-3.30pm, and admission is S$4 adult, S$2 child under 12.

Fort Canning Park

The Fort was established in 1859 to protect the port of Singapore, and the park covers old Government Hill, once known to the Malays as Forbidden Hill. Its history dates back to the 14th century and includes an old Christian cemetery and a Malay grave believed to be the tomb of the last king of 14th century Temasek. The park is open daily and admission is free. (Dhoby Ghaut station (N1).)

Fort Canning Aquarium

The former Van Kleef Aquarium, and World of Aquarium, has been transformed into the Fort Canning Aquarium and is in Central Park on River Valley Road. The aquarium is open daily 9am-9.30pm and admission is S$4 adult, S$2.50 student, S$2 child under 12 years.

Parliament House

Originally a private mansion, this magnificent building is Singapore's oldest government building, and was designed by the renowned colonial architect, George Coleman. The bronze elephant in front of the building was a gift from King Chulalongkorn of Siam in 1871. Parliament House is in North Boat Quay, and is open by appointment only, made at least a week in advance, with the Clerk-of-Parliament, ph 330 8517.

Empress Place Building

One of Singapore's finest neo-classical buildings, Empress Place has served many roles since it was built in 1854. Extended several times, each addition remained faithful to the original design. Today it is a venue for international cultural and historical exhibitions. The building includes a shopping arcade, a restaurant, and indoor/outdoor function areas with seating capacity for 40 to 1000 guests. Open daily 9am-6.30pm, admission is S$6 adults, S$3 child below 12 years, ph 336 7633.

Merlion Park

A mythical beast, said to be half-lion, half-fish, the Merlion has become the symbol of Singapore. A fountain-statue stands guard at the mouth of the Singapore River. (Raffles Place MRT station (C1).)

Chinatown

Chinatown is bordered by Upper Pickering Street, Cantonment Road, New Bridge and South Bridge Roads, behind the financial district. It is a very colourful part of town that has changed little over the decades. The goods offered are pretty much the same as in any other Chinatown in the world, but it is possible that they will be at better prices here.

The area also has some modern shopping venues - Chinatown Point, People's Park Complex, Chinatown Plaza and Chinatown Complex.

Chinaman Scholar's Gallery

This a faithful re-creation of the home of a Chinese scholar of the 1920s, and it is at 14B Trengganu Street, ph 222 9554. It has a kitchen, bedroom, dining and living areas, with furniture, porcelain, musical instruments and photographs from the period. Open Mon-Sat 9am-4pm, admission is S$4 adult, S$2 child under 12. From Chinatown, walk towards the Sri Mariamman Temple, then take the first street on the right, then first on the left.

Mount Faber

The Mount has landscaped gardens and offers great panoramic views of the harbour, Sentosa and the other southern islands. A cable car service leaves from here for the island of Sentosa. From Orchard Road take SBS 65, 124 or 143.

Guinness World of Records Exhibition

For the first time in Asia, facts and feats from the *Guinness Book of World Records* are displayed in a fascinating exhibition in the World Trade Centre, 1 Maritime Square #02-70, ph 271 8344. Using 3-D life-sized replicas and audio-visual presentations, spectacular human endeavours and amazing facts are presented.

The exhibition is open Mon-Fri 10am-7pm, Sat-Sun and public holidays 9.30am-7pm, and admission is S$5.50 adults, S$3.50 children under 12 years.

On the sea side of the World Trade Centre is the Singapore Cruise Centre, from where domestic and regional ferries and international cruises depart. From Orchard Road, take SBS bus 143.

Singapore Maritime Showcase

On the Harbour Promenade, at #02-131, is the Singapore Maritime Showcase, where there are computer interactive terminals, multi-media movies and an exciting ride that depicts the world's busiest port in the past, the present and the future. It is open Tues-Sun 11am-8pm (until 9pm on Sun and public holidays) and admission is S$5 adult, S$3 child.

Marina City Park

The park offers fine views of the sea, acres of space for kite flying, and some unusual works of art amidst its rolling greenery. These include sculptures of Confucius and seven other Chinese legendary heroes, and a 13m high brass and stainless steel expression of Singapore's aspirations called *Spirit of Youth and Sculpture Fountain*.

Singapore Botanic Gardens

Situated in Cluny Road, the gardens are spread over 52ha and include some 2000 perennial species, and 4ha of jungle. One of the main attractions is the orchid pavilion which has some 12,000 plants, including Singapore's national bloom, the *Vanda Miss Joaquim*. The gardens are open daily 5am-midnight and admission is free. From Orchard Boulevard, take SBS bus 7, 105, 106, 123 or 174.

JURONG

Haw Par Villa

Originally known as the Tiger Balm Gardens, the park reopened in 1990 after a S$80 million expansion program. It now combines ancient Chinese legends with modern technical wizardry. There are exciting rides and a covered amphitheatre where musicals are staged.

Haw Par Villa is open daily 9am-6pm and admission is S$16 adult, S$10 child under 12 years. From Orchard Road take SBS bus 143 to Haw Par, and expect to spend at least three hours visiting.

Royal Selangor Pewter Factory

Pewter, an alloy of tin, copper and antimony, is a specialty of both Singapore and Malaysia and just about every visitor goes home with at least one piece in his/her luggage. At this factory, at 32 Pandan Road, ph 265 7711, you can see the whole process from melting to casting, soldering, polishing and hammering, and then you will have a chance to buy. If you are not interested in spending you can spend some time in the private collection of antique pewter pieces. The factory is open daily 8.30am-5.30pm and to get there, take the MRT to Clementi (W8), then a taxi or SBS bus 78.

New Ming Village

It was during the Ming and Qing dynasties of ancient China that the art of Porcelain-making reached its peak, and pieces from those periods are worth a fortune. The New Ming Village, 32 Pandan Road, ph 265 7711, has exhibitions of craftsmen at work on reproductions of those valuable works of art, and visitors can buy affordable porcelain from their shop. Open daily 9am-5.30pm, access is by the MRT to Clementi (W8), then a taxi or SBS bus 78.

Singapore Science Centre

The centre has over 600 exhibits that explain the world of science, with specially built Crazy Rooms where visitors can explore the effects of scientific principles. A highlight is the Aviation Gallery which introduces the principles of flight. Throughout the centre computers present fun ways to test your knowledge of science, and all information is presented in easily understood forms.

The centre is open Tues-Sun 10am-6pm and admission is S$3 adult, S$1.50 child under 16 years. The **Omnimax** shows range from S$8-10 adult, and S$4-5 child under 12, and showtimes are noon, 1pm, 2pm, 4pm, 7pm and 8pm. The **Planetarium** shows cost S$8 adult, S$3 child under 12. Singapore Science Centre is on Science Centre Road, ph 560 3316, and can be reached to taking the MRT to Jurong East (W9), then SBS bus 335.

Chinese & Japanese Gardens

The two gardens are side by side in Yuan Ching Road, and they reveal two very different styles of landscaping. The Chinese Garden recalls the style favoured in the imperial Sung Dynasty, and is very grand. The Japanese Garden has a minimalist landscaping style in keeping with its name, the Garden of Tranquillity.

The gardens are open Mon-Fri 9am-7pm, Sat-Sun 8.30am-7pm, and admission is S$4.50 adult, S$2 child under 12 years. The address is Jurong Park, Yuan Ching Road, ph 264 3455, a five minute walk from the Chinese Garden MRT station (W10).

Tang Dynasty City

Asia's largest cultural and historical theme park, Tang Dynasty City is a recreation of Chang-An, the capital of 7th century Tang China. Attractions include the Great Wall, a gallery of life-sized terracotta Xian warriors, and over 100 life-sized historical figures such as Confucius, Genghis Khan, Dr Sun Yat Sen and Mao Zedong. The Silk Road Market Place features merchants, live processions and performances and historical re-enactments of events from the Tang Dynasty.

The City is open daily 9.30am-6.30pm and admission is S$15 adult, S$10 child under 12 years. To get there take the MRT to Lakeside (W11), then from opposite the station take SBS bus 154 or 240.

Mint Coin Gallery

The gallery has an impressive collection of coins, medals and medallions from all over the world. Visitors can mint their own souvenir coin at the press here. Situated at 249 Jalan Boon Lay, ph 261 4749, the gallery is open Mon-Fri 9am-4pm and there is no admission fee. Take the MRT to Boon Lay (W12).

Jurong Crocodile Paradise

Landscaped streams and enclosures create a natural habitat for over 2500 crocodiles. There are underwater viewing areas, and the breeding enclosure has watchful mothers guarding nests of eggs. Situated at 241 Jalan Ahmad Ibrahim, ph 261 8866, the park is open daily 9am-6pm and admission is S$4.50 adult, S$2.50 child under 12 years. Show times are: **Crocodile Feeding** - 10.15am, 5pm; **Crocodile Wrestling** - 11.45am, 2pm (and 4pm on Sun and public holidays); **Dundee Show** - 10.45am, 3pm. To get there take the MRT to Boon Lay (W12), then take SBS bus 251, 253 or 255.

Jurong BirdPark

Next to the Crocodile Paradise is the largest bird park in South-East Asia, with over 8000 birds of some 600 species. Attractions include the world's largest collection of South-East Asian Hornbills and South American Toucans, and the world's second largest penguin exhibit. The best way to see the entire park is to board the air-conditioned monorail system called the Panorail.

Daily shows include Breakfast with the Birds (9am-11am), Birds of Prey, Penguin Feeding Time, and the JBP All Stars Birdshow. The park is open daily 9am-6pm (Panorail 9am-5.30pm) and admission is S$9 adult, S$3 child under 12 years, ph 265 0022. Panorail fares are S$2 adult, S$1 child, and Breakfast with the Birds costs S$12 adult, S$10 child. See the Jurong Crocodile Paradise for information on getting to the Birdpark.

NORTH

Bukit Timah Nature Reserve

The reserve is on Hindhede Drive and can be reached by taking the MRT to Newton station (N4), then SBS bus 67, 170 or 171, or TIBS bus 182. It is only 12km from the city centre and is one of the last remaining areas of primary rainforest in Singapore, containing more species of trees than the entire North American continent.

At the heart of the reserve lies Bukit Timah Hill, the highest point in Singapore at 165m. The reserve is open daily and admission is free.

Singapore Zoological Gardens

The zoo is in Mandai Lake Road, ph 269 3411, and is open daily

8.30am-6pm. It is acclaimed as one of the world's most spectacular zoos, with streams, rock walls and vegetation replacing the old walls and bars to separate the more than 2000 animals. The zoo has many endangered species, including the world's largest colony of orang-utans, with whom visitors can have breakfast or afternoon tea if bookings are made in advance through hotels.

Admission is S$9 adult, S$4 child (3-12 years); Breakfast with an orang-utan costs S$15 adult, S$11 child (plus admission); High tea with an orang-utan (except Sun and public holidays) costs S$10 adult, S$8 child (plus admission).

A new adventure offered by the zoo is the **Night Safari**, which is laid out in eight zones within the 40ha of secondary jungle adjacent to the zoo. It features animals from the Himalayan foothills, the Malaysian rainforest, Africa, the Nepalese river valley, India, tropical Africa and the Indo-Malayan region. It is open daily 7.30pm-midnight. Admission is S$15 adult, S$10 children below 12.

To get to the zoo take the MRT to Ang Mo Kio (N9) station, then SBS bus 138.

Check with your hotel tour desk about express bus/zoo trips that can work out cheaper, especially if you are travelling with kids.

A regular tram service that covers the entire zoo gives an excellent overview of the complex, complemented by a taped commentary.

Mandai Orchid Gardens

A whole hillside is covered in brilliant blooms, some of which are over 2m high. The gardens are open daily 8.30am-5.30pm, and admission is S$2 adult, S$0.50 child under 12 years.

The gardens are on Mandai Lake Road, ph 269 1036, and to get there take the MRT to Ang Mo Kio (N9) station, then SBS bus 138.

Kranji War Memorial

Situated in Woodlands, an hour's drive from Orchard Road (TIBS bus 182 from Hill Street), are the beautifully landscaped grounds and peaceful environment of Kranji War Memorial. The park is dedicated to the Allied troops who died in the defence and fall of Singapore during the second world war. The memorial's walls are inscribed with the names of those who died, and a register is available for inspection from the custodian.

EAST COAST

Arab Street

Arab Street was a thriving trading district in the 1800s, and is still going strong today. In fact, Arab Street runs through the middle of a rough square bounded by Beach Road, Ophir Road, Victoria Street and Jalan Sultan, and has gives its name to the whole area. Many shops still specialise in Muslim products such as prayer rugs, skull caps, etc, but there is still much to tempt the Westerner - luxurious fabrics, genuine batik, & at the top end near North Bridge Rd, goldsmiths & jewellers.

Take the MRT to Bugis station (E1) and walk along Victoria Street towards Arab Street.

Little India

The area around Serangoon Road is home to Singapore's Indian community, and is therefore called Little India. All things Indian are available and the scent of spices will greet you before you actually arrive. This part of Singapore really comes into its own during Deepavali, the Hindu Festival of Lights. From Orchard Road take SBS bus 64, 65, 106 or 111.

Singapore Crocodilarium

Over 1000 live crocodiles at close range, and a shop with products made from crocodile skins at even closer range, are to be found at 730 East Coast Parkway, ph 447 3722. It is open daily 9am-5pm and feeding time is 11am on Tues, Thurs and Sat.

Take the MRT to Paya Lebar (E5) or Eunos (E6) and a taxi from there.

East Coast Park

Located off the East Coast Parkway, the park is a favourite with Singaporeans. There is a beach, landscaped gardens, bike tracks, water slide, bowling alley, golf driving range, tennis and squash complexes, watersports centre, swimming lagoon, the East Coast Sailing Centre, and a number of fine seafood restaurants and fast food outlets. From Orchard Road, take SBS bus 16.

Malay Village

Also accessible from MRT station Paya Lebar (E5) is Malay Village, the cultural showcase of Singapore's Malay community. The low-rise complex in Geylang Serai has restaurants and shops specialising in Malay cuisine, goods, arts and crafts.

Changi Prison Chapel and Museum

The Changi Prison Chapel is a replica of the original built by Allied POWs during World War II, with a simple thatched roof and outdoor pews. The museum has sketches, watercolours, photographs and other memorabilia, including a pair of rail spikes from the Thai-Burma railway, and a photograph of the quilt made by women inmates. Embroidered with their names, it was the only signal that they were still alive.

The museum is open 9.30am-4.30pm Mon-Sat, and admission is free. There is a service in the chapel at 5.30pm on Sundays, ph 743 7885. It is situated 20km Upper Changi Road North, and can be access by MRT to Tanah Merah (E9), then SBS bus 2.

Singapore Air Force Museum

Situated at Block 78 Cranwell Road, off Loyang Avenue, ph 540 1537, this museum is open Tues-Sun 10am-4.30pm and admission is free. It shows exhibits from the growth of the force from the Malayan Volunteer Air Force in 1939, to the Royal Singapore Air Force, to the present Republic of Singapore Air Force. Take the MRT to Tanah Merah (E9), then SBS bus 2 or 9.

Pasir Ris Park

The park is bounded by Pasir Ris Drive, Pasir Ris Drive 3 and Sungei Tampines, and its 17ha includes a 6ha mangrove swamp. The swamp is crossed by boardwalks enabling visitors to get a close-up look at mangrove flora and fauna. Pasir Ris Park is a favourite with the locals who come here to birdwatch, cycle, fly kites, swim and picnic.

SENTOSA

Sentosa is Singapore's holiday resort island, and there is a choice of how to get there: by cable car from Mount Faber and the World Trade Centre; by ferry from the World Trade Centre; or overland by the Causeway-bridge.

There is so much to see that many visitors check into either the Beaufort Sentosa or the Shangri-La Rasa Sentosa Beach Resort for at least one night. Of course, it is not hard to take the luxury of these two hotels, with their watersports and golf courses.

A monorail track operates in the north-western part of the island, allowing easy access to the various attractions.

Asian Village

The village showcases ethnic foods, architecture, arts and crafts from around the region. It also offers eleven exhilarating rides at its Family Entertainment Centre. Open daily 10am-9pm, admission is S$5 adult, S$3 child. Showtimes: 11am, 3.30pm.

Underwater World

Asia's largest tropical oceanarium houses over 2000 species of fish that can be viewed from a submerged perspex walkway. A special inhabitant is the Weedy Seadragon, a fish that resembles the mythical dragons in Chinese folklore. Underwater World is open daily 9am-9pm and admission is S$10 adult, S$5 child.

Fort Siloso

The 19th century fort has underground tunnels and cannons and was the last bastion of the British forces during the Japanese invasion of Singapore. A S$6 million upgrading enables visitors to experience the harsh living conditions of the soldiers stationed at the fort during the period from 1885 to 1942. Due to the use of special liquid scents, this "experience" includes the smells as well as the sights of barracks life.

A new exhibit is called *Behind Bars*, and it shows what life was like for the Allied POWs in Changi Prison during World War II.

Fort Siloso is open daily 9am-7pm and admission is S$3 adult, S$2 child.

Butterfly Park

This park has 2500 live butterflies from over 50 species, and an insectarium with lots of creepy crawlies. Open Mon-Sat 9am-6pm, Sun and public holidays 9am-6.30pm, and admission is $4 adult, $2 child.

Rare Stone Museum

Claimed to be the only one of its kind in the world, this museum has over 4000 stones that have been shaped by nature. It is worth having a short visit. Open 9am-7pm daily and admission is S$2 adult, S$1 child.

Pioneers of Singapore & Surrender Chamber

This exhibition features 89 figures in tableaux of people who were important in the history of Singapore, as well as those who were involved in the Japanese invasion and the Allied surrender. Open daily 9am-9pm and admission is S$3 adult, S$1 child.

Maritime Museum

This museum features vessels from the earliest primitive craft to the latest tankers, battleships and luxury cruisers. It is open daily 10am-7pm and admission is S$1 adult, S$0.50 child.

Fantasy Island

Asia's largest water theme park, Fantasy Island covers an area of 71,000 sq m, and around 1.4 million gallons of water flow constantly through the park's 32 slides and 13 water rides.

Every conceivable type of ride and slide has been included in the S$50 million facility. Visitors can choose their method of descent - feet-first, head-first, on their backs or on tubes, mats or rafts. And they can select the speed - from drifting to 36km per hour, and even if they wish to be above ground or underground.

It wouldn't be Singapore if there weren't shops and restaurants to cater for your every need, and of course there are. Fantasy Island is open daily 9.30am-7pm and admission is S$16 adult, S$10 child under 12 and over 3.

Cinemania

A new attraction is Cinemania, a S$2.4 million 48-seat theatre that takes visitors on the "Devil's Mine Ride", a terrifying 3-4 minute adventure that has won two major international awards. No, it is not all done with mirrors. The theatre has equipment that can run a 70mm film at 60 frames a second, with special sound systems that surround the audience, and seats that will jolt, dip, skid, heave and sway as the action on the screen unfolds. This adventure is not recommended for small children or people with special health problems. Admission is S$6 adult, S$4 child under 12.

VolcanoLand

This is a multi-sensory experience where you can discover aspects of the extinct Mayan civilisation, fossils, archaeological digs and where a "pit cage" can transport you to the centre of the world's most active volcano - guaranteed to erupt every half-hour. The "eruption" produces a 30m column of smoke that can be seen from the World Trade Centre. Open daily 9am-9pm, and admission is S$10 adults, S$5 child.

Mississippi River-Boat

This turn-of-the-century river-boat has a fast food outlet and a seafood restaurant, and is ideal for relaxing after a busy day enjoying the delights of Sentosa.

Musical Fountain

An unusual feature where the water formations respond to the different sounds.

Travel to Sentosa

Firstly, it must be mentioned that there is an entry fee to the island of S$5 adult, S$3 child, and then there are separate entry fees for each attraction. A visit to Sentosa can be an expensive day, so if you are travelling with children a picnic lunch could be a very good idea. There are day and evening tour packages with pick-up from your hotel, or you can travel independently on public transport.

From Orchard Road, take SBS bus 65 or 143, and from Chinatown take SBS bus 61, 84, 143, 145 or 166, to the World Trade Centre. From there you can take either the Sentosa Bus Service A, the Sentosa Ferry, the Cable Car, or walk across the causeway bridge to Sentosa.

Alternatively, take the MRT to Tiong Bahru (W3) and transfer to Sentosa Bus Service B or C.

Sentosa Bus Service A - World Trade Centre to Underwater World - Mon-Thurs 7.15am-11.30pm (until 12.30am Fri-Sun and public holidays - return fares are S$6 adult, S$4 child, includes basic admission to the island.

Sentosa Bus Service B - Tiong Bahru MRT to Central Beach - weekends, public holidays and school holidays only 8.20am-7.30pm - return fares are S$6 adult, S$4 child, and include basic admission to the island.

Sentosa Bus Service C - Tiong Bahru MRT to Sentosa Ferry Terminal - daily - 7.20am-11.30pm - return fares are S$6 adult, S$4 child, and include basic admission to the island.

Orchard Service E - from Orchard Road to Sentosa's Coach Park - return fares are S$7 adult, S$3 child, and include basic admission to the island.

Sentosa Ferry - daily - 10am-9pm - return fare is S$1.20 adult/child. The entry fee to the island must then be paid.

Cable Car - daily - 8.30am-9pm - 1 station S$5 adult; 2 stations S$5.50 adult; scenic trip S$6.50 adult. There is a flat S$3 rate for children. The entry fee to the island must then be paid.

KUSU ISLAND

Kusu is 30 minutes away by ferry from the Singapore Cruise Centre, and the warm waters of its lagoon are ideal for swimming. From its beaches and its hilltop you can get quite stunning views of the mainland.

The island has a Malay shrine and a Chinese temple which are part of an interesting legend. A giant sea turtle is believed to have turned into an island to save two shipwrecked sailors, a Malay and a Chinese.

Ferries depart at 10am and 1.30pm Mon-Sat, and 9.45am-5pm Sun and public holidays, at 1 1/2 hour intervals. Return fares are S$6 adult, S$3 child. For more information, ph 270 7888.

PULAU UBIN

If you want to know what Singapore looked like 30 years ago, take a trip to Pulau Ubin. It has thatched huts, backyard orchards, dirt tracks, vegetation gone wild, and traditional fishing huts called kelongs that are built on stilts over the water.

The island also has some interesting wildlife, including bats, monkeys, squirrels, and the Purple Jungle Fowl, the bird from which all the world's domestic chickens are descended.

Attractions include several Chinese temples, including one in a cave that is only accessible at low tide, a traditional mosque, a quarry lake and a Buddhist meditation centre. More distant parts of the island can be explored by bicycle, which can be hired.

There are no regular ferry services to Pulau Ubin, but boats can be hired or shared at Changi Jetty. Costs are about S$2-3 for the 10 minute trip. For more information, ph 320 9913.

ST JOHN'S ISLAND

St John's is an hour ferry trip from the Cruise Centre, and was formerly a penal settlement. It is now a resort island with swimming lagoons, beaches, camping and picnic grounds, hiking routes, holiday hostels and soccer fields - perfect for a break away from it all.

Ferries department from the Singapore Cruise Centre at 10am and 1.30pm Mon-Sat and 9.45-5.15pm Sun and public holidays at 1 1/2 hour intervals. Return fares are S$6 adult, S$3 child. For more information, ph 270 7888.

SOUTHERN ISLANDS

Pulau Hantu, Pulau Seking, Lazarus and Sisters Islands are tiny islands with sandy beaches and waters that are recommended for swimming, snorkelling and scuba diving. **Note that it is recommended that only experienced divers try the waters off Lazarus and Sisters Islands.**

Ferries leave from the World Trade Centre's Jardine Steps or Clifford Pier. Cost of the ferry ride is S$15-20 per person, return, and there is a minimum of 10-15 passengers. The trip takes about one hour. For more information contact the World Trade Centre Information Centre, ph 321 1972.

PLACES OF WORSHIP

Churches
St Gregory the Illuminator, 60 Hill St, ph 334 0141 - Singapore's oldest church-Armenian-a short walk from City Hall MRT station (C2).
Cathedral of the Good Shepherd, Queen Street, ph 337 6870 - Catholic - a short walk from City Hall MRT station (C2).
St Andrew's Cathedral, Coleman Street, ph 337 6104 - Anglican - a short walk from City Hall MRT station (C2).
St Joseph's Church, 143 Victoria Street, ph 338 3167 - Catholic - a short walk from Bugis MRT station (E1).

Mosques
Abdul Gaffoor Mosque, 41 Dunlop Street, ph 295 4209 - a short walk from Bugis MRT station (E1).

Hajjah Fatimah Mosque, 4001 Beach Road - a short walk from Lavender MRT station (E2).

Nagore Durgha Shrine, 140 Telok Ayer Street - a short walk from Raffles Place MRT station (C1).

Sultan Mosque, North Bridge Road, ph 293 4405 - between Bugis (E1) and Lavender (E2) MRT stations.

Synagogue

Maghain Aboth Synagogue, 24 Waterloo Street, ph 336 0692 - a short walk from Bugis MRT station (E1).

Temples

Central Sikh Temple, 731 Serangoon Road, ph 299 3855 - take a taxi from Dhoby Ghaut MRT station (N1).

Fuk Tak Ch'i Temple, 76 Telok Ayer Street, ph 253 4107 - Shentoist - a short walk from Raffles Place MRT station (C1).

Kong Meng San Phor Kark See Temple, 88 Bright Hill Drive, ph 452 4223 - Buddhist - take a taxi from Bishan MRT station (N8).

Siong Lim Temple, 184E Jalan Toa Payoh - Buddhist - a short walk from Toa Payoh MRT station (N6).

Sri Mariamman Temple, 244 South Bridge Road, ph 223 0464 - Hindu - a short walk from Tanjong Pagar MRT station (W1).

Sri Thandayuthapani Temple, 15 Tank Road - Hindu - a short walk from Dhoby Ghaut MRT (M1).

Tan Si Chong Su Temple, Magazine Road - Hokkien - take a taxi from Raffles Place (C2) or Dhoby Ghaut (N1) MRT stations.

Temple of 1000 Lights, 366 Race Course Road, ph 294 0714 - Buddhist - take a taxi from Dhoby Ghaut MRT station (N1).

Thian Hock Kheng Temple, 158 Telok Ayer Street, ph 222 2651 - Taoist-Buddhist - a short walk from Raffles Place MRT station (C1).

NOTES

TOURS

Tours offered in Singapore range from city sights to island hopping and wining and dining. Bookings and pick-up times can be arranged through your hotel desk. The prices in the following selection should be used as a guide only.

City Tours

The routes of these vary from company to company, but generally they visit the ethnic quarters, the downtown area, the housing estates, and the Botanic Gardens. The duration ranges from 3 to 3 1/5 hours, and the prices are S$20-25 adult, S$10-14 child.

Island Tours

Sunday Special by Singapore Sightseeing Tour East.

Drive through Little India and browse through the quaint shophouses of Chinatown. Visit specialised factories, Kwong Min Hill Chinese Temple and the orchid nursery in Mandai forest reserve. On then to Malaysia and Johor Bahru to visit a typical Malay village, watch songket weaving and batik painting. Last attraction - the Central Market to practise haggling skills. Note that Passports are required. The duration is 7 hours - S$69 adult, S$35 child.

Round Island Tour by Singapore Sightseeing Tour East.

Visit wholesale market, then Ming Village, Jurong Crocodile Paradise, then lunch at a seafood restaurant. Next stop is a modern housing estate, a Buddhist temple complex, a trip by bumboat from Changi Creek, past the fish traps perched above the waters of the Johor Straits. Duration is 7 1/2 hours - S$67 adult, S$34 child.

Sentosa Tour by most tour operators.

Tours usually include a cable car ride across the harbour to/from Sentosa. Attractions visited on the island include the Butterfly Park, Insectarium, Fountain Gardens and the Pioneers of Singapore Exhibition and Surrender Chambers. Some tours also visit Fort Siloso. Duration is 3 1/2 to 4 hours - $37-40 adult, S$18-20 child.

Underwater World, Sentosa by RMG Tours, Holiday Tours and Grayline.

Travel on a moving walkway through a perspex tunnel and see the marine creatures up close. Children will like the touch pool and adults the anemones in the tidal pool. The tour takes in the others attractions of Sentosa, including the Musical Fountain Show and the Surrender Chambers. Duration is 3 1/2 to 4 hours - S$47-49 adult, S$24-26 child.

Attractions Tours

Haw Par Villa - 3 1/2 hours - S$27-29 adult, S$14-18 child.

Jurong Extension - 7 hours - S$54 adult, S$30 child, includes lunch.

Jurong BirdPark & Ming Village - 3 1/2 hours - S429-31 adult, S$15-17 child.

Jurong BirdPark & Crocodile Paradise - 3 1/2 hours - S$34 adult, $19 child.

Night Safari - 3 1/2 hours - S$38-43 adult, S$2021 child.

Tang Dynasty Tour - 3 1/2 hours - S$31-32 adult, S$17-18 child.

Tang Discovery Tour - 3 1/2 hours - S$57 adult, S$43 child (includes lunch).

Zoo Tours - 4 1/2 hours - S$51 adult, S$26 child (includes breakfast. There are many other Zoo Tours run by different companies.

Night Tours

ASEAN Night - 2 hours - S$46 adult, S$27 child (includes dinner).

Sentosa Evening Tour - 3 1/2 to 4 1/2 hours - S$49-52 adult, S$26-27 child.

Singapore By Night - 3 1/2 to 4 hours - S$51-53 adult, S$26-31 child.

Special Interest Tours

Battlefield Tours of Singapore - 4 hours - S$39 adult, S$25 child.

Shop Till U Drop - 3 1/2 hours - $21 adult, $11 child.

Boat Quay Wine and Dine Passport - free and easy tour - S$35-56 adult (no children).

Helicopter Sightseeing Tour - 1/2 hour Mon-Fri (min 4 pax) - S$150 adult, S$75 child.

Horse Racing Tour - 6 hours - S$70 adult (no children) includes lunch.

The above is really only the tip of the iceberg. Make sure you pick up some brochures and check out all the available tours.

NOTES

SPORT

Singapore has excellent sporting facilities, and the preferred sports of the locals are golf, tennis, soccer, and watersports of all kinds.

Bowling

There are about 16 bowling centres in Singapore, each offering more than 20 lanes. Most centres open at 9am and close between 1am and 2am. Prices range from S$2 to S$4 per game, and are usually higher are 6pm and on the weekends. For more information contact Singapore Tenpin Bowling Congress, 400 Balestier Road, #01-01 Balestier Plaza, ph 355 0136, fax 355 0390.

Canoeing

There are various private hire companies at Changi Point, East Coast Park and on Sentosa Island. Operating hours are usually 9am-6pm every day, and costs are S$6-10 single seaters, S$8-12 double seaters.

Cycling

Bicycle renting places are found at a number of public parks, including East Coast Parkway, Sentosa, Pasir Ris, Bishan and Pulau Ubin. They are usually open daily 8am-6pm and charges are around S$5-8 per hour. Sometimes a refundable deposit is required.

Golf

Generally clubs are open daily 7am-7pm, with some offering night golfing until 11pm. It is difficult for visitors to get a game on the weekends, and some clubs also require a handicap or proficiency certificate from a recognised club in your home country. Fees range between S$50 and S$200. Here are some names and numbers.

Changi Golf Club, ph 545 5133
Executive Golf Club, ph 453 2700
Green Fairways (driving range only), ph 468 8409.
Jurong Country Club (including driving range), ph 560 5655.
Keppel Club (including driving range), ph 273 5522.
Marina Bay Golf & Country Club, ph 221 2811.
Orchid Country Club (including driving range), ph 755 9811.
Parkland Golf Driving Range (driving range only), ph 440 6726.
Raffles Country Club (including driving range), ph 861 7655.
Seletar Country Club (including driving range), ph 481 4745.
Sembawang Country Club (including driving range), ph 257 0642.
Sentosa Golf Club, ph 275 0022.

Singapore Island Country Club, ph 459 2222.
Warren Golf Club (including driving range), ph 777 6533.

Horse Racing

Contact the Singapore Turf Club, ph 469 3611, for details of on-course racing dates. Meetings are held on Saturdays and Sundays only, but not every week.

Scuba Diving

Day and night diving in local waters and off the Malaysian coast are available. Costs range between S$380-S$480, including all equipment. Some names and numbers:

Asia Aquatic, ph 738 8158.
Great Blue Dive Shop, ph 467 0767.
Leeway Sub-Aquatic Paradise, ph 743 1208.
Mako Sub-Aquatics, ph 774 1440.
Pro Diving Services, ph 291 2261.
Sharkeys Scubanauts, ph 337 4836.

Snooker

There are many snooker parlours in Singapore and to find out the one nearest to you, look in the Yellow Pages of the telephone directory, or contact Singapore Billiards & Snooker Council, ph 440 5155.

Water Skiing

The locals water ski off Sembawang, and on the Kallang River. Costs range from S$65 to S$85 per hour. Some names and numbers:

William Water Sports, ph 282 6879.
Bernatt Boating & Skiing, ph 257 5859.
Cowabunga Ski Centre, ph 344 8813.

Windsurfing/Sailing

Contact *East Coast Sailing Centre*, ph 449 5118. Operating hours are 9.30am-6.30pm daily, and costs are around S$20 per hour for Lasers/Sailing, and S$20 for 2 hours for a windsurfer. A refundable deposit is required.

Malaysia

Malaysia is situated in the central part of South-East Asia, just north of the Equator. To the north are Myanma, Thailand, Laos, Kampuchea and Vietnam; to the south are Singapore and Indonesia; and to the east are the islands of the Philippines.

The land mass of Malaysia is made up of two parts, the Malay Peninsula and the states of Sabah and Sarawak on the island of Borneo. The total land area is 330,434 sq km, with 131,587 sq km in Peninsular Malaysia and 198,847 sq km in Sabah and Sarawak.

Malaysia is divided into thirteen states, eleven in Peninsular Malaysia and two on the island of Borneo, and two federal territories - Kuala Lumpur and Labuan, an island off the coast of Sabah. Nine of the states have hereditary rulers, and the Supreme Head of State, the Yang Di Pertuan Agong (King), is elected every five years from among these rulers. The thirteen states are listed below with their capitals.

Perlis - Kangar
Kedah - Alor Setar
Penang - Georgetown
Perak - Ipoh
Negeri Selangor Darul Ehsan - Shah Alam
Negeri Sembilan - Seremban
Melaka - Melaka
Johor - Johor Bahru
Negeri Pahang Darul Makmur - Kuantan
Terengganu - Kuala Terengganu
Kelantan - Kota Bharu
Sabah - Kota Kinabalu
Sarawak - Kuching.

The head of government is the Prime Minister, who must be a member of the Dewan Rakyat (House of Representatives). The Parliament itself comprises two houses: the Dewan Rakyat, which is fully elective, and the Dewan Negara (Senate) to which members are nominated by the King from among citizens who have rendered distinguished public service, or have achieved distinction in the professions, or are representatives of racial minorities, or are capable of

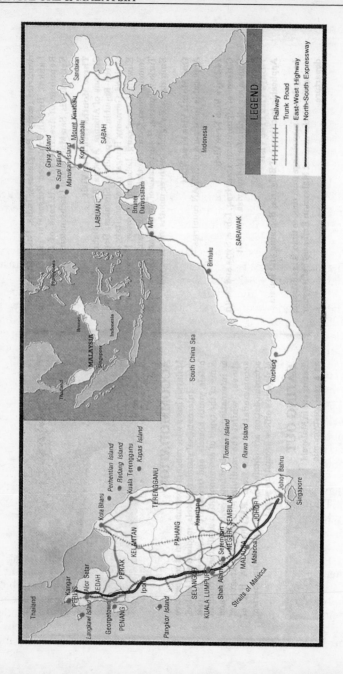

representing the interests of the aborigines.

As Head of Government, the Prime Minister leads the Cabinet, which is made up of the various Ministers of Government. Each of the thirteen states also has its own Chief Minister, or Menteri Besar, who is also elected to office, and its own (elected) State Assembly.

Malaysia is among the world's largest producers of tin, rubber and palm oil. Other major products are petroleum (exploration and production are under the supervision of the national oil corporation, Petronas), timber and pepper. A number of agencies have also been set up to speed industrialization, and the implementation of the New Economic Policy (NEP).

Transportation is a fast-growing industry, with Malaysian Airline System (MAS) leading the field in air services. Tourism is another growing and important industry and a special agency, Tourism Malaysia, has been set up to promote Malaysia as a destination. It has offices throughout the country and overseas in Australia, Canada, France, Germany, Hong Kong, Italy, Japan, Singapore, South Africa, South Korea, Sweden, Taiwan, Thailand, UK and the USA.

The **national flag** of Malaysia has 14 red and white horizontal stripes of equal width and a yellow 14-pointed star in a dark blue canton, representing the equal membership of the 13 States and the Federal Government. The canton also contains a yellow crescent, the symbol of Islam. Yellow is considered to be the royal colour.

Malaysia's **national flower** is the *Bunga Raya* - the hibiscus. Although there are many varieties of this flower, the one chosen is red in colour with five petals, and can be found throughout the country.

HISTORY

Because of its strategic position between the Indian Ocean and the South China Sea, Malaysia has long been a meeting place for traders and travellers from the West and the East. Hence, its history is one of continual interaction with foreign powers and influences.

The earliest known kingdom was that of Kedah, mentioned in Chinese and Sanskrit records as early as 600 to 700AD. Hindu-Buddhist influence was strong in the centuries before the coming of Islam. By 1400, when the Malacca Malay Kingdom was at the height of its power, Islam had become a major influence. By 1511, however, Melaka (Malacca) fell to the Portuguese.

Hard on the heels of the Portuguese came the Dutch. With the help of Johor and Naning Malays, the Dutch attacked and defeated the Portuguese in 1641. Melaka was under Dutch control until 1824, when the Anglo-Dutch Treaty saw it exchanged for Bencoolen, the English-held territory on the other side of the Straits.

The first English ship to arrive in Malayan waters was the *Edward Bonaventure*, commanded by Edward Lancaster. She anchored off

Penang from June to August 1592 to take on fresh provisions. Thereafter came Francis Light and Stamford Raffles, of Singapore fame, who stayed in Melaka in the early 1800s when Dutch power fell to Napoleon's armies. By the time the English officially occupied Melaka, they had two other ports under their control. Francis Light had founded Penang for the East India Company, and Stamford Raffles had established Singapore. From these three ports the English penetrated inland. Through friendly treaties, relentless persuasion and negotiations with powerful Thailand in the north, the English slowly extended their control over all the states of the Malay Peninsula.

Sarawak, once part of the Sultan of Brunei's empire, had been ruled since 1841 by a British adventurer, James Brooke, and his descendants. In 1888 Sarawak and North Borneo (Sabah) became British protectorates. By the 1920s all states that eventually comprised Malaysia were under English control.

The British period saw the construction of roads and many fine colonial buildings, but the most important things they left behind were the established system of government offices and the use of the English language, the language of business and diplomacy world-wide. The first stirrings of Malaysian nationalism were felt as early as the 1930s, and following the end of World War II, the momentum of nationalism resumed, culminating in independence for the Federation of Malaya in 1957.

In 1963 Malaysia was formed, bringing together the States of Malaya, Singapore, Sabah and Sarawak. Singapore however, left the federation in 1965.

Today Malaysia is a member of the six-nation Association of South East Asian Nations (ASEAN). This association, comprising Malaysia, Thailand, Indonesia, Singapore, Brunei Darussalam and the Philippines, was formed to promote greater economic, social and cultural co-operation among these nations.

CLIMATE

There are no distinct seasons and temperatures vary little throughout the year, ranging from 21C to 32C, with cooler temperatures in the hill resorts. Humidity is high all year, and can be oppressive if visitors are not dressed for it. Cotton fabrics that can breathe are recommended, and a hat is essential. Average annual rainfall varies from 2000 to 2500mm.

POPULATION

Malaysia is a multi-racial country with a population of around 19 million. Malays, Chinese, Indians and the indigenous people of Sabah and Sarawak form the majority of the population, however Muslim

Malays dominate government and the bureaucracy.

All schools in Malaysia follow a common curriculum and syllabus.

LANGUAGE

Bahasa Melayu is the national language, and is the medium of instruction in all schools. English is widely used all over the country, especially in business, and is a compulsory subject in school. Other languages used are Chinese (Mandarin) and Tamil.

Here are some words and phrases that might come in handy. Pronunciation guide - 'a' as in far, 'c' as in chip, 'sy' as in shut, 'g' as in girl.

Greetings

Welcome	Selamat datang
Hello	Hello
How do you do?	Apa khabar?
Good morning	Selamat pagi
Good afternoon	Selamat petang
Good night	Selamat malam
Good bye	Selamat tinggal
Fine	Baik

Pronouns

I	Saya
You	Anda/Awak
We	Kami
He/She	Dia
They	Mereka

Questions

Can you help me?	Bolehkah encik tolong saya?
How do I get there	Bagaimanakah saya boleh ke sana?
How far?	Berapa Jauh?
How long will it take?	Berapa lama?
How much (price)	Berapa Harganya?
What is this/that	Apakah ini/itu?
What is your name sir?	Siapa nama encik?
When?	Bila?
Where?	Di mana?
Why?	Mengapa?

Useful Words and Expressions

A little	Sedikit
A lot	Banyak
Beef	Daging lembu

Chicken	Ayam	Mutton	daging kaming
Cold	Sejuk	No	Tidak
Crab	Ketam	Please	Tolong/Sila
Drink	Minum	Pork	Daging babi
Do not have	Tiada	Prawn	Udang
Eat	Makan	Salt	Garam
Excuse me	Maafkan saya	Shop	Kedai
Female	Perempuan	Sugar	Gula
Fish	Ikan	Thank you	Terima Kasih
Fruit	Buah	Toilet	Tandas/bilik air
Have	Ada	Trishaw	beca
Hot	Panas	Wait	Tunggu
I am sorry	Saya minta maaf	Want	Mahu
Meat	Daging	Water	Air
Money	Wang/duit	Yes	Ya

Map References

Bukit	Hill	Padang	Open space
Changkat	Hillock	Pantai	Beach
Charuk	Small stream	Parit	Drain/Canal
Gunung	Mountain	Perhentian	Halt
Jeram	Rapids	Pengkalan	Wharf
Kampung	Village	Pulau	Island
Kangkar	River mouth	Sungai	River
Kuala	River mouth	Tanjong	Promontory
Ladang	Clearing/Plantation	Teluk	Bay

Numbers

One	Satu	Eight	Lapan
Two	Dua	Nine	Sembilan
Three	Tiga	Ten	Sepuluh
Four	Empat	Eleven	Sebelas
Five	Lima	Twelve	Dua belas
Six	Enam	Twenty	Dua puluh
Seven	Tujuh	One hundred	Seratus

Directions

Go up	Naik	Front	Hadapan
Go down	Turun	Behind	Belakang
Turn	Belok	North	Utara
Right	Kanan	South	Selatan
Left	Kiri	East	Timur
		West	Barat

RELIGION

Islam is the official religion of the country. but freedom of worship is guaranteed. Buddhism, Taoism, Hinduism and Christianity are among other religions practised in Malaysia.

FESTIVALS

Malaysia celebrates many festivals, as each of the different racial communities has its own customs and traditions. Usually everyone joins in the festivities, regardless of their own race or religion, and a good time is had by all.

A major event each year is **Hari Raya Aidil Fitri** which marks the end of the Muslim fasting month (Ramadan). It starts with daybreak visits to the cemetery, followed by thanksgiving prayers at all mosques. Adults and children alike are dressed in their Sunday best. Malaysian muslims hold "open-house" where relatives and friends call on one another. A variety of local dishes is served throughout the day. Tourists are welcome at Seri Perdana, the Prime Minister's residence, during its open-house on Hari Raya.

Thaipusam, in late January or early February, is a day when offerings are made to the Hindu diety, Lord Murugan, also called Lord Subramaniam. People carry a *kavadi*, a frame decorated with coloured papers, tinsel, flowers and fruits, and deposit it at the feet of the deity and they are forgiven their sins.

Chinese New Year is another major festival and this means the exchange of gifts, visits to the temples and holding "open-house" for relatives and friends. Children look forward to the "ang pow" - the gift of money in bright red envelopes.

Wesak Day, May 25, is the most important day of the Buddhist year as it commemorates the birth, enlightenment and death of Buddha. The followers gather in temples to pray, and during the day many doves are released and alms are given to monks.

Kaamatan Festival is held in Sabah during the entire month of May, and is a celebration of the bountiful harvest. Activities range from cultural rituals to beauty contests.

Gawai Festival is held in Sarawak around the end of May/early June, and also celebrates the harvest. It is a festival of much dancing, and drinking of *tuak*, a very potent wine made from rice.

The **Festival of San Pedro** is celebrated in Malacca which has retained its Portuguese custom; in June on the birthday of the patron saint of fishermen.

Malaysia's **Flora Fest** is held in July, when the exotic blooms are at their very best. The festival lasts for a week and finishes with a spectacular Floral Parade through the main streets of Kuala Lumpur, with marching bands, floats, horses and dancers.

Pesta Malaysia, or Malaysia Fest, is a two week celebration of culture, craft and cuisine that is held in September every year.

Also held in September is the **Mooncake Festival** that celebrates the overthrow of the Mongols during the end of the Yuan Dynasty (1206-1341 AD) in China.

Malaysia's Indian community celebrates **Deepavali**. The name means "festival of lights", and the homes are decorated with candles and oil lamps. As with the other major festivals, the Hindus visit relatives and friends at this time.

Christmas is celebrated with the usual carolling and thanksgiving, and it is the Christians' turn to hold "open-house" for relatives and friends.

Some of these festivals incorporate public holidays, others do not, but following is a list of gazetted holidays that apply to the whole country.

January	New Year's Day
	Thaipusam *
	Chinese New Year *
	Hari Raya Aidil Fitri *
May	Labour Day
	Wesak Day *
June	King's Birthday
	Awal Muharam *
	Hari Raya Aidil Adha *
August	National Day
	Deepavali *
December -	Christmas

* Dates vary from year to year

Merdeka
(National) Day

In addition to these each state has a few holidays and special celebrations of its own so it is best to check with a Tourism Malaysia office before you leave home. Visitors intending to spend a week in one town would find it less than normal if they arrived in the middle of a week long festival.

ENTRY REGULATIONS

Visitors to Malaysia must be in possession of a valid passport or other internationally recognised travel document.

Citizens of Commonwealth countries (except Bangladesh/India, Pakistan and Sri Lanka), West Germany, The Netherlands and the United States of America do not require a visa to visit Malaysia for social or business reasons.

Items such as video equipment, cameras, watches, pens, lighters, cosmetics and perfume are duty-free in Malaysia. Visitors bringing in dutiable goods may have to pay a deposit for temporary importation, refundable when they leave. This is normally up to 50% of the value.

The importation of illegal drugs into Malaysia carries the death penalty.

International airports in Malaysia are staffed by customs officers, and normal checks of baggage are made on all international arrivals. Standard security checks are also in operation at all Malaysian airports.

> Airport departure tax is collected at all airports. For domestic flights the tax is RM5, and for international flights it is RM20.

EMBASSIES

Australia: Jalan Yap, ph 242 3122, fax 241 5773.
Canada: ph 261 2000, fax 261 3428.
New Zealand: Jalan Tun Razak, ph 238 2533, fax 238 0387.
Singapore: Jalan Tun Razak, ph 251 6277, fax 261 6343.
United Kingdom: ph 248 2122, fax 248 0880.
USA: Jalan Tun Razak, ph 248 9011, fax 242 2207.

MONEY

The unit of currency is the Malaysian Ringgit (RM), which is divided into 100 sen. Notes are issued in denominations of RM1, RM5, RM10, RM50, RM100, RM500 and RM1000, and coins are 1 sen, 5 sen, 1 sen, 20 sen, 50 sen and RM1.

Approximate rates of exchange are:

A$	=RM1.85	S$	=RM1.90
Can$	=RM1.85	UK£	=RM4.10
NZ$	=RM1.65	US$	=RM2.50

When changing foreign currency or travellers cheques, the best rate will be obtained from a registered Money Changer. There are plenty of them around and although it seems strange to westerners (even slightly illegal), they definitely will offer you a better rate than a bank. Of course, changing cheques or money at hotels is only to be done in cases of extreme emergency as they will offer the lowest exchange rate of all.

COMMUNICATIONS
Telephones
Local calls can be made from public phones, whether coin or card operated. International calls can be made from booths that have phonecard facilities or from Telecom offices. Relevant numbers are:

Operator - 102 *Operator Assisted Trunk Calls - 101*
Directory - 103 *Telegrams Service - 104*
International calls - 108 *Time Check - 1051.*

Newspapers
English language newspapers that are available are: *New Straits Times*, *The Star*, *Business Times*, *Malay Mail*, *Daily Express*, *Sabah Daily News* and *Sarawak Tribune*. The content of these is mostly local interest stories, but they do cover international sporting fixtures, eg US Open Golf, and the Rugby World Cup.

International newspapers can be purchased at most bookshops and news stands, and some carry English language paperbacks but they are expensive. Expect to pay at least 50% more than the equivalent recommended prices printed on the back of the book.

Post
Postcards and Aerogrammes to all countries cost 50 sen, and can take more than two weeks to reach their destination.

Radio and Television
There are four television stations with TV1 and TV2 being government owned and the other two private. A flick around the channels will usually provide visitors with an English language program. Radio networks broadcast in various languages, including English.

MISCELLANEOUS
Credit Cards
Most large establishments in Malaysia will accept the internationally-known credit cards.

Opening Hours
Banks are open Mon-Fri 9.30am-3pm, Sat 9.30am-11.30am. Post offices

are usually open Mon-Fri 8am-5pm, Sat 8am-noon.

Government offices are open Mon-Fri 8am-4.15pm, Sat 8am-12.45pm, with lunch breaks Mon-Fri 12.45-2pm, Sat 12.15-2.45pm. Note that in the states of Kelantan, Kedah and Terengganu the Government office hours are Sat-Wed 8am-4.15pm, Thurs 8am-12.45pm, Fri closed.

> **Department stores and supermarkets are usually open daily 10am-10pm.**

Electricity
Mains voltage in Malaysia is 220 volts, 50-cycle system. Appliances wired for other voltages will need a converter.

Health
Private clinics are easily found even in the smallest towns. In major cities medical centres offer the best facilities. It is very inexpensive to visit a private doctor, and they dispense medicine on the spot. There are government hospitals throughout the country, but apart from emergencies they are more geared to serve the local population. Spectacles and contact lens practitioners, most of whom have trained overseas, make excellent products. Spectacle frames from France, Germany and other countries are available at a much lower price than in their countries of origin.

Chemist shops (drug stores) are found all over the country and apart from western medicine they also dispense traditional Chinese herbs and potions.

Tap water is generally regarded as safe, at least in the main cities, but for those who don't like to run the risk of stomach upsets bottled water is widely available.

Laundry and Dry Cleaning
Most major hotels offer same-day service for laundry, cleaning and dry cleaning. Laundrettes, where you do your own washing, are hard to find but shops where they'll do it for you are available. The service is usually quite inexpensive, but is not known for its speed.

Time
Malaysia is 8 hours ahead of GMT and 16 hours ahead of United States Pacific Standard Time.

Tipping
A service charge of 10% is added automatically to restaurant and hotel bills, plus a 5% government tax, so tipping is unnecessary unless service is exceptionally good.

Tourist Police

These are found around the main tourist centres and are easily recognisable. They wear dark blue shirts and trousers, with the letter "i" on a red and blue badge on their breast pocket. Also, their hats have chequered hat bands. If you feel that you need their assistance and there isn't one around, the following telephone numbers will put you in touch with them.

Kuala Lumpur   (03) 241 5522
Johor Bahru   - (07) 223 2227
Malacca   - (06) 222 222
Penang   - (04) 615 522
Pulau Langkawi -(04) 966 6031
Kuantan   - (09) 552 2222

Kuala Terengganu (09) 622 222
Kota Bahru   - (09) 747 2222
Kuching   - (082) 245 522
Kota Kinabalu - (088) 212 222.

Etiquette

There are a few rules of behaviour to keep in mind so as not to upset the locals:

Remove your shoes when entering homes and places of worship.

Arms and legs must be covered when visiting places of worship.

Always handle food with your right hand.

Do not point with your foot.

People being openly affectionate tend to embarrass the local people.

Ladies should note that topless bathing is not permitted in Malaysia.

NOTES

TRAVEL INFORMATION

HOW TO GET THERE

By Air
More than 30 international airlines fly in and out of Malaysia. Airports at Kuala Lumpur, Penang, Kuantan, Kota Kinabalu and Kuching cater for international flights.

By Sea
There is a ferry service from Changi Point in Singapore to Tanjung Belungkor in Desaru, Johor.

By Road
A road network from Singapore to Thailand means you can drive, or catch a bus, from either of these points into Malaysia.

By Rail
Train services extend from Singapore to Padang Besar at the Thai border, linking up with Thai Railways to Bangkok.

ACCOMMODATION
Malaysia offers a range of accommodation from international class hotels to simple government rest-houses and chalets.

Hotels
Rates for a night in an international hotel, twin/share, start at around RM250 (US$100) per person; economy hotels at RM175 (US$70); and budget hotels at RM120. (US$55)

Condominiums/Apartments
These are ideal for those who like to live in a little luxury, but have facilities to prepare their meals. A one bedroom apartment costs around RM175 (US$70) per night.

Government Rest-Houses
These are usually old colonial buildings that have been converted into accommodation units with private bathrooms. Rates are less than

RM100 (US$40) per room, and bookings can be made through the district information offices.

Chalets
Only found at island and beach resorts, chalets provide something different in accommodation style and are usually around RM100 (US$40) per night.

Budget Accommodation
Lower priced accommodation ranges from youth hostels to A-frame huts, to guest houses, which are usually found in the popular beach areas. Costs range from RM10 to RM25 per person per night.

Homestay
This is a new concept in Malaysia, and can be arranged through your travel agent. Prices are very competitive.

LOCAL TRANSPORT

Air
Apart from Malaysia Airlines, there are several other airlines that provide domestic services within Malaysia, including Pelangi Air, Berjaya Air and Mofaz Air.

Rail
Malayan Railways, or Keretapi Tanah Melayu (KTM), provide a comfortable and economical rail service. There are two main lines being operated for passenger service. One line leaves Singapore and runs northward through Kuala Lumpur and Butterworth and meets the Thai railways at the border. The other line branches off from the west coast line at the town of Gemas and travels up to the north-eastern part of the peninsula near Kota Bharu. This line also meets the State Railway of Thailand line at the border.

For foreign visitors, KTM offers a Railpass which entitles the holder to unlimited travel on any passenger train in Malaysia and Singapore for the duration of the pass. The price for adults is US$55 for 10 days and US$120 for 30 days. For children between 4 and 12 years of age, the Railpass is US$28 for 10 days and US$60 for 30 days.

The Eurotrain Explorer Pass-Malaysia is valid for second or economy class travel on all KTM services in Peninsular Malaysia, including Singapore.

Malaysia also has a luxury train service, the Eastern and Oriental Express, modelled on the famous Orient Express. The 41-hour round trip journey travels from Singapore through Kuala Lumpur to Bangkok and return.

Foreign visitors under 30 years of age that hold either the ISIC, the YIEE or the Youth Hostel Card can have unlimited travel for 7 days for only US$32.

Ferries

Ferry or hydrofoil services are available from the mainland to the island resorts of Langkawi, Penang, Pangkor and Tioman.

Buses

Air-conditioned and nonair-conditioned buses are available from Kuala Lumpur to other towns in Peninsular Malaysia. Buses that operate within a city charge fares according to the distance covered, with the exception of the mini buses in Kuala Lumpur which charge a standard fare of 60 sen to any destination within their routes.

Taxis

Interstate taxis can be hired from a stand on Level 2 of the Pudu Raya Bus Terminal in Kuala Lumpur. This is an inexpensive form of transport, with the prices fixed by the government. Meters are not used.

City taxis, on the other hand, have meters and the fares are RM1.50 flag fall and the first 2km, with 10 sen for every 200m thereafter.

Cars

The roads are good in Malaysia, and driving yourself is the obvious way to see the "off the beaten track" parts of the country. But, driving in the crowded areas is nerve-wracking to say the least.

It is not just the amount of traffic, it is the hundreds, dare I say thousands, of small motor bike riders who seem to have some sort of death wish. Admittedly, they can weave in and out of the traffic and so probably arrive at their destination before a car would, but you have to wonder how many of these daredevils get killed each year. (For that matter it would be interesting to know how many pedestrians are hit by these cyclists in a twelve month period.)

To hire a car, visitors need an international driving permit, or a valid licence issued in their home country.

All international rules apply, traffic drives on the left and gives way to that on the right. Seat belts are compulsory for the driver and front seat passenger, and the speed limit in built-up areas is 50kph.

Malaysian drivers have developed a few signals of their own, which they say is for safety. The driver in front flashing his Right Indicator is signalling "Do Not Overtake". Flashing of the Left Indicator signals "Overtake With Caution". A driver flashing his headlights is claiming the right of way.

Some local road signs are:

Awas	-	Caution
Ikut Kiri	-	Keep Left
Kurang-kanaju-		Down
Jalan Sehala	-	One Way in direction of arrow
Utara	-	North
Selatan	-	South
Timur	-	East

To give an idea of the amount of driving involved in getting around Malaysia, following is a list of distances from Kuala Lumpur -

Alor Setar -	481km		Muar -	192km
Ayer Hitam -	278km		Port Dickson -	90km
Butterworth -	381km		Segamat -	201km
Cameron Highlands -	229km		Seremban -	68km
Fraser's Hill -	103km		Singapore -	394km
Ipoh -	217km		Sungai Petani	420km
Johor Bahru -	367km		Taiping -	302km
Klang -	32km		Tanjong Malim	84km
Kluang -	295km		Tapah -	159km
Kota Bahru -	658km		Teluk Intan -	198km.
Kuala Terengganu -	492km			
Kuantan -	277km			
Malacca -	148km			
Mersing -	399km			

FOOD

If variety is the spice of life, when it comes to eating Malaysia has few equals. Each state in the country has its own distinctive flavour, with Malay food being on the spicy side. Chinese food in its endless variety is available almost everywhere. Indian food from both north and south India is widely available. Outside hotels, European food from sizzling steaks to fast foods from the US can be obtained in the larger towns, although you may have to search and ask around.

Tropical fruit such as durian (you'll either love it or hate it), ciku, mangosteen, rambutan, guavas, watermelons, papayas and bananas, can be bought from fruit stalls along highways, as well as in towns. Around cinemas and other entertainment areas there are also fruit-sellers with a variety of fruits that have been cut up and stored in cool display cases. Try them, they are delicious.

SHOPPING

One popular pastime all travellers enjoy in Malaysia is shopping, because many of the things you can buy are unique to Malaysia. Whether you shop at supermarkets, department stores or open markets, you'll delight in the range of pewter, batik, jewellery, pottery and antiques.

There are good duty-free shops at Kuala Lumpur and Penang airports, as well as in all the large centres. Cameras, watches, pens, lighters, cosmetics, perfume and electronic goods are duty-free in Malaysia. Many people are now saying that the shopping in Malaysia is closely rivalling the opportunities in Singapore.

In the markets bargaining is still popular, so if a stall-holder asks a price that you think is too expensive, make an offer. In department stores, however, "fixed price" is a general rule, so bargaining is not possible.

BEACHES

If it is beautiful, secluded beaches you are seeking, then Malaysia has many. There are approximately 700km of beaches on the East Coast, and the islands off shore have some magnificent strips of coastline. The only good beaches on the West Coast are in Port Dickson and Malacca, otherwise try the off-shore islands.

NATIONAL PARKS

The tropical rain forests of Malaysia are very, very old. While other areas were subjected to the ravages of the Ice Age and climatic changes that destroyed their vegetation, the Malaysian rain forests, as represented by the national parks, have become storehouses of flora and fauna that can no longer be found elsewhere.

The more popular national parks are the Taman Negara in Peninsular Malaysia, Niah National Park in Sarawak, and Kinabalu National Park in Sabah. Each offers its own unique attractions. Taman Negara is particularly favoured for its fishing and animal observation hides. Niah National Park has caves ranking among the largest in the world, and Kinabalu National Park has Mount Kinabalu which can be climbed by the anyone of average fitness. **More detailed information on these parks is found in a later chapter.**

SPORT AND RECREATION

The Malay art of self-defence is called *Silat*, and it has been practised in the Malay Archipelago for hundreds of years. Apart from the physical aspect, it is believed that participants in this art develop spiritual strength according to the tenets of Islam. Silat demonstrations are held during national celebrations, and at important family gatherings, such as weddings.

Sepak Takraw is the Malay form of volleyball, except that they use every part of their body except their hands to keep a small rattan ball from touching the ground.

Kite-Flying originated as a pastime for padi farmers after the harvest had been brought in. Nowadays it is an international event with competitors coming from The Netherlands, Japan, Germany, Belgium and Singapore.

Another post harvest pastime was *Top Spinning*, and this too has become a national sport. A *Gasing* (spinning top) can be as big as a dinner plate and weigh around 4kg.

One of the most popular sports in Malaysia is **golf**, and there are about 200 courses to tempt locals and visitors alike. Night-time golfing is becoming popular as more and more courses install the facilities.

Other sports - tennis, horse racing, motor racing, soccer, cricket and squash - are well catered for in Malaysia.

Petaling Street
Kuala Lumpur

KUALA LUMPUR

Kuala Lumpur (KL), the capital of Malaysia, has an area of 244 sq km and a population of around 1.3 million. It is situated on the west coast of Peninsular Malaysia, about 35km inland, and roughly midway between the north and south extremities.

KL, as it is known, is a bustling cosmopolitan city with a rich mix of architectural styles from Moorish to Tudor. It is a modern city, but still preserves a charm from another era.

The city had its beginnings in 1857 when a group of miners found tin near the junction of the Klang and Gombak Rivers in the state of Selangor. It began as a small trading post and meeting place for the miners, and grew in size and importance as the tin trade prospered. Then came the British and the formation of the Federated Malay States in 1896, with Kuala Lumpur as the capital. It was during the period of British administration that the city gained its system of roads and its fine examples of colonial architecture.

In 1957 the Federation of Malaya gained its independence, and Kuala Lumpur was declared the Federal capital. In 1972 it achieved city status, but was still part of Selangor until February 1, 1974, when Kuala Lumpur was declared a Federal Territory.

HOW TO GET THERE

By Air

The Subang Kuala Lumpur International Airport is 24km from the city centre. It has three terminals - Terminal 1 for international flights, Terminal 2 for flights to/from Singapore, and Terminal 3 for domestic flights. Terminal 1 is very modern with motorised walkways and plenty of duty-free shops, eateries and bars, but due to the expected increase in tourism in the next decade, a new international airport is being constructed at Sepang, Selangor. It will have one of the most sophisticated passenger facilities in the region and is expected to be ready for operation in early 1998.

Malaysia Airlines, the national flag carrier, has flights to Kuala Lumpur from:

Adelaide -	daily, via Sydney or Melbourne
Auckland -	Thurs & Sun, via Brisbane
Brisbane -	Thurs & Sun direct,
	other days via Sydney or Melbourne.

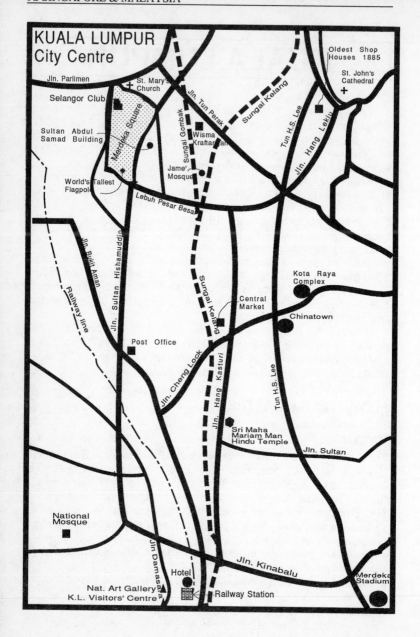

Darwin -	Mon direct
Frankfurt -	Mon & Sat direct
Hong Kong -	daily direct
London -	daily direct
Los Angeles -	Tues, Thurs, Sat, Sun, via Taipei
Melbourne -	Mon, Tues, Thurs, Fri, Sun direct, other days via Sydney
Perth -	Tues, Thurs-Sun direct
Singapore -	daily direct
Sydney -	Wed, Sat direct, other days via Melbourne.

Malaysia Airlines also has domestic flights from every airport in Malaysia to Kuala Lumpur.

Flight confirmations -ph (03) 746 3000.

British Airways has direct flights to Kuala Lumpur from London - Mon, Wed, Fri & Sun.

Flight confirmations - ph (03) 232 5797.

Qantas has direct flights to Kuala Lumpur from Sydney - Tues, Thurs & Sat. Flights from other cities call at Singapore &/or Sydney.

Flight confirmations - ph (03) 238 9133

Singapore Airlines has daily direct flights to KL from Singapore.

Flight confirmations - ph (03) 244 9211.

By Rail

The rail journey from Singapore takes approximately 6 1/2 hours by Express train and costs RM68 1st class, RM34 2nd class and RM19 third class. The trip from Padang Besar, the northernmost station in Malaysia, to Kuala Lumpur takes approximately 12 1/2 hours and costs RM40 for a seat, RM190-100 for a first class berth, and RM43.50-46 for a second class berth.

By Bus

The main bus terminal in KL is Pudu Raya Terminal on Jalan Pudu, where buses from Singapore arrive, ph (03) 230 0145.

Other terminals are: Putra Bus Station, opposite the PutraWorld Trade Centre, ph (03) 442 9530 - east coast express bus service.

Pekeliling Bus Station - east coast bound buses, ph (03) 442 1256.

Medan Mara - south bound buses.

Fares are charged according to distance, and air-conditioned express bus fares are higher than regular buses.

By Interstate Taxi

This are an inexpensive and fast way to travel from one state to another. Fares are fixed and so meters are not used. The taxi stand in Kuala Lumpur is on level 2 of the Pudu Raya Bus Terminal.

TOURIST INFORMATION

Tourist information offices are found at:

Jalan Parlimen, ph (03) 293 6661.

Kuala Lumpur Railway Station, Jalan Sultan Hishamuddin, ph (03) 274 6063.

Level 2, Menata Dato' Onn, Putra World Trade Centre, 45 Jalan Tun Ismail, ph (03) 441 1295.

Malaysia Tourist Information Complex (MATIC), 109 Jalan Ampang, ph (03) 264 3929.

Terminal 1, Subang International Airport, ph (03) 746 5707.

ACCOMMODATION

Kuala Lumpur has a wide range of hotels, including most of the top international chains. Prices quoted here are for a double room per night, and should be used as a guide only.

The telephone area code is 03.

International

Shangri-La, 11 Jalan Sultan Ismail, ph 232 2388 - 720 rooms, 9 restaurants, cocktail lounge, coffee shop, swimming pool, sauna - RM195.

The Regent, 160 Jalan Bukit Bintang, ph 241 8000 - 469 rooms, 4 restaurants, cocktail lounge, coffee shop, pool, sauna - RM180.

Hotel Istana, 73 Jalan Raja Chulan, ph 241 9988 - 516 rooms, 5 restaurants, cocktail lounge, coffee shop, pool, sauna - RM178.

Hilton, Jalan Sultan Ismail, ph 242 2322 - 581 rooms, 5 restaurants, cocktail lounge, coffee shop, swimming pool, sauna - RM175.

Hyatt Regency Saujana, 2km off Subang International Airport Highway, Saujana, ph 746 1234 - 386 rooms, 5 restaurants, cocktail lounge, coffee shop, swimming pool, sauna - RM169.

Park Royal, Jalan Sultan Ismail, ph 242 5588 - 333 rooms, 3 restaurants, cocktail lounge, coffee shop, swimming pool, sauna - RM162.

The Legend Hotel & Apartment, Basement 1, The Mall, Putra Place, 100 Jalan Putra, ph 442 9888 - 613 rooms, 6 restaurants, cocktail lounge, coffee shop, swimming pool, sauna - RM156.

Pan Pacific, Jalan Putra, ph 442 5555 - 571 rooms, 1 restaurant, cocktail lounge, coffee shop, swimming pool, sauna - RM153.

Equatorial, Jalan Sultan Ismail, ph 261 7777 - 300 rooms, 3 restaurants, cocktail lounge, coffee shop, swimming pool, sauna - RM153.

Crown Princess, City Square Centre, Jalan Tun Razak, ph 262 5522 - 576 rooms, 3 restaurants, cocktail lounge, coffee shop, swimming pool, sauna - RM151.

Ming Court, Jalan Ampang, ph 261 8888 - 447 rooms, 1 restaurant, cocktail lounge, coffee shop, swimming pool, sauna - RM140.

Concorde, 2 Jalan Sultan Ismail, ph 244 2200 - 610 rooms, 3 restaurants, cocktail lounge, coffee shop, swimming pool, sauna - RM137.

Holiday Inn on the Park, Jalan Pinang, ph 248 1066 - 200 rooms, 2 restaurants, cocktail lounge, coffee shop, pool, sauna - RM137.

Holiday Inn City Centre, Jalan Raja Laut, ph 293 9233 - 250 rooms, 1 restaurant, cocktail lounge, coffee shop, pool, sauna - RM137.

Melia Kuala Lumpur, 16 Jalan Imbi, ph 242 8333 - 302 rooms, 4 restaurants, cocktail lounge, coffee shop, pool, sauna - RM130.

Swiss Garden, 117 Jalan Pudu, ph 241 3333 - 308 rooms, 1 restaurant, cocktail lounge, coffee shop, swimming pool - RM120.

Federal Kuala Lumpur, 35 Jalan Bukit Bintang, ph 248 9166 - 450 rooms, 5 restaurants, cocktail lounge, coffee shop, pool sauna - RM116.

Tourist

Chamtan Hotel, 62 Jalan Masjid India, ph 293 0144 - 44 rooms - RM66-88.

Embassy Hotel, 205-211 Jalan Imbi, ph 984 1288 - 35 rooms - RM42-88.

Wilayah Sdn Bhd Hotel, 53-59 Jalan Tiong Nam, ph 291 2233 - 44 rooms - RM47-86.

Emerald Hotel, 166-168 Jalan Pudu (off Jalan Bukit Bintang), ph 242 9233 - 45 rooms - RM67-78.

Lock Ann Hotel, 113A Jalan Petaling, ph 238 9544 - 21 rooms - RM60-74.

New Sin Ma Hotel, 16-18 Jalan Brunei Barat, ph 242 6644 - 28 rooms - RM44-69.

Kok Ping Hotel, 36-36A Lorong Haji Hussein Satu, ph 298 7273 - 23 rooms - RM45-60.

Dashrun Hotel, 285-287 Jalan Tuanku Abdul Rahman, ph 292 5596 - 40 rooms - RM40-64.

Lido Hotel, 7A Jalan Marsh Brickfield, ph 274 1258 - 34 rooms - RM30-60.

Budget

Fuji Hotel, 45 Jalan Barat (off Jalan Imbi), ph 242 9333 - 24 rooms - RM46-50.

Omar Khayam Hotel, 5 Jalan Medan Tuanku, ph 298 8744 - 14 rooms - RM36-45.

Palace Hotel, 38 Batu 2 1/2, Jalan Kelang, ph 274 2304 - 27 rooms - RM34-45.

New Cylinmen Hotel, 110 Jalan Raja Laut, ph 442 5905 - 40 rooms - RM27-45.
Rome Hotel, 380A Jalan Raja Laut, ph 441 241 - 21 rooms - RM25-45.
Star Hotel, 107A Jalan Raja Laut, ph 441 2844 - 22 rooms - RM23-45.
Golden Hill Hotel, 58 Batu 2 1/2, Jalan Kelang Lama, ph 274 2441 - 18 rooms - RM20-40.
Colonial Hotel, 29-45 Jalan Sultan, ph 238 0336 - 36 rooms - RM19-28.
Kawana Tourist Inn, 68 Jalan Pudu, ph 238 6714 - 20 rooms - RM12-45.

Hostels

YMCA of Kuala Lumpur, Jalan Tun Sambanthan, ph 274 1439 - 60 rooms - RM24-77.
YWCA, 12 Jalan Hang Jebat, ph 238 3225 - 12 rooms - RM30-80.
Alpine Hostel, 17 Jalan Tun Sambanthan 4, Brickfields, ph 273 1227 - 8 rooms - RM12-29.
Meridian International Youth Hostel, 36 Jalan Hang Kasturi, ph 232 5819 - 4 rooms - Rm12-15.
M'sian Youth Hostel Association, 21 Jalan Kg Attap, ph 230 6870 - 14 rooms - from RM10 per bed.

LOCAL TRANSPORT

KL has an efficient transport system comprising of buses and taxis.

Bus

There are two types of buses operating in the city area - regular buses and mini buses. Regular buses charge 20 sen for the first kilometre and 5 sen for each additional kilometre. Mini buses charge a standard 60 sen to any destination within their routes. Always ensure that you have the correct fare, or plenty of loose change.

Bus terminals within the city are for specific areas both inside and outside the city. They are:

* **Kelang Bus Station** - Petaling, Jaya, Subang Airport, Shah Alam, Port Klang.

* **Jalan Sultan Mohamed Bus Station** - Taman Bangsar, Petaling Jaya (Old Town), Kelana Jaya, Pantai, Bukit Damansara, Subang.

* **Kota Raya Shopping Complex/Menara Maybank** - Jalan Cheras, Sri Petaling, Serdang Lama, Taman Goodwood, Salak South, Sungei Besi, Kampung Pandan, Bandar Tun Razak, Taman Maluri.

* **Pudu Raya Bus Station** - Seri Kembangan, Sungai Besi Camp, Balakong, Taman Seri Serdang, Kajang.

* **Lebuh Ampang Bus Stand** - Taman Greenwood, Kampung Air Panas, Sri Gombak, Taman Setapak, 12th mile Gombak.

* **Chow Kit Road Bus Stand** - Kampung Datuk Keramat, Ulu Kelang, Ampang, Cheras, Salak South, Sungai Besi, Petaling Jaya, Jalan

Kelang Lama, Bangsar, Damansara, Kepong, Jinjang, Segambut, Selayang, Sentul, Gombak, Jalan Genting Kelang.

Taxi

Taxis can be hailed in the street or hired at designated taxi stands along major roads. It is also possible to phone for a cab, but this involves an extra fare of RM1 above the normal RM1.50 for the first 1km and 10 sen for each subsequent 200m. Between midnight and 6am an additional 50% charge is levied. **To get from the airport to your hotel by taxi you must first purchase a fixed price voucher from the Taxi counter at the airport concourse. This should be given to the driver at the start of the journey.**

Car Hire

ACME Rent-A-Car, 2nd Floor, Ming Court Hotel, Jalan Ampang, ph 261 1136.

Avis Rent-A-Car, 40 Jalan Sultan Ismail, ph 241 7144.

Budget Rent-A-Car, 29 Jalan Yap Kwan Seng, ph 242 5166.

Thrifty Car Rental, Ground Floor, LPPKN Building, Jalan Raja Laut, ph 293 2388.

Toyota Rent-A-Car, Ground Floor, Federal Hotel, Jalan Bukit Bintang, ph 243 8142.

Sintat Rent-A-Car, 22, Jalan Inai, ph 982 1988.

National Car Rental, G47, Wisma HLA, Jalan Raja Chulan, ph 248 0522.

Orix Car Rental, 5 Jalan Leiu Weng Chee, ph 248 8553.

SMAS Rent-A-Car, Lot 9, 1st Floor, UBN Tower, Jalan P Ramiee, ph 230 7788.

EATING OUT

There is no shortage of good food and service in Kuala Lumpur. There are wayside stalls and restaurants serving a variety of Malay, Chinese, Indian and Western food.

Eating in the open air is a distinctive Malaysian experience. A number of car parking areas are turned into colourful eating areas at night. If you are interested in visiting a typical open air food stall, you will find many at Jalan Brickfields, Jalan Bukit Bintang, Jalan Imbi, off Jalan Raja, Jalan Kampung Baru, and on the top floor of Central Market.

Those who prefer to dine in comfort will find many air-conditioned restaurants that serve local and Western food. Some restaurants even have Malaysian cultural shows to entertain their dinner guests. Most of the international hotels in the city have restaurants, some of which serve local cuisine.

Following is a selection of restaurants.

Malay

Bunga Raya Restaurant, Level 2, Putra World Trade Centre, ph 442 2999.
Rasa Utara, BB Plaza, Jalan Bukit Bintang, ph 248 8639.
Satay Anika, BB Plaza, Jalan Bukit Bintang, ph 248 3113.
Yazmin Restaurant, 6 Jalan Kia Peng, ph 241 5655.
Restoran Sri Melayu, 1 Jalan Conlay, ph 245 1833.

Chinese

Dynasty Garden Chinese Restaurant, Lot M72-75, Mezzanine Floor, Plaza Yow Chuan, ph 262 1411
Tai Thong Seafood, 32 Jalan Sultain Ismail, ph 244 1939.
Marco Polo Restaurant, 1st Floor, Wisma Lim Foo Yong, Jalan Raja Chulan, ph 242 5595.
Regent Court Chinese Restaurant, Jalan Sultan Ismail, ph 242 2232.
Restaurant Teochew, 270 Jalan Changkat Thambi Dollah, ph 248 3452.
Shang Palace, Shangri-La Hotel, Jalan Sultan Ismail, ph 232 2388.

Indian and Pakistani

Bangles Restaurant, 60A Jalan Tuanku Abdul Rahman, ph 298 3780.
Bilal Restaurant, 33 Jalan Ampang, ph 238 0804.
Shiraz Restaurant, 1 Jalan Medan Tuanku, ph 291 0035.
Yusoof Restaurant, Merdeka Stadium, ph 230 7411.
Omar Khayam Restaurant, 5 Jalan Medan Tuanku, ph 291 1016.

Thai

Chili Padi Restaurant, 2nd Floor, The Mall, Jalan Putra, ph 442 9543.
Sawasdee Thai Restaurant, Holiday Inn On The Park, ph 248 1066.

Japanese

Chikuyo-tei, Basement, Plaza See Hoy Chan, ph 230 0729.
Munakata Japanese Restaurant, 2nd Floor, Menara Promet, Jalan Sultan Ismail, ph 241 7441.
Hoshigaoka Restaurant, 2nd Floor, Lot 10, Jalan Sultan Ismail, ph 244 2585.
Hatsuhana, 1 Jalan Yap Kwan Seng, ph 242 0771.
Kamogawa, Ming Court Hotel, Jalan Ampang, ph 261 9066.
Nadaman, Shangri-La Hotel, Jalan Sultain Ismail, ph 232 2388.
Edo Kirin, Regent Kuala Lumpur, Jalan Bukit Bintang, ph 241 8000.

Korean

Koryo-Won, Komplek Antarabangsa, Jalan Sultan Ismail,
ph 242 7655.
Seoul Garden, 37 Jalan Sultan Ismail, ph 242 0425.

Western

Castell Grill, 81 Jalan Bukit Bintang, ph 242 8328.
Decânter Restaurant, 7 Jalan Setiakasih 5, ph 255 2507.
Esquire Kitchen, 1st Floor, Sungai Wang Plaza, ph 248 4506.
The Ship, 40/1 Jalan Sultan Ismail, ph 241 8805.

French

Restaurant Lafite, Shangri-La Hotel, Jalan Sultan Ismail,
ph 232 2388.
Chez Bidou, Ming Court Hotel, Jalan Ampang, ph 261 9066.

Italian/Mediterranean

Mario's, Holiday Inn On The Park, ph 248 1066.
Trebotti, MiCasa Hotel Apartment, ph 261 8833.

Kuala Lumpur Skyline

ENTERTAINMENT

When the sun sets Kuala Lumpur comes alive with entertainment as the night clubs, discos and cabarets open for business. No one will every expire from boredom in KL

Cinemas

The cinemas show Malay, Indonesian, Hindi, Cantonese and Western movies, so it is wise to check the local newspapers to see what is screening or you might not understand a word.

Odeon, Jalan Tuanku Abdul Rahman, ph 292 0084.
Odeon Cineplex, Central Square, ph 230 8548.
Cathay, Jalan Bukit Bintang, ph 242 9942.
Cathay Cineplex, The Mall, ph 442 6122.
Federal, Jalan Raja Laut, ph 442 5014.
Rex, Jalan Sultan Ismail, ph 238 3021.
Capitol, Jalan Raja Laut, ph 442 9051.
Coliseum, Jalan Tuanku Abdul Rahman, ph 292 5995.

Pubs

Cee Jay's, 6 Jalan P. Ramlee, ph 232 4437.
Riverbank, Central Market, ph 274 6652.
7th Avenue KTV Lounge, Menara Apera ULG, Jalan Raja Chulan, ph 261 5448.
Tatlers, Jalan Telawi Lima, Bangsar.
Castell Pub & Grill, 81 Jalan Bukit Bintang, ph 242 8328.

Piano Lounges

Kencana Lounge, Ming Court Hotel, Jalan Ampang, ph 261 8888.
Lobby Lounge, Shangri-La Hotel, Jalan Sultan Ismail, ph 232 2388.
Rama Rama Lounge, Holiday Inn On The Park, Jalan Pinang, ph 248 1066.
Aviary Bar, Hilton Hotel, Jalan Sultan Ismail, ph 242 2222.
Tanners Lounge, Fortuna Hotel, Jalan Berangan, ph 241 9111.

Discos

Copperfield, Pan Pacific Hotel, Jalan Putra, ph 442 5555.
Club OZ, Shangri-La Hotel, Jalan Sultan Ismail, ph 232 2388.
Blue Moon, Equatorial Hotel, Jalan Sultan Ismail, ph 261 7777.
Tin Mine, Kuala Lumpur Hilton, Jalan Sultan Ismail, ph 242 2222.

The Musictheque, Hotel Istana, 73 Jalan Raja Chulan,
ph 241 9988.
Tsim Sha Tsui Disco, 1 Jalan Kia Peng, ph 241 4929.
Renaissance, Plaza Yow Chuan, ph 242 0540.
Hard Rock Cafe, Wisma Concorde, 2 Jalan Sultan Ismail,
ph 244 4152.

Karaoke Lounges
Life Entertainment Hall, Jalan Sultan Ismail, ph 262 2570.
Oriental Club, Grand Continental, Jalan Beliaj, ph 291 1728.
Club 10, MCB Plaza, Changkat Raja Chulan, ph 232 3866.
Deluxe Nite Club, Ampang Park, Jalan Ampang, ph 262 1399.

Night Clubs
City Night MTV/KTV Nite Club, The Mall, 37-39 Jalan Putra,
ph 441 8660.
Pertama Cabaret Nite Club, Pertama Complex, Jalan Tuanku Abdul
Rahman, ph 298 2533.
Copacabana, Federal Hotel, Jalan Bukit Bintang, ph 241 8006.
Shangri-La Nite Club & Cabaret, 4th Floor, Puduraya,
ph 232 1695.

SHOPPING
Kuala Lumpur has plenty to keep the dedicated shopper interested,
from oriental art to local handicrafts through designer gear and
electrical equipment. The prices in the bigger shops are usually fixed,
although it never hurts to ask for a discount, but at the smaller shops
and stalls bargaining is the only way to go.

Shopping Complexes
Pekeliling Plaza, cnr Jalan Ipoh & Jalan Tun Tazak.
The Mall, Jalan Putra (opposite the Pan Pacific Hotel).
Hankyu Jaya Store, Jalan Tuanku Abdul Rahman.
Ampang Park, Jalan Ampang.
City Square Centre, Jalan Tun Razak.
Yow Chuan Plaza, Jalan Tun Razak.
Campbell Complex, Jalan Dang Wangi.
Semua House, adjacent to Campbell Complex.
Komplex Pemas Sogo, Jalan Dang Wangi.
Wilayah Complex, Jalan Dang Wangi.
Pertama Complex, Jalan Raja Laut.
Pudu Plaza, Jalan Landak.
Dataran Merdeka Kompleks, Jalan Raja Laut.

Infokraf, Leboh Pasar Besar (also the weekend craft market).
Central Market, Jalan Hang Nadim.
Kota Raya Complex, Jalan Cheng Lock.
Karyaneka Handicraft Centre, Jalan Raja Chulan
Kuala Lumpur Plaza, Jalan Bukit Bintang.
Bukit Bintang Plaza, Jalan Sultan Ismail.
Lot 10, Jalan Sultan Ismail.
Sungai Wang Plaza, cnr Jalan Imbi & Jalan Sultan Ismail.
Imbi Plaza, Jalan Imbi.
The Weld, Jalan P. Ramlee.

Shopping Areas

Jalan Bukit Bintang - once the centre of KL's night life, it is now home to modern shopping complexes, international hotels and commercial banks.

Jalan Tuanku Abdul Rahman - a mixture of old and new shopping establishments and a good area for oriental antiques, curios, carpets and fabrics.

Chinatown - with Petaling Street as its centre, this centre offers the same goods and services as all the other Chinatowns you have ever visited (including the one in your own home city).

Central Market - also known as "Pasar Seni", this was once the wet market for the central city area. Extensive conservation efforts have changed it into a centre for handicrafts, souvenirs and curios. Also, here are found many local artists who paint portraits, and personalised T-shirts, cards, plaques and plates.

Pasar Malam - or "night markets", give a fascinating insight into Malaysia and its people. The market along Jalan Tuanku Abdul Rahman is held every Saturday after 6pm, but that in Petaling Street happens every night.

Pasar Tani - a weekly farmers' market, this is not really for visitors, but it is interesting to see the wide range of produce.

The Royal Selangor Factory Complex - the largest pewter factory in the world. The address is 4 Jalan Usahawan Enam, Setapak Jaya, ph 422 1000, and it is open Mon-Sat 8.45am-4.45pm, Sun 9am-4pm. Royal Selangor is also available at the leading department stores, but here you can take a complimentary tour of the factory, see master craftsmen at work, and choose from a much larger range of goods.

Duty Free Shopping

The duty free shops at the airport can hardly be missed by anyone arriving or leaving by plane, but there are also a few outlets in the downtown area.

Agate Sdn Bhd, 209-212 Jalan Bunus, Off Jalan Masjid India, ph 293 1473.

Agate Duty Free (BB) Sdn Bhd, Ground and Mezzanine Floors, 47-49 Wisma Bintang, Jalan Bukit Bintang, ph 242 5337.

Golden Boutique, 2nd Floor, Bangunan MAS, Jalan Sultan Ismail, ph 265 5324.

Wealthouse Sdn Bhd, Emporium Bebas Cukai, Kawasan Musium Negara, Jalan Damansara, ph 282 2705.

SIGHTSEEING

Sightseeing around Kuala Lumpur is made easy by the fact that a large number of interesting places are concentrated within the city centre. You can set forth armed with a map, camera, comfortable walking shoes and light clothing, or you may opt for one of the city tours that introduce visitors to the varied attractions of the city in air-conditioned comfort.

To assist in you, the city's attractions have been grouped here in convenient clusters. Almost a dozen points of interest lie along a roughly circular route in the heart of the city, easily accessible from several major hotels. If you have difficulty in finding your way around, do ask for help - you will find Malaysians, even in this bustling city, are friendly and eager to show you the way.

Kuala Lumpur Lake Gardens (Taman Tasik Perdana)

Built in the 1880s, the city's most popular park has an area of 91.6ha and surrounds an artificial lake. Facilities in the park include a children's playground, jogging tracks, exercise stations and rowing boats. Many musical and cultural performances are held in a valley in the park.

The *Kuala Lumpur Orchid Garden* is also in the park, and it has over 800 species of exotic Malaysian orchids. On the weekends an orchid bazaar is held. Within walking distance of the orchid garden is the *Bird Park*, a beautifully landscaped are with trees, flowering shrubs, miniature waterfalls, and of course, hundreds of birds. Admission is RM3 adult, RM1 child.

Nearby is the *Hibiscus Garden*, but next to the Bird Park is the *Kuala Lumpur Butterfly Park*, with over 6000 specimens from around 120 species. Admission to this park is RM4 adult, RM2 child, and there is a restaurant, a showroom and an insect museum.

The next attraction, down the slopes towards the lake, is the *Deer Park*. Here these gentle animals roam free, and try to cadge food from visitors. Further down the road is the *Memorial Tun Razak*, formerly the official residence of Malaysia's second Prime Minister, who was known as The Father of Development. The memorial has a vast collection of his personal and official memorabilia, and is open Tues-Sun 9am-6pm (closed noon-3pm on Fri). No admission charge.

National Art Gallery

Housed at the former Hotel Majestic on Jalan Sultan Hishamuddin, it has a permanent collection of fine works by Malaysian artists. Various exhibitions of both local and international artists are held throughout the year. It is open daily 10am-6pm (closed Fri noon-3pm) and admission is free.

National Monument

Across the road from the Lake Gardens the monument was built in 1966 in honour of the nation's fallen heroes. It was designed by Felix de Weldon, who was also responsible for Washington's Iwo Jima Memorial. The monument depicts seven men from the Malayan security forces, symbolising the seven qualities of leadership, and is surrounded by a moat filled with fountains and water-lilies. Nearby is the **ASEAN Sculpture Garden**, with a collection of prize-winning sculptures by some of the finest artists in the ASEAN region.

Parliament House

The building stands on elevated ground, and commands a panoramic view of the Lake Gardens. An 18-storey office tower dominates the complex which includes a three-storey building containing the two houses of Parliament, various offices, a library, a Banquet Hall and committee rooms. When Parliament is in session visitors may enter only by prior arrangement with the authorities.

National Museum

A magnificent building based on the old Malay style of architecture. Two immense murals in Italian glass mosaic, each 35m in length and 5m high, flank the main entrance, and they depict historical episodes and cultural activities in the country. Displays within the Museum relate to Malaysian history, arts and crafts, weapons, currency, birds and mammals, entomological specimens, and major economic activities - rubber industry and tin mining, among others. Open daily 9am-6pm, admission is RM1.

Kuala Lumpur Railway Station

Designed by architect A.B. Hubback, and built in 1910, the station is a fine example of Moorish inspired architecture. The basic design, beneath the Islamic exterior, resembles the large glass and iron train sheds constructed in England toward the close of the 19th Century.

Part of the building houses the Malayan Railway Administration.

In 1986 extensive renovations were carried out and the station was linked to the General Post Office at Dayabumi.

National Mosque (Masjid Negara)

Across the road from Dayabumi, and connected by an underground passage, the National Mosque is a very modern building with an unusual multi-fold roof, and a 73m minaret. The **Islamic Centre** is a short walk away, built into the hillside behind the Malayan Railway Administrative Building. It is a centre for Islamic learning, culture and art, and has a fine collection of Islamic texts, artifacts, porcelain and weaponry.

Sultan Abdul Samad Building

Built in 1894-97, the building was used by the British as a Government administrative building. It is the most photographed building in KL, and now houses the Supreme and High Courts. Nearby on Jalan Raja is the two storey **Kuala Lumpur Memorial Library**.

Merdeka Square

Opposite the Sultan Abdul Samad Building is Merdeka Square, the scene of the annual celebration of Independence. Formerly the venue for Cricket, Hockey, Tennis and Rugby matches, the field in front of the Selangor Club has been returfed and a black marble plaque marks the spot where the Union Jack was lowered at midnight on August 30, 1957. At the southern end of the square is the world's tallest flagpole (100m) flying the Malaysian flag, and at the northern end there are some fountains. Underneath the square is a shopping centre. The Malaysians are very proud of Merdeka Square.

Sultan Abdul Samad Building

Masjid Jamek (Jame Mosque)

Situated at the confluence of the Klang and Gombak rivers, the site of the beginnings of Kuala Lumpur, the mosque nestles within a grove of coconut palms with its two minarets rising to the height of the trees. It was designed by A.B. Hubback and was built in 1909.

Chinatown

Concentrated in one of the city's busiest areas, bounded roughly by Jalan Petaling, Jalan Sultan and Jalan Bandar, this is a hive of activity day and night. Wares on sale and display range from textiles, household goods, herbs and ancient remedies, to vegetables, fruits, flowers, cakes, delicacies such as roast duck and birds' nests, and a myriad of other intriguing items. At dusk the mid-section of Jalan Petaling is closed to motor vehicles and the entire area is transformed into an open-air night bazaar.

Chan See Shu Yuen Temple

Situated at the end of Jalan Petaling, this temple was built in 1906. It has all the features typical of a Chinese temple - open courtyards and symmetrically organised pavilions. It serves as the venue for both religious ceremonies and meetings. Paintings and wood carvings provide interior decor while elaborate glazed ceramic sculptures decorate the facade and roof ridges, resulting in an extremely ornate over-all effect.

Sri Mahamariamman Temple

This Hindu Temple, on Jalan Tun H.S. Lee close to Chinatown, was built in 1873. It is said to be the most ornate and elaborate Hindu temple in the country. Its elaborate decor incorporates gold, precious stones, and Spanish and Italian tiles.

Merdeka Stadium

The stadium has a seating capacity of 50,000, and is the venue for national and international sporting events.

Istana Negara

The official residence of the king, Istana Negara is located on a hillock at Jalan Istana. The formal grounds are beautifully landscaped, and there is a lily-filled pond to add to the atmosphere of tranquillity. But all visitors can do is take a photograph of the guards at the palace gates, or try to snap the building through the iron bars.

KL Tower

Located at Bukit Nanas, the KL Tower is reputed to be the third highest in the world. Literature on the design of the tower says that it is based on Islamic minarets, but to this jaded traveller, a tower is a tower is a tower.

Malaysia Tourist Information Complex

Formerly known as the Tuanku Abdul Rahman Hall, but originally built in 1935 as a mansion for a Malaysian planter and tin-miner. The building was the headquarters of the British Army in 1941, and later for the Japanese Imperial Army, and it was where the first Yang Di Pertuan Agong was installed. It has now been restored and houses the tourist information complex which includes an exhibition hall, information counter, mini auditorium, a souvenir shop, a restaurant and travel services counters.

Titiwangsa Lake Gardens

North of the city centre, and accessible from both Jalan Pahang and Jalan Tun Razak, is Taman Tasik Titiwangsa, a popular park amongst city folk. It has a jogging track, tennis courts, a children's playground and rowing boats for hire.

A short distance away along Jalan Tun Razak is **Bakatkraf**, an exhibition and sales centre for handicraft items produced by the wives of Armed Forces personnel.

Negeri Selangor Darul Ehsan

The state of Selangor Darul Ehsan is on the west coast of Peninsular Malaysia and has an area of 124,450 sq km. The capital is Shah Alam. Local buses operate from Kuala Lumpur to Selangor, but a car is really needed to get around after arriving.

Selangor Pewter Factory

Travelling out of KL along Jalan Pahang you arrive first at the world's biggest pewter factory. Malaysian pewter is made from refined tin, antimony and copper. The demonstration showroom is open to visitors Mon-Sat 8.45am-4.45pm, Sun 9am-4pm.

Visitors can see how the pewter is worked into beautiful articles, and also watch demonstrations of batik making and silverware crafting. Duty-free shopping is available.

Kutang Kraf Batik Factory

Located 15km off Jalan Damanmsara, in Kampong Sungei Pencala, the factory specialises in exclusive hand-drawn and block-printed batik. Here skilled craftsmen give a step-by-step demonstration of the batik making process. Lengths of batik are on sale, and the factory is open Mon-Fri 9.30am-5pm, Sat 9.30am-4pm. Demonstrations are possible at any time during these hours, except from 1 to 2pm.

The Mines Wonderland

The Wonderland is located 15km south of Kuala Lumpur in the Sungei Besi area. It is a delightful theme park that is extremely popular with the locals. Attractions include:

Chinese Fortune Garden, Magic Turtle Lake
Roller Coaster, Mini-Golf
A Snow House (temperatures between 10C and -20C with falling snow)
Aqua Screen Show, Musical Fountain
Lights Fantasy on Water.

The park is open daily 11am-11pm and admission is RM8 adult and RM4 child (weekdays), RM12 and RM6 on weekends, plus separate charges for all rides and the Snow House.

Buses serving the general area include Minibus no. 65 from Kota Raya, and Toong Foong Bus nos. 107 and 110 from Puduraya Bus Terminal. Travel agents in KL who operate tours to the Wonderland include Genting Holiday Travel Sdn Bhd, ph 242 1566, and Mayflower Acme Tours Sdn Bhd, ph 622 1888.

National Zoo and Aquarium

The complex spans 62ha at Ulu Kelang on the outskirts of KL. It is one of the new open-range plan zoos and is home to about 1000 species of flora and fauna from Malaysia and other parts of the world. The aquarium has some 82 species of marine life. There are elephant, camel and donkey-cart rides for the children, a zoo train, and shows featuring elephants, orang-utans and sea-lions. Open daily 9am-5pm, admission is RM5 adult, RM1 child.

Batu Caves

The northbound road, Jalan Ipoh, leads to these caves, 13km from the city centre. They are a massive outcrop of limestone cliffs, which is mainland Asia's southernmost limestone formation. This is the location of a Hindu shrine, and the destination of an annual pilgrimage by thousands of Hindu devotees during Thaipusam. Access to the caves is by means of 272 steps.

Board bus no 70 at Lebuh Pudu, or mini bus no 11 at the Bangkok Bank. The buses run every half hour and travel time is 45 minutes.

National Rubber Museum

The museum is at the Rubber Research Institute's Experimental Station in Sungai Buloh, and was officially opened on February 11, 1992. It traces the history and development of the rubber industry in Malaysia, and is open Mon-Thurs and Sat 10am-4pm. Admission is gratis.

SPORT & RECREATION

Kuala Lumpur has several sports complexes that cater for **court and racquet** games. They are:

Bangsar Sports Complex, ph 254 6065 - badminton, squash, tennis, table tennis, volleyball.

MSN (National Sports Council) Complex, ph 292 9377 - badminton, squash, tennis, table tennis.

Jalan Tun Razak Multipurpose Hall, ph 423 1158 - badminton, table tennis.

Kampung Datuk Keramat Multipurpose Hall, ph 456 4853 - badminton, tennis, basketball, table tennis.

Taman Tasik Titiwangsa, ph 423 9558 - squash, tennis.

Bandar Tun Razak Sports Complex - badminton, squash, table tennis.

Ten Pin Bowling

Pekeliling Bowl, Yow Chuan Plaza, Jalan Tun Tazak, ph 243 0953.

Kent Bowl, 3rd Floor, Asia Jaya Complex, Lorong Utara C, Petaling Jaya, ph 755 7930.

Federal Bowls, Jalan Bukit Bintang, ph 248 9166.

Pin & Balls, 9 Jalan SS 12/1, Subang Jaya, ph 733 8788.

Mirama Bowling Centre, 5th Floor, Wisma Mirama, Jalan Wisma Putra, ph 242 1863.

Jogging

Parts of the main roads around the Lake Garden are closed to make way for joggers, and jogging tracks are also available at Taman Tasik Perdana, Taman Tasik Titiwangsa, Taman Tasik Permaisuri and at the National Sport Council sports complex at Jalan Duta.

Golf

Visitors are welcome at the following golf clubs:

Sentul Golf Club, ph 442 4278, *Armed Forces Golf Club*, ph 241 1113, *The Royal Selangor Golf Club*, ph 984 8433, *Darul Ehsan Golf Club*, ph 457 2333, *Saujana Golf & Country Club*, ph 746 1466, *Kelab Golf Negara Subang*, ph 776 0388, *Sultan Abdul Aziz Shah Golf Club*, ph 550 5872, *Palm Garden Golf Club*, ph 943 7160, *Kelab Rekreasi UKM*, ph 825 7685, *Titiwangsa Golf Club*, ph 293 4964.

NEGERI SEMBILAN

Negeri Sembilan in the national language means "nine states" - as the state comprises a loose federation of nine districts. With a total area of 6645 sq km and a 43km long coastline, this small but pretty state is renowned for its Minangkabau-styled architecture, characterised by sweeping buffalo-horn shaped roof peaks. These reflect the influence of the first inhabitants who came from Minangkabau in Sumatra.

Negeri Sembilan offers attractive beach resorts, historical sights and recreational areas. It is the only state in the country that practises a matrilineal (through the female line) social system (*Adat Perpateh*).

Today Negeri Sembilan is headed by the Yang DiPertuan, who exercises legislative powers on the advice of the Executive Council headed by the Menteri Besar (Chief Minister).

Official business is conducted in Bahasa Malaysia, the national language, however English is widely spoken.

SEREMBAN

Seremban, the state capital, is 64km south of Malaysia's capital city of Kuala Lumpur.

HOW TO GET THERE

An air-conditioned bus from Kuala Lumpur costs RM3 per person, and an air-conditioned taxi costs RM8 per person.

The rail service between Singapore and Kuala Lumpur stops at Seremban.

ACCOMMODATION

Accommodation is available in the town or near the beaches. The higher-priced rooms usually offer better facilities such as air-conditioning, hot and cold water, telephone and television. The bigger hotels and resorts also have bars, restaurants and water sports facilities. There are enough hotels for you to be able to choose to suit your budget.

The telephone area code is 06.

Hotels
Alison Klana Resort, PT4388 Jalan Penghulu Cantik, Tasman Tasik Seremban, ph 729 600.
Carlton Hotel, 47 Off Jalan Dato' Sheikh Ahmad, ph 725 336.
Majestic Hotel, 1 Jalan Dato Lee Fong Yee, ph 722 506.
Tasik Hotel, Jalan Tetamu, ph 730 994.
Mee Lee Hotel, 16/17 Jalan Tuanku Hassan, ph 730 162.
Milo Hotel, 24 Jalan Dato Abdul Rahman, ph 723 451.
Nam Yong Hotel, 5 Jalan Tuanku Munawir, ph 720 155.
New International Hotel, 126 Jalan Tan Sri Manickavasagam, ph 734 957.

Government Rest Houses
Kuala Pilah District - Jalan Bukit.
Jempol District - Lake Garden, Bahau, ph 844 788.
Jelebu District - Jalan Pertang, Kuala Klawang.
Tampin District - Jalan Seremban, Tampin, ph 411 924.
Rembau District - Jalan Kampung Muda, Rembau, ph 652 466.

LOCAL TRANSPORT
Seremban has a good taxi and bus service to take you around town and to attractions outside the town area.

EATING OUT
Negeri Sembilan usually prepares its food heavily chillied and spiced, following the tradition of its early inhabitants from Minangkabau, and the most popular dishes are *Lemak Cili Api* and *Rendang Minang*. *Lemang* (glutinous rice cooked in bamboo) is tasty by itself, but more often eaten with *Rendang*, a dry curried meat dish.

There are plenty of restaurants in Seremban, and the major hotels serve Western, Malay, Chinese and Indian dishes, to suit a variety of tastes. Here are some popular restaurants in the town.

Malay
Tom Yam Corner, Taman Seni Budaya, Jalan Sungai Ujong.
Flamingo Inn, 1A Jalan Zaaba.
Bilal Restaurant, 100 Jalan Dato' Bandar Tunggal.
Fatimah Restaurant, 419 Jalan Tuanku Munawir.
Negeri Restaurant, Jalan Tuanku Munawir.

Chinese
Suntori Restaurant, 10/11 Jalan Dato' Sheikh Ahmad.
Regent Restaurant, 2391-2392 Taman Bukit Labu.
Seafood Restaurant, 2017-2018 Blossom Heights, Jalan Tok Ungku.
Happy Restaurant, 1 Jalan Dato' Bandar Tunggal.

Indian
Samy Restaurant (banana leaf), 120 Jalan Yam Tuan.
Aura Restaurant, 97 Jalan Tuanku Antah.

Food Stalls
Jalan Tuanku Antah - near the Post Office.
Jalan Tun Dr. Ismail - near the Market.

ENTERTAINMENT
For evening entertainment in Seremban there are a few pubs along Jalan Dato' Bandar Tunggal and Jalan Tuanku Munawir, and a nightclub at Jalan Dato' Abdul Rahman.

SHOPPING
The most popular shopping area is in Jalan Dato' Bandar Tunggal, where you can buy almost anything.

SIGHTSEEING

Lake Gardens
Situated in the heart of Seremban there are two lakes surrounded by tropical fauna and flora. Every weekend cultural performances are held, and there are also jogging tracks and a children's playground.

State Mosque
This modern building, built with nine pillars to symbolise the nine districts of Negeri Sembilan, is situated by the Lake Gardens.

State Library
Built in 1912, and designed by Englishman A.B. Habback, this building was originally the State Secretariat. It is quiet near the Lake Gardens.

Cultural Handicraft Complex
The *Kompleks Taman Seni Budaya* is on a 4ha site at the junction of Jalan Sungai Ujong and the Kuala Lumpur-Seremban expressway, about 1km from the heart of Seremban. Built in the style of Minangkabau houses of old, it houses handicrafts and historic items of state. Demonstrations of crafts are held here, and traditional games are performed.

State Museum
The museum is also situated in the Cultural Handicraft Complex, and it built entirely of wood. It houses historical state artifacts and was formerly the old palace at Kampong Ampang-Tinggi. Next to the museum is the *Rumah Minang*, an old Minangkabau house.

OUTLYING ATTRACTIONS

Padas Hot Spring

Located to the south of Seremban on the way to Malacca, the warm waters of the spring are a popular attraction with locals and visitors alike. Refreshment and bathing facilities are available, and there are some good restaurants.

Sri Menanti

This is the state's royal town, and it is east of Seremban. The Sri Menanti Palace was built in 1902, and has 99 pillars depicting the 99 warriors of the various *Luak-luak* (clans). Made entirely of wood, the palace's main attractions include beautiful intricate carvings bearing varied local motifs. The building ceased to be a royal residence in 1931, and current plans are for it to become a Royal Museum.

Ulu Bendol

This forest reserve, about 16km east of Seremban on the way to Kuala Pilah, is a great picnic spot. It lies near the foot of Mount Angsana (762m), and fresh water flows into a man-made lake. Facilities include long-cabins, hiking tracks and jungle paths.

Port Dickson

Situated about 32km south-west of Seremban, Port Dickson has 18km of the best beaches along the west coast of Peninsular Malaysia. It is a favourite playground for Malaysians during holidays and weekends,

A Malay House

and has its share of international standard hotels, motels, bungalows, rest houses and condominiums. The town also has a good choice of restaurants, but it will be no surprise that seafood is usually the specialty of the house.

Cape Rachado overlooks the Straits of Malacca, and is close to the Blue Lagoon Resort. The British built a lighthouse here, and it is worth visiting for the incredible views of the beaches and, on a clear day, the outline of Sumatra. The area is a haven for monkeys, so if it is not a clear day you can watch their antics.

Fort Lukut was built in 1826-27 in a tin mining area. Now visitors can see the palace site, the old well, the drainage around the fort, and the site where the art of Malay defence was practised.

Fort Kempas is 23km from Port Dickson and has an old grave - *Keramat Sungai Ujong* - that marks the last resting place of one of the state's leading historical figures, Ulama Sheikh Ahmad Majnun. Arabic writings found on the megalithic stones behind the grave tell the story of his struggles.

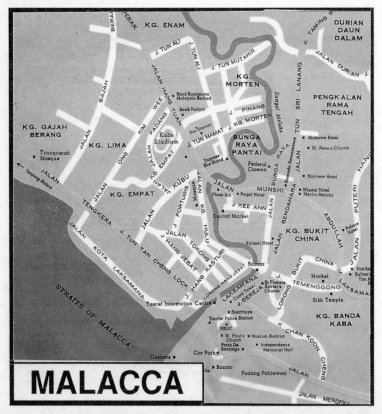

MALACCA

MALACCA

Malacca is situated on the western coast of Peninsular Malaysia, facing the Straits of Malacca, about 147km from Kuala Lumpur and 245km from Singapore. Malacca is sandwiched between the states of Negeri Sembilan and Johor, and covers an area of 658 sq km. It is divided into three districts - Alor Gajah, Malacca Tengah and Jasin.

HISTORY

A refugee prince called Parameswara sought sanctuary in a fishing village around six hundred years ago, and decreed that a city be built where he stood. He named it Malacca from the Malacca tree. The city became a prosperous and powerful nerve centre of trade between the East and West, and eventually became an empire. It was here that gold, silk, tea, opium, tobacco, perfumes and countless other items from nearby countries, and from as far away as Europe and South America, changed ships.

Fame of course attracted conquerors who coveted monopoly of the spice trade, and the Portuguese, the Dutch and the English, at different times, took control of the empire until Malaysia obtained her independence in 1957 and Malacca was handed over to its first local Governor.

Each conquering nation left its mark on the city, and today every street tells its own story of conquest and valour, avarice and victory.

HOW TO GET THERE

By Air

Malacca has a small airport at Batu Berendam, ph (06) 351 175, which is 9km from town. Pelangi Air operates a regular shuttle service between the following destinations:

Malacca/Singapore - daily - RM236 return;
Malacca/Ipoh - daily - RM200 return;
Malacca/Ipoh/Langkawi - Mon, Wed, Fri - RM300 return.
One-way fares are half the above.

By Bus

Several companies operate express bus services between Malacca and other parts of the country. Contact the Tourist Information Office for timetables and fares.

By Rail

There is no rail service to Malacca, but the nearest station is at Tampin, only 38km to the north. For schedules and fares contact the Malacca Office, ph (06) 282 3091, or Tampin Station, ph (06) 411 034.

By Ferry

Ferry services connect Dumai, Sumatra, with Malacca, and the one-way fare is RM80. Companies to contact are: Madai Shipping, 321A Jalan Tun Ali, Malacca, ph (06) 284 0671; Tunas Rupat Utama Express, 17A Jalan Merdeka, ph (06) 283 2506; Ferry Malaysia Sdn Bhd, T-472 Jetty Quayside, Jalan Quayside, ph (06) 284 4344.

Ferries from Malacca to Pulau Besar leave from the Umbai Jetty, ph (06) 261 0492 at least 24 hours in advance. Fares are RM10 per person return, or RM80 per boat (8 people) return.

Ferries to Pulau Upeh leave from the TIC Jetty, Jalan Kota, at 8.30am, 3.30pm, 5pm and 11.30pm. Departures from the island are at 9am, 4pm, 5.30pm and midnight.

By Road

Malacca is 148km from Kuala Lumpur

TOURIST INFORMATION

The Malacca Tourist Information Centre is in Jalan Kota, ph (07) 283 6538.

ACCOMMODATION

Listed below is a sample of the accommodation available. The prices are for a double room per night in Malaysian Ringgit, and should be used as a guide only. The telephone area code is 06.

Malacca Village Park Plaza Resort, Ayer Keroh, ph 323 600 - 146 rooms, 3 restaurants, cocktail lounge, coffee shop, swimming pool, sauna - RM178.

Malacca Renaissance, Jalan Bendahara, ph 248 888 - 295 rooms, restaurant, cocktail lounge, coffee shop, pool, sauna - RM188.

Budget

Ayer Keroh Country Resort, Ayer Keroh, ph 325 210 - from RM80.
Lotus Inn, 2846 Jalan Semabok, ph 237 211 - RM28-58.
Malacca Hotel, 27A Jalan Munshi Abdullah, ph 222 499 - RM26.
Majestic Hotel, 188 Jalan Bunga Raya, ph 222 367 - RM21-42.
Bachang Hotel, 91F Jalan Bachang, ph 351 799 - RM16-28.
Chong Hoe Hotel, 26 Tukang Emas, ph 226 102 - RM16-28.
Hong Kong Hotel, 154-A1 Jalan Bunga Raya, ph 223 392 - RM16-26.
Merryland Hotel, 49 Jalan Pasar Baru, ph 220 371 - RM16-24.

Rest Houses
Seri Jasin Rest House, JKR 1777 7700 Jasin, ph 593 413 - RM35.
Seri Gajah Rest House, 2052 Alor Gajah, ph 563 217 - RM30.
Paradise Hostel, 4 Jalan Tengkera, ph 230 821 - RM6-20.
Eastern Lodging Hotel, 85 Jalan Bendahara, ph 231 541 - RM10-16.

LOCAL TRANSPORT

Taxi
Taxis are comfortable and quick. During the day they will be metered, but between the hours of midnight and 6am an additional 50% of the normal rate will be charged.

Bus
The Historical Melaka Shuttle offers unlimited travel all day and starts from TIC Jalan Kota 8.30am weekends, 9.30am weekdays, and after at hourly intervals. Fares are RM5 adult, RM3 child.

Trishaws
Once a common method of transportation, the trishaw - a bicycle with a side car - is now more popular with tourists. A ride is a novel way to explore parts of the city.

EATING OUT

Malay
Restoran Anda, 8A Jalan Hang Tuah - open for lunch and dinner.
Restoran 35, 35 Jalan Merdeka, Banda Hilir - open 11am-3pm.
Hawkers Stall at Malacca Tourist Market, Jalan Tun Sri Lanang - open 7.30pm-midnight.
Hawkers Stall along Jalan Hang Tuah - open 7.30pm-midnight.
Restoran Sri Pandan, Jalan Kota - Hawkers Stall.
Kedai Makan dan Minuman, Hj. Mohd. Abdullah bin Sulaiman, 517 Jalan Munshi Abdullah - open 11am-3pm.
Mata Kuching Restoran, Jalan Taming Sari - open moon-3pm, closed Sunday.

Nyonya
My Baba's, 164 Jalan Munshi Abdullah.
Peranakan Restaurant, 107 Jalan Tun Tan Cheng Lok.
Ole Sayang Restaurant, 198 & 199 Taman Melaka Raya.
Nyonya Makko Restaurant, 123 Taman Melaka Raya.

Portuguese
San Pedro Restaurant, Portuguese Settlement.

Restaurant d'Lisbon, Portuguese Settlement.

Chinese
New Good World Restaurant, 133-2B Tmn Melaka Raya.
Hiking Restaurant, 112 Taman Melaka, Raya.
Bei Tang Restaurant, 502, 503 & 504 Taman Melaka Raya.

Indian
Banana Leaf Restaurant, 42 Jalan Munshi Abdullah.
Veni Restaurant, 34 Jalan Temenggong.

Japanese
Kiraku Restaurant, Park Plaza Resort, Air Keroh.

Fast Food
Pizza Hut, 114 Jalan Bendahara. *Kentucky Fried Chicken*, 52 Jalan Taming Sari; Plaza Melaka, Jalan Gajah Berang; Jaya Jusco, 4991 Mukim Bukit Baru, Daerah Tengah Melaka.
McDonald's, Lot 165 Soon Seng Plaza, Jalan Tun Ali; Mahkota Parade, Jalan Melaka Raya; Jaya Jusco, 4991 Mukim Bukit Baru, Daerah Tengah Melaka.
Eighteen Carrot Coffee House Restaurant, Plaza Melaka, Jalan Gajah Berang. *Shakey's Pizza Melaka*, Lot G-11, Ground Floor, Jaya Jusco Melaka, Ayer Keroh.

SHOPPING
With its ancient history as the main port of South-East Asia, it is natural that many fine antiques have come to roost in Malacca.

Its narrow, picturesque streets are full of old treasures, but remember that it is necessary to have an export permit to take antiques out of the country. This is available from the office of the Director General of Museums, Malaysia, in Kuala Lumpur.

Jalan Hang Jebat, formerly known as Jonker Street, is the place to visit for antiques. Authentic artifacts dating back nearly 300 years can be found in shops here, and can be purchased at reasonable prices.

Prices at shopping complexes are fixed, but bargaining is welcomed at smaller retail shops and roadside stalls.

Shopping Complexes
Parkson Grand Mahkota Parade, Jalan Merdeka.
Jaya Jusco Store, Bukit Beruang.
Madam King's (Departmental, 126, 128 & 133 Jalan Bunga Raya.
Fajar Departmental Store & Supermarket, 165 Jalan Hang Tuah.
Great Wall Shopping Centre, Plaza Melaka, Jalan Gajah Berang.
Store Holding, 12A Jalan Kilang.

Emporium Formosa, Jalan Bunga Raya.
Orchard Square, Off Jalan Ong Kim Wee.
City Bayview Hotel Arcade, Jalan Bendahara.

Duty Free Shops
Melaka Duty Free Shop, Jalan Munshi Abdullah.
Duty Free Shop, Batu Berendam, Airport 1.

Souvenirs
Handicraft Stalls, Taman Merdeka, Bandar Hilir.
Orang Utan House, 59 Jalan Hang Jebat.
Jade House Jewellery 564 Tmn Melaka Raya.
Malacca Souvenir House, 22 Jalan Tokong.

Handicrafts
Sykt Pemasaran Karyaneka, 1 Jalan Laksamana.
Pusat Kraftangan, Taman Mini Malaysia, Air Keroh.

SIGHTSEEING

The Stadthuys
Situated in the Dutch square and solid testimony to Dutch masonry and woodwork skills, the Stadthuys were built as the official residence of Dutch Governors and their officers.

Completed in 1650, only one room still has the original wooden floral ceiling of that period. The building now houses the Historic Museum and Ethnography Museum. On display daily are traditional bridal costumes and relics from Malacca's colourful past.

Christ Church
This is an exquisite piece of Dutch architecture, completed in 1753. The ceiling beams were each cut from one single tree and have no joints at all. The handmade pews are the originals dating back over 200 years. Over the altar there is a frieze of the Last Supper in glazed tiles. The brass bible rest dates back to 173 and in the centre is inscribed the first verse of St John. On the floor are tombstones in Armenian Script.

St Francis Xavier's Church
This twin Gothic towered church was built in 1849 by a French priest, Fr Farve, on the site of a former Portuguese Church. It is dedicated to St Francis Xavier known as the Apostle of the East, who spread Catholicism in South East Asia during the 16th century.

St Paul's Church
Built in 1521, this was known as Duarte Coelho, the leading church for Catholics at that time.

The Dutch renamed the church St Paul's and eventually made it an extension of the fortress. Evidence of gun embrasures with holes for gun-recoilers can still be seen today. When the Dutch completed the Christ Church in the red-painted Dutch Square in 1753, they made St Paul's Hill into a burial ground for their noble dead.

St Paul's Hill Fort.

One can see tombstones, some with Latin and Portuguese inscriptions. The open grave inside St Paul's is where St Francis Xavier was buried in 1553 before his body was moved to Goa in India.

A Famosa (Porta De Santiago)

This gateway is the remaining ruin of the once strong fortress built by the Portuguese in 1511 and known as A Famosa. During the Dutch attack the fortress was badly damaged and had to be repaired. The Dutch did this in 1670 and renamed this great fortress "Voc", with the crest above the gateway that can be seen till this day. Had it not been for Sir Stamford Raffles' intervention in 1810, the gateway would not still exist.

Light and Sound Show

This is the first of this kind of entertainment in South-East Asia, and it is well worth visiting. It is held at Bandar Hilir, Padang Pahlawan and is a great insight into the history of Malacca. Local literature compares the show with those held at the Pyramids at Giza and the Acropolis at Athens, but that may be carrying things a bit far. The Tourist Information Centre has details of current show times and prices.

Malacca Sultanate Palace

This wooden replica of the Sultanate's Palace is situated at the foot of St Paul's Hill. The architectural design of the palace is based on the description of "Malay Annals" or "Serjarah Melayu" and is one of its kind in Malaysia. The palace now houses the Malacca Cultural Museum.

Proclamation of Independence Memorial

Built in 1912 this hall was formerly known as the Malacca Club. Today it houses pictures portraying events leading to the attainment of Malaysia's Independence and the struggles and efforts of leaders like Tunku Abdul Rahman Putra Al-Haj, Malaysia's first Prime Minister. Visitors can also view a wide range of exhibits that include historical documents, maps, treaties, videos, films, minutes of meetings, news scripts, etc, all relating to the Independence struggle.

Hang Jebat's Mausoleum

Hang Jebat, along with four of his closest friends, took lessons in the Malay art of self defence, until they had perfected every movement. They saved the life of Bendahara Paduka Raja, Prime Minister of the Sultan Shah. As a reward they were made attendants at court.

Hang Jebat was killed by his friend Hang Tuah in a duel of honour that lasted three days and three nights. He ran amok after suffering a fatal wound from Hang Tuah's dagger. In the name of justice to avenge the Sultan's hasty punishment against Hang Tuah for a crime he didn't commit, Hang Jebat was accused by Hang Tuah of "durhaka" (insubordination).

The duel between two of Malacca's most prominent knights has left a permanent question as to the moral behind Hang Jebat's aberrant reaction against the authority, and the conventions by which Hang Tuah exercised his conduct as a loyal subject of the Sultan. (I think there are a lot of questions left unanswered in the above story. For one, who on earth was in the right?)

Sri Poyyatha Vinayagar Moorthi Temple

One of the first Hindu temples built in the country at the turn of the century. It was built on the plot given by the Dutch.

Kampong Kling's Mosque

One of the oldest mosques in the country with Sumatran architectural features. Instead of a conventional dome, a three-tier roof rises like a pyramid. The minaret is built like a pagoda, showing a mixture of East and West influences.

The Baba Nyonya Heritage

Straits Chinese, or the Baba and Nyonya, are Chinese of noble blood who have adopted much of the Malay culture into theirs. The public can now view their unique heritage at a private museum in Jalan Tun Tan Cheng Lock.

Cheng Hoon Teng's Temple

This temple is the oldest Chinese temple in Malaysia, founded in 1646. It covers an area of 4600 sq m, and its eaves are decorated with figures of mythology. The wood carvings and lacquer work inside the temple are magnificent.

The main altar houses the "Goddess of Mercy", and on the left altar is the "Queen of Heaven", the special guardian of fishermen and voyagers on the high seas. The railings above the altars depict the life of Buddha. Outside is the courtyard where you can see the "Three Doctrinal Systems" of Buddhism, Confucianism and Taoism, beautifully blended.

All the materials used to build the temple came from China.

Hang Kasturi's Mausoleum

Hang Kasturi was one of the friends of Hang Jebat who became a knight of the Sultan. However, Hang Kasturi remained loyal to the ruler until his dying day.

Kampong Hulu's Mosque

This mosque is the oldest in Malaysia. It was built in 1728 by Dato Shamsuddin. The unique architectural style of this mosque can only be found in Malacca.

St Peter's Church

Built in 1710 by the Portuguese with a mixture of Oriental and Occidental architectural styles, the church contains a life-size alabaster statue of *The Dead Lord Before the Resurrection*. The interior is unique in Iberian design with several Corinthian pillars supporting the curved ceiling above the aisle.

Sam Po Kong Temple

The temple is dedicated to Admiral Cheng Ho, but named after a fish that miraculously saved the admiral's ship from sinking after it had been hit by a storm enroute to Malacca from Chins. The fish placed itself against a damaged hull preventing the ship from taking on water.

Hang Li Poh's Well

Built in 1459 by the following of Hang Li Poh, the Chinese princess who married the Sultan of Malacca, the well never dried up during days of old and was the only source of water during long droughts.
It has been turned into a wishing well, and it is said that people who throw coins into it will return to Malacca again and again.

Bukit China

Chinese Hill was the official settlement of the Chinese retinue that arrived with Princess Hang Li Poh. They stayed on here until the Portuguese arrived in 1511. Today Bukit China is the largest Chinese cemetery outside China, and many of the tombs date back to the Ming Dynasty.

St John's Fort
The fort, built on St John's Hill 3km from town, was constructed by the Dutch during the latter part of the 18th century, but was once a private Portuguese chapel dedicated to St John the Baptist. It is interesting to note that the gun embrasures of the fort face inland and not toward the seas, as regular attacks came from the hinterland.

Portuguese Square
Located in the Portuguese Settlement, this is where their descendants live in a close-knit group. The architectural design of the square resembles that of Lisbon. Besides the availability of authentic Portuguese dishes, cultural shows are performed every Saturday.

Tranquerah Mosque
A unique mosque that bears testimony to the fact that Islam was present in Malacca almost 600 years ago. The tomb of Sultan Hussain of Johore is in the compound of the mosque. He was the ruler who signed the cession of Singapore with Sir Stamford Raffles in 1819.

OUTLYING ATTRACTIONS

Butterfly Farm, Air Keroh
One of the world's most comprehensive butterfly and insect farms, it has well over 200 local species, including the rare Raja Brooke and Birdwing. There is also a collection of more than 400 insect specimens.

Mini Malaysia, Air Keroh
Step into Mini Malaysia and experience the rich Malaysian arts and culture, a heritage moulded by its diverse races, rivalled by few in this part of the world. See the thirteen types of attractively crafted Malaysian traditional state houses, each containing works of art and culture. Colourful cultural shows and traditional games staged in the open prove intriguing.

Mini ASEAN, Air Keroh
A theme park conceived as the summary of prominent cultural elements of the countries that make up ASEAN - Malaysia, Thailand, Philippines, Singapore, Indonesia and Brunei. The park is open daily 9am-6pm.

Ayer Keroh Recreational Forest
Set amidst a splendid forest about 11km from town, visitors can walk through an tropical haven. The trees are labelled, giving a quick lesson in Malaysia's flora and fauna. There are also marked routes for trekking, hiking, jogging and cycling. The forest is open 7am-6pm.

Crocodile Farm, Air Keroh
The largest crocodile farm in the country, with more than 100 species, is a short way off the Air Keroh Road.

Malacca Zoo, Air Keroh
The zoo has more than 44 species of animals found in South-East Asia and Africa, set in natural surroundings.

Ayer Keroh Lake
This scenic lake has various water sport facilities such as boating and canoeing, coupled with refreshment kiosk and a children's playground.

Gadek Hot Spring
The Gadek Hot Spring is a popular spot on the route to Tampin, about 25km from Malacca Town. The sulphur water is believed to possess curative elements for a number of skin diseases. Handicraft shops and playgrounds make this a perfect outing for the family.

Megalithic Stones
There are over 90 separate sites for these century old stones, mostly found in Alor Gajah and on the road to Tampin. These components form part of a large cluster that spreads in Negeri Sembilan.

Hang Tuah's Mausoleum
Hang Tuah was an admiral of Malacca's naval forces who successfully defended attacks by the Siamese and Achenese fleets. His outstanding performance as an officer made him a legend throughout the land.

His bravery, however, was discovered during his adolescence, when he single-handedly arrested a man who had ran amok in the village of Kampong Duyong. This act was reported to the Sultan who knighted Hang Tuah, making him the youngest person to be so honoured.

Hang Tuah's Well
This is a sacred well in Kampong Duyong that is believed to be the abode of Hang Tuah's soul. The soul is believed to take the form of a white crocodile, but only the most holy of people can see it, so maybe a visit would be a waste of time.

Tun Teja's Mausoleum
Situated about 24km from Malacca Town in Merlimau, this is the grave of Tun Teja, the daughter of Sri Amar Di Raja Pahang. She was taken to Malacca by Hang Tuah to marry Sultan Mahmud Shah, and died a queen while retreating with the Sultan from a Portuguese attack in 1511.

Malacca Traditional House

This colourful, intricately carved wooden house was built in the 19th century by a Chieftain. It is the only one of its kind in this zone. Situated 5km from Merlimau Town on the way to Muar.

Dutch Fort

The fort is located at Kuala Linggi, 49km from Malacca Town on the way to Port Dickson. It was used as an outpost to enforce the collection of taxes, and was manned by a small garrison of Dutch officers. It was abandoned when mining in the Naning area ceased.

British Graveyard

Located in Alor Gajah town, this graveyard was for British officers killed during the Naning War.

Dol Said's Grave

Dato Dol Said was the ninth ruler of Naning who opposed the imposition of tax on the district by the British. The Naning War, waged in 1834, made him a hero to his people, and earned him a place in the history of Malacca. His grave is at Taboh Naning, about 32km from Malacca Town.

Cape Rachado

This enclave is in Negeri Sembilan, 57km from Malacca. The headland forest forms an important guideline for migratory birds like sparrows, hawks, honey buzzard, eagles and swifts. In September/October and again in March/April, large concentrations of hawks and eagles can be seen. There is also a blue lagoon that has interesting marine life, and a beautiful beach. The lighthouse towers over the cape.

Pulau Besar

The island is located in the Straits of Malacca, 13 nautical miles off the mainland of Umbai jetty and 10 nautical miles from Malacca Port. The sandy beaches provide ample opportunities for swimming, fishing, picnicking, camping and snorkelling.

SPORT AND RECREATION

Golf

Ayer Keroh Country Club is one of the most challenging courses in the country - 18 holes. *Jasin Golf Club* was once an exclusive and prestigious British planters' club, but is now confined within an army camp - 9 holes.

Golden Valley Golf and Country Club can only be described as big - 54 holes, ie three 18-hole courses.

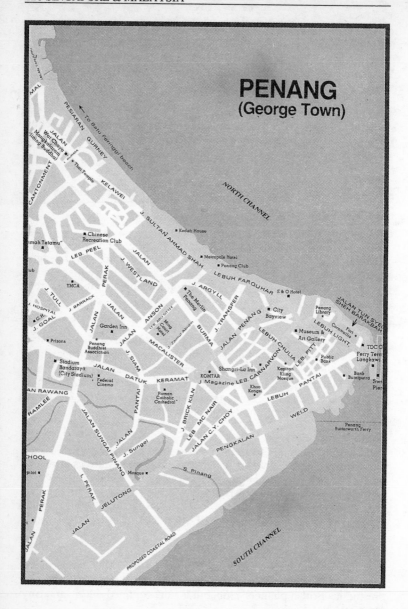

PENANG

Penang, the Pearl of the Orient, is situated on the north-western coast of Peninsular Malaysia. It is bounded to the north and east by the state of Kedah, to the south by the state of Perak, and to the west by the Straits of Malacca and Sumatra (Indonesia).

Penang consists of the island of Penang (*Pulau Pinang*) and a coastal strip on the mainland called Province Wellesley. The island covers an area of 284 sq km, and its shape resembles a swimming turtle. It is approximately 24km north to south and 14.5km east to west. The mainland and the island are separated by a channel 3km wide at the closest point and 13km at the farthest, and are linked by the Penang Bridge and a 24-hour ferry service.

The capital city of Penang is Georgetown.

HISTORY

In the early 1700s, Penang was viewed as an excellent location for a harbour to repair British ships damaged in monsoons in the Bay of Bengal. In 1786 Captain Francis Light of the British East India Company arrived on the island and formally took possession of it for England on August 11, following negotiations with the Sultan of Kedah, to whom he promised protection. Penang was the first British settlement in the Far East.

As August 11 was the birthday of the then Prince of Wales, Light renamed the island Prince of Wales Island. He named the capital Georgetown after the reigning monarch, George III. Today Georgetown still retains its name but the island is called *Pulau Pinang* or Island of the Betel Nut, a palm commonly found in the State.

A strip of land on the mainland was ceded by the Sultan of Kedah in 1800 and named Province Wellesley after the then Governor of India - Richard, Marquis of Wellesley. In 1805, Penang's status was raised to that of Presidency and in 1832 it became part of the Straits Settlements, together with Malacca and Singapore.

Penang became a State of Independent Malaya on August 31, 1957. When Malaysia was formed in September 1963, following the merging of Malaya with the former Borneo states of Sabah and Sarawak, Penang became one of its 13 states.

CLIMATE

Penang has an equatorial climate which is warm and humid throughout the year. Average temperature is between 33C and 24C.

Mean annual rainfall of approximately 267cm is evenly distributed, with the wettest months from September to November.

HOW TO GET THERE

By Air
Penang's International Airport at Bayan Lepas is about 20km from the centre of Georgetown. Malaysia Airlines has several daily flights from Kuala Lumpur to Penang, and the airport is also serviced by Singapore Airlines, Cathay Pacific and Air New Zealand, among others.

The airport telephone number is (04) 830 811.

By Rail
The train journey from Kuala Lumpur to Butterworth takes approximately 6 hours, and first and second class passengers travel in air-conditioned coaches.

By Ferry
From Butterworth there is an around-the-clock car ferry service to Penang Island. Tickets are available at the Butterworth terminal and return fares are RM0.40 adult, RM0.20 child. Rates charged for vehicles are based on the engine capacity and the number of passengers -
Cars below 1200cc - RM4 + RM0.40 per passenger.
Cars above 1200cc - RM5 + RM0.40 per passenger.

By Road
There is a toll of RM7 for cars driving across the Penang Bridge from the mainland to the island, payable at the toll plaza in Perai. There is no charge for the return journey.

TOURIST INFORMATION
Thee are a few information offices in Penang -

Penang International Airport, ph (04) 830 501.

Penang Development Corporation, Tourism Division, 1 Pesiaran Mahsuri, Bayan Baru, ph (04) 832 111.

Penang Tourist Centre, Bangunan Penang Port Commission, ph (04) 616 663.

ACCOMMODATION
There is no shortage of accommodation in Penang and a selection follows. Prices quoted are for a double room per night and should be used as a guide only. The telephone area code is 04.

Hotels - City
Shangri-La, Jalan Megazine, ph 262 2622 - 447 rooms, 1 restaurant,

cocktail lounge, coffee shop, swimming pool, sauna - from RM345.

Equatorial, 1 Jalan Bukit, 11900 Bayan Lepas, ph 643 8111 - 413 rooms, 1 restaurant, cocktail lounge, swimming pool, sauna - RM256

City Bayview, 25A Farquhar Street, ph 263 3161 - 160 rooms, 4 restaurants, cocktail lounge, coffee shop, swimming pool - RM192.

Eastern & Oriental (E & O), 10 Farquhar Street, ph 263 0630 - 100 rooms, 1 restaurant, cocktail lounge, coffee shop, swimming pool - RM185.

Hotels - Beach

Rasa Sayang, Batu Ferringhi Beach, ph 881 1811 - 514 rooms, 3 restaurants, cocktail lounge, coffee shop, swimming pool, sauna, fitness centre - RM302-400.

Golden Sands, Batu Ferringhi Beach, ph 881 1911 - 395 rooms, 3 restaurants, cocktail lounge, coffee shop, swimming pool, fitness centre - RM240-340.

ParkRoyal Penang, Batu Ferringhi Beach, ph 881 1113 - 333 rooms, 4 restaurants, cocktail lounge, coffee shop, swimming pool, fitness centre - RM247-270.

Crown Prince Hotel, Tanjung Bungah, ph 890 4111 - 280 rooms, 2 restaurants, cocktail lounge, coffee shop, swimming pool, fitness centre - RM235.

Bayview Beach, Batu Ferringhi Beach, ph 881 2123 - 396 rooms, 4 restaurants, cocktail lounge, coffee shop, swimming pool, sauna, fitness centre - RM209-225.

Casuarina Beach Hotel, Batu Ferringhi, ph 881 1711 - 180 rooms, 2 restaurants, cocktail lounge, swimming pool - RM215.

Holiday Inn, 72 Batu Ferringhi, ph 881 1601 - 350 rooms, 2 restaurants, cocktail lounge, coffee shop, swimming pool, fitness centre - RM181.

Palm Beach, Batu Ferringhi Beach, ph 881 1621 - 143 rooms, 1 restaurant, cocktail lounge, swimming pool - RM194.

Ferringhi Beach Hotel, 12.5km Jalan Batu Ferringhi, Batu Ferringhi, ph 890 5999 - 350 rooms, 2 restaurants, cocktail lounge, coffee shop - RM181.

Novotel, Tanjung Bungah, ph 890 3333 - 323 rooms, 2 restaurants, cocktail lounge, coffee shop, swimming pool, sauna - RM165.

Budget

Bellevue Penang Hill Hotel, ph 699 500 - RM88-110.

Central Hotel, 404 Penang Road, ph 366 411 - RM69-80.

Cathay Hotel, 15 Lebuh Leith, ph 626 271 - RM46-58.

Lum Thean Hotel, 422 Chulia Street, ph 614 117 - RM23-28.

Eng Aun Hotel, 380 Chulia Street, ph 612 333 - RM20-22.

Hostel

YMCA of Penang, Jalan Macalister, ph 362 211 - RM48-80.

Penang Youth Hostel, 8 Leboh Farquhar, ph 630 558 - dormitory RM8;

apartments RM50-70.

Rest House
Government Rest House, Jesselton Road, ph 281 343 - RM39-44.

LOCAL TRANSPORT

Bus
The Penang Yellow Bus Co operates an hourly service between the airport and Pengkalan Weld in the city, between 6am and 10pm daily (bus no. 83).

Other bus companies ply different routes within the city, and fares range from RM0.30 to RM2.05.

Kenderaan Juara Sdn Bhd buses leave from Lebuh Victoria Terminal and travel to:

Bus1	Air Itam
2	Bagan Jermal
3	Jelutong
4	Jalan Yeap Chor Ee via Jalan Perak
5	Jalan Mesjid Negeri via Dhoby Ghaut
6	Jalan Mesjid Negeri via Jalan Patani
7	Jalan Kebun Bunga
8	Penang Hill Railway
9	Green Lane via Jalan Penang/Jalan Dato Keramat
10	Kampung Melayu
11	Bukit Gelugor via Jalan Mesjid Negeri
12	Jelutong to Air Itam Village

Sri Negara Bus Transport Services Co buses leave from Jalan Dr Lim Chwee Leong Terminal and serve the following destinations:

Bus 136 Pengkalan Weld to Pepper Estate
136 Pengkalan Weld to Tanjung Tokong

Hin Bus Co (Blue Buses) leaves from Dr Lim Chwee Leong Terminal as follows:

Bus 93 Pengkalan Weld to Teluk Bahang
94 & 102 Pengkalan Weld to Tanjung Bunga

Lim Seng Seng Bus Co (Green Buses) leaves from Dr Lim Chwee Leong Terminal.

Bus 91 & 92 Pengkalan Weld to Air Itam

Penang Yellow Bus Co leaves from Dr Lim Chwee Leong Terminal.

Bus66	Pengkalan Weld to Balik Pulau
67	Pengkalan Weld to Gertak Sanggul
68 & 69	Pengkalan Weld to Batu Maung
77	Pengkalan Weld to Minden Heights
78	Pengkalan Weld to Sg Ara (Snake Temple)
79	Pengkalan Weld to Air Itam via Paya Terubong

83	Pengkalan Weld to Penang Airport
84	Pengkalan Weld to Bayan Baru
86	Pengkalan Weld to Mayang Pasir

Taxi

Airport taxis follow the coupon system with fixed fares. The fare from the airport to Batu Ferringhi is RM35. Most city taxis do not generally use the meter, but you can insist it be turned on, or you can settle on a price before beginning the journey. The usual charge for short distances within the city is between RM3 and RM6. Radio taxi telephone numbers are 229 0501, 378 501 and 228 9368.

Trishaw

A ride on one of these is a novel way to see the sights of Penang, but be sure to fix a price first. The normal rate is about RM15 per hour.

Car Hire

The following companies have offices in Penang:

Avis Rent-A-Car, E & O Hotel, Lebuh Farquhar, ph 631 685; Rasa Sayang Hotel Lobby, ph 811 522.

Bakar Rent-A-Car, ph228 1541.

Herz Rent-A-Car, Penang Bowl Building, Lebuh Farquhar, ph 635 914; Bayan Lepas International Airport, ph 830 208; Casuarina Hotel, ph 811 711.

Kasina Baru (M) Sdn Bhd, Bayan Lepas International Airport, ph 847 901.

Sintat Rent-A-Car, Bayan Lepas International Airport, ph 830 958.

National Rent-A-Car, 1 Weld Quay, ph 629 404; Bayan Lepas International Airport, ph 834 205.

Seraya Mutiara Rent-A-Car, 394 Batu Ferringhi, ph 811 394; ParkRoyal Penang, ph 811 133; Golden Sands Resort, ph 811 911; Bayan Lepas International Airport, ph 848 313.

Orix Rent-A-Car, City Bayview Hotel, ph 618 608.

SMAS Rent-A-Car, Bayan Lepas Internat. Airport, ph 852 288.

EATING OUT

The main hotels have at least one restaurant, usually more, and there are plenty of other restaurants and coffee shops offering fine food. Present on every bill of fare is seafood, which the local fisherman deliver daily.

Hawker Stalls are found at the following locations:

Lebuh Carnarvon (morning only), Pengkalan Weld (morning only); Lebuh Cintra; Lebuh Kimberley; Jalan Macalister, near Jalan Penang; Jalan Burma; Lorong Selamat; Lorong Swatow; Jalan Kampong Malabar; Lebuh Chulia; Pesiaran Gurney; Esplanade; Padang Brown.

ENTERTAINMENT

Penang has discos with the latest sound and light effects, cocktail lounges with live artists, cultural shows, and everything in between.

Air-conditioned cinemas screen English, Malay, Chinese and Indian movies and tickets range from RM4 to RM7. Details of programs can be found in the daily newspapers.

Drama performances and concerts are advertised in the daily newspapers, and the venues are: Dewan Sri Pinang, Lebuh Light; Fort Cornwallis Amphitheatre; and Geodesic Dome, Komtar.

SHOPPING

The main shopping areas in Penang are Jalan Penang, Lebuh Campbell, Lebuh Kapitan Kling, Lebuh Chulia and Lebuh Pantai.

Batik is available at factories in Teluk Bahang, souvenir shops at Batu Ferringhi, specialist shops in Jalan Penang, department stores; in short, just about everywhere.

Chinese embroidery, lacquer screens and jade and ivory carvings can be found in shops along Jalan Penang and Lebuh Bishop.

The majority of jewellery outlets are found on Lebuh Campbell, Lebuh Kapitan Kling and Jalan Penang, and pewter goods are available in department stores and shops along Jalan Penang.

For antique lovers a trip to Rope Walk (Jalan Pintal Tali) is well worthwhile, but remember that you have to have a licence from the Director General of Museums, Malaysia, to export antiques.

Most shops are open daily 10am-10pm, and bargaining is definitely the way to go.

> Remember that you may not be allowed to take goods made from ivory into your home country.

SIGHTSEEING

Georgetown

Acheen Street Mosque

This is one of the oldest mosques in Penang, built by Syed Sheriff Tengku Syed Hussain Aidid, who came to the island in 1792 from Acheh, Sumatra. In a will made in 1820, Syed Hussain left a piece of land for the mosque, which was built next to his tomb. The mosque is reminiscent of Egyptian architecture, and half-way up the minaret is a round window which, according to popular belief, was originally a hole made by a cannon ball fired during fighting between two secret societies during the Penang riots in 1867. It is necessary to obtain permission from Mosque official to enter.

Khoo Kongsi

Kongsis, or clan houses, are associations which originated in China centuries ago for people of the same surname. Today they look after the affairs of members and also safeguard the principles of ancestral worship.

The first Khoos emigrated from South China, and the first clan-house they erected burned down in 1894, apparently because some people thought it too closely resembled the Emperor's palace. The present smaller version was built in 1902, and it contains intricate carvings and richly ornamented beams that bear the mark of master craftsmen from China. In a side room there are plaques commemorating Khoos that have made their mark on society.

Situated in Lebuh Cannon, the complex is open Mon-Fri 9am-5pm, Sat 9am-1pm, and although brochures say that permission must be obtained from the Kongsi office to enter, when I was there everyone simply walked in and looked around.

Kapital Kling Mosque

Built about 1800 by an Indian Muslim merchant, Caudeer Mohudeen, who was the Kapitan Kling (headman) at that time. Situated in Lebuh Pitt, the dome-shaped and well placed minaret reflect Islamic architecture with Indian influence.

Sri Mariamman Temple

Built in 1883, and situated in Lebuh Queen, this temple contains a priceless statue of Lord Subramaniam that is decorated in gold, diamonds, emeralds and other precious stones. The statue is led in a chariot procession to the temple at Jalan Waterfall during the Thaipusam festival.

Kuan Yin Temple

Popularly known as the Temple of the Goddess of Mercy, it was built in 1800 through the joint efforts of the first Chinese settlers - the Hokkien and Cantonese communities.

Situated in Lebuh Pitt, this temple is one of the busiest in Penang, especially during the Goddess' birthday celebrations in March, and in October when puppet shows are stage in the vicinity.

St George's Church

Built by convict labour in 1818, it was the first Anglican Church to be built in Singapore and Malaya.

St George's, in Lebuh Farquhar, is more than a Christian edifice, it is one of the oldest landmarks in Malaysia. Apart from the original flat roof, which was altered to its gable shape, the church still looks as it did in the old days. The first marriage to be conducted here was on June 20, 1818, between the Governor of the East India Company, W.E.

Phillips, and Janet, daughter of Colonel Bannerman.

The church is also a symbol of Penang's early history, for in the grounds stands a monument to the memory of Captain Francis Light, founder of Penang.

Penang Museum & Art Gallery

Formerly the Penang Free School, it was built in 1816 in Lebuh Farquhar. When the Free School moved to its present premises in 1928, the building was taken over by the Hutchings School.

During the Pacific War (1941-45), the building was badly damaged, leaving only the main block, which currently houses the Penang Museum and Art Gallery. During the war, the school was occupied by the Japanese Navy, and the playground was used for planting tapioca and vegetables.

The museum has a good collection of old photographs, maps, charts and historical exhibits, as well as Malay daggers, Chinese furniture, and embroidery and paintings of old Penang.

It is open daily 9am-5pm (closed Fri 12.15-2.45pm).

Cathedral of the Assumption

One of the oldest Roman Catholic churches in Malaysia, the cathedral is in Lebuh Farquhar. It has a rather simple interior, especially for a Catholic cathedral, but it does exude an atmosphere of "holiness".

Logan Memorial and High Court

The marble statue that stands in the compound of the High Court in Lebuh Farquhar, is dedicated to James Richardson Logan, a prominent lawyer and one-time editor of the *Penang Gazette*. Logan devoted his life to serving the public and advocating freedom of speech, and law and order till his death in 1869. The Memorial and High Court are in front of the Museum & Art Gallery.

Cheong Fatt Tze Mansion

This mansion of 18th and 19th century Chinese architecture is believed to be one of the only three such buildings remaining outside China. The others are in Manila and Jakarta.

The mansion is in Lebuh Leith and was built by Cheong Fatt Tze, a Kwantung business man, and son of the Grand Taifung, a scholar.

Clock Tower

The tower was presented to the town in 1897 by Mr Cheah Chen Eok, a Penang millionaire, to commemorate the Diamond Jubilee of Queen Victoria. It is 60 feet high - a foot for each of the years of the Queen's reign. It is situated in Jalan Tun Syed Sheh Barakbah.

Fort Cornwallis

A city landmark built where Captain Francis Light landed in 1786. Originally a wooden stockade, it was replaced by a concrete structure built by convict labour in 1804. Today there is an open-air amphitheatre, and a history gallery and a handicraft and souvenir centre occupy the interior. The walls are moss-covered, and protruding from the ramparts are several age-old cannons retrieved by the British from pirates who had captured them from the Johore Sultanate, then a Dutch protectorate.

The main cannon "Seri Rambai" is said to date back to 1618, and if you happen to see flowers and joss-sticks near it, do not be surprised. According to local belief, childless women can conceive by placing flowers in its barrel and offering special prayers. The fort is in Lebuh Light and is open daily 8.30am-7pm. Admission is RM1 per person.

Komtar

The 65-storey Complex Tun Abdul Razak is in the main street, Jalan Penang, and houses government departments, commercial offices, department stores, shops, restaurants, theatres, squash courts and a geodesic dome that serves as a multi-purpose hall. A trip to the 55th floor offers great views of the city and, on clear days, of Gunung Jerai in Kedah.

BEYOND GEORGETOWN

Botanic Gardens

Occupying 30ha, the gardens have a fine collection of the flora and fauna of Malaysia and other parts of the tropics. They are well-known for their friendly Rhesus monkeys.

Located off Jalan Waterfall in Botanical Gardens Road.

Natukkotai Chettiar Temple

This is the largest Hindu temple in Penang, dedicated to the deity Lord Bala Subramaniam. Before the shrine is a peacock given to Subramaniam by his mother, Parvathi, as his attendant *vakanan* (vehicle). Located at the Jalan Waterfall, the temple is one of the important centres of rites and ceremonies during the Thaipusam festival.

Penang Hill

A popular spot for locals and visitors, Penang Hill is 830m above sea level and 3C cooler than the lowlands. A 30-minute funicular train ride takes visitors to the summit, which affords a magnificent panoramic view of Georgetown and the mainland's coastal areas. There is also a hotel, a children's playground and a kiosk.

The funicular rail service begins at 6.30am and ends at 9.30pm and the fares are RM4 adult, RM2 child. For the more energetic there is a good walking track up the hill that begins at the "moongate" at Jalan Waterfall, approximately 300m from the Botanic Gardens entrance. The walk takes about four hours, one way. For more information see the section on Hill Resorts.

Street scene in Penang

Butterfly Farm

The farm occupies 0.8ha and is home to 3000 living specimens of over 50 species. It has a garden enclosure, breeding area, laboratory, exhibition area, souvenir shop and information centre. Other interesting features include a lily pond, artificial waterfalls, a rock garden, a tunnel and a bubbling mud pool.

Located at Teluk Bahang, the farm is open daily 9am-5pm Admission is RM4 adult, RM1.50 child.

Kek Lok Si

The largest Buddhist Temple complex in Malaysia is situated at Air Itam. Work on the Kek Lok Si started in 1890 and took more than two decades to complete. The temple is dominated by the seven-tier Ban Po Thar pagoda, which rises 30m. The pagoda combines Chinese, Thai and Burmese architecture and craftsmanship. The octagonal base is typically Chinese, the middle tiers Thai, and the spiral dome Burmese.

Snake Temple

Built in 1850, it is dedicated to the deity Chor Soo Kong and is a sanctuary for pit vipers which can be seen coiled around vases, beams and potted plants. Although poisonous, they are not known to bite. Devotees refer to these snakes as "officers" of the deity and regard them as "holy and harmless".

Tourists who feel they must experience everything offered may pose for photographs with a pit viper coiled around their neck, but this is not necessarily recommended. The temple is located in Bayan Lepas.

State Mosque

Completed in 1980, it stands on a 4.5ha site at the Jalan Air Item/Jalan Masjid Negeri junction. The mosque, which took more than four years to build, can accommodate 5000 worshippers.

Always remember when visiting a mosque or temple to dress accordingly, and to remove your shoes.

Wat Chayamangkalaram

This Buddhist temple of Thai architecture in Lorong Burmah houses the world's third largest reclining Buddha, measuring 33m. Behind the statue are niches where urns containing the ashes of the dead are stored.

Photography is not allowed inside the Temple, but you can pay the caretaker to take your photograph in front of the statue. I don't know what the procedure is, whether they are instant photos or if you have to arrange to have the prints sent to you, because frankly I thought it was a rort. I fail to see why my camera is going to damage the statue any more than his is.

Beaches

The northern shoreline of the island is famous for its beaches of golden sand and deep blue seas. The Tanjung Bunga, Batu Ferringhi and Teluk Bahang beaches have stretches of sand interspersed with coves sheltered by gigantic rocks. It is along this famous coastline that international resorts have been built.

However there are secluded beaches in other parts of Penang and the tourist information offices have full details. The only catch with most of them is you have to hike along jungle trails to get to them.

MAINLAND ATTRACTIONS

Penang Bird Park

The park covers 2ha and has a good collection of about 800 birds from over 100 species from all over the world. It is attractively landscaped and features a walk-in aviary, ponds with ducks and swans, ornamental ponds with water-lilies and Japanese carp. The park is in Seberang Jaya, and it is open daily 9am-7pm. Admission is RM3 adult, RM1 child.

Sacred Heart Church (Pagar Teras, Bukit Mertajam)

Built by the French Mission in 1882, the church used to be the focal point for Roman Catholics in the area until it was abandoned during the Emergency when the residents of Pagar Teras were resettled. A flight of stairs leads to the ruins of the Church which was designed after the famous Notre Dame Cathedral in Paris.

Cherok To'kun Relic (Bukit Mertajam)
A large smooth block of granite bearing inscriptions in Chinese, Jawi, Tamil, English and classical Indian writing (probably Pali), believed to have been written in the 4th and 5th centuries.

Mengkuang Dam
The largest dam in the state has a storage capacity of about 24 million litres. Situated north of Bukit Mertajam, it has a large recreational area with gardens, sporting facilities, and walking and jogging tracks.

SPORT AND RECREATION

Horse Racing
Races are held at Jalan Batu Gantung on two consecutive weekends every two months. On other weekends, when the races are held at Ipoh, Kuala Lumpur and Singapore, the turf club is open for off-course betting.

Tennis and Squash
Courts are available at most of the leading hotels. Hourly rates are inclusive of the use of racquets and balls.

Water Sports
The beaches along the north coast are suitable for most watersports. Facilities for para-sailing, water skiing, windsurfing, sailing, etc, are available at most beach hotels, or from private operators. The uninhabited islands of Pulau Bidan, Pulau Telur and Pulau Song Song off Batu Ferringhi are ideal for all water sports.

Golf
Visitors are welcome at the following golf clubs:
Bukit Jambul Golf and Country Club, ph 842 255.
* Green fees RM100 + 5% (weekdays)
        RM120 (weekends and public holidays)
* Caddies fees RM20 for 18 holes.
Penang Turf Club, ph 370 246.
* Green fees RM80 (weekdays)
        RM120 (weekends and public holidays)
* Caddies fees RM20 for 18 holes.
Air Force Golf Club Butterworth, ph 322 632 - 9-hole course.
* Green fees RM20 (weekdays)
        RM30 (weekends and public holidays)
* Caddies fees RM5.

Bukit Jawi Golf Resort, ph 582 2612.
* Green fees RM70 (weekdays)
        RM100 (weekends and public holidays)
* Caddies fees RM15 for 18 holes.
Kristal Golf Resort, ph 398 661.
* Green fees RM70 (weekends)
        RM110 (weekends and public holidays)
* Caddies fees RM20 for 18 holes.

MAS International Dragon Boat Race

The race that originated in China attracts teams from all over the world to compete in June each year. Over 50,000 spectators gather to watch and cheer. Each boat bears a dragon's head and has a 27 man crew, comprising 24 oarsmen, a coxswain, a gong beater and a cheerleader.

Looking north from Fort Cornwallis
(see page 135)

PERLIS

Perlis, the northern-most state, lies close to the border with Thailand, 56km north-west of Alor Setar in Kedah. It is an important rice-growing state and its capital, Kangar, is a bustling town with another picturesque mosque.

HOW TO GET THERE

By Bus
There are services from Butterworth and Alor Setar to Kangar.

By Train
The International Express train stops at Arau and Padang Besar.

By Car
Kangar is 56km north-west of Alor Setar, in Kedah, on the main road north to Thailand.

By Taxi
Taxis will take passengers from Butterworth or Alor Setar to Kangar.

TOURIST INFORMATION
Perlis Tourist Association, c/- Perlis Inn, Kangar, ph (04) 752 266/7.

ACCOMMODATION
There is not a wide choice of accommodation in Kangar. Perlis is mostly a border state for people travelling between Malaysia and Thailand. Here is a selection, with prices for a double room per night, which should be used as a guide only. The telephone area code is 04.
Pens Hotel, 138 Main Road, ph 760 487 - RM92-172.
Federal Hotel, 104 Jalan Kangar, ph 766 288 - RM26-60.
Hotel Malaysia, 65-67 Jalan Jubli Perak, ph 751 365 - RM23-39.
Hotel Ban Cheong, 79A Jalan Besar, ph 761 184 - RM18-24.
Hotel Asia, 18 Jalan Taman Sentosa, ph 755 322 - RM16-20.

SIGHTSEEING

Arau
The royal town of Perlis, Arau has a fine Istana (royal palace).

Padang Besar

Padang Besar is the border town straddling the Malaysian-Thai border. It is very popular with locals and visitors alike with a two-way flow across the border. There is an Immigration and Customs post here for entry and exit formalities.

Kuala Perlis

A small market town at the mouth of the Sungei Perlis, 14km from Kangar and the jump-off point for the island of Langkawi.

Kaki Bukit

This is a tin mining town. Tin is taken from underground caves and crevices in the limestone cliffs.

Harvesting Rice

KEDAH

Kedah, with an area of 9425 sq km, is north-west of Perak, south-east of Perlis, and south of Thailand. Known as the "Rice Bowl of Malaysia", Kedah produces approximately 44% of the country's rice needs. Interesting and beautiful sights abound in this state, whether you visit the mountains, the beaches, an island, a Malay village, or one of Kedah's small rural towns. Alor Setar, the state capital, is 96km from Butterworth.

HISTORY

Kedah is thought to be the most ancient state in the country. Archaeological evidence has revealed that the state was once a prosperous trade centre, and numerous temple sites found in the Bujang Valley have provided further proof of the existence of a Hindu-Buddhist period in early Malaysian history.

Throughout its history Kedah has had several periods of foreign dominance. In the 7th and 8th century the Sumatran Kingdom of Sri Vijaya took control, then came the Thais, then the Malacca Sultanate, which brought Islam to Kedah. When their influence waned there were successive attacks from the Portuguese and the Chinese in the 17th century. Towards the end of the 18th century the fear of a Thai threat resulted in Penang being offered to the British, but Kedah was not included and fell to the Thais in 1821. In 1826 the Sultan was restored, and in 1909 the Thais transferred their sovereignty over Kedah to the British. After the Japanese occupation during World War II, Kedah joined the Malayan Union and subsequently the Federation of Malaya.

ALOR SETAR

HOW TO GET THERE

By Air

Malaysia Airlines have several daily flights from Kuala Lumpur.

By Rail

There are services from Kuala Lumpur, Bangkok and Haadyai,

Thailand, to Kedah. For more information contact Malayan Railway, ph (03) 274 7435.

By Bus

Buses also travel from Kuala Lumpur, Bangkok and Haadyai, and if you are travelling from Thailand you enter Kedah through Bukit Kayu Hitam, a town that has a duty free shopping complex.

By Road

The drive from Kuala Lumpur to Alor Setar takes about 5 hours on the North South highway.

TOURIST INFORMATION

State Tourism Department - Kedah Darul Aman, State Secretariat Office, Wisma Darul Aman, 05503, Alor Setar, ph (04) 740 957.

ACCOMMODATION

Here is a selection of budget accommodation, with prices for a double room per night, which should be used as a guide only. The telephone area code is 04.

Samila Hotel, 27 Jalan Kancut, ph 722 344 - RM66.

Royale Hotel, 97 Jalan Putra, ph 730 922 - RM54-58.

Regent Hotel, 1536G Jalan Sultan Badlishah, ph 711 900 - RM37-63.

Miramar Hotel, 246 Jalan Putra, ph 738 144 - RM29-55.

Mahawangsa Hotel, 449 Jalan Raja, ph 721 433 - RM28-42.

Putera Jaya Hotel, 250B & C Jalan Putera, ph 730 344 - RM23-37.

Federal Hotel, 429 Lebohraya Darulaman, Jalan Kancut, ph 730 055 - RM25-30.

Station Hotel, 2nd Floor Transport Building, Jalan Langgar, ph 733 786 - RM17-32.

Rest House

Alor Setar Rest House, 75 Jalan Pumpong,
ph 710 422 - RM20-33.

SHOPPING

Opposite the Government Offices building is a market which is called *Pekan Rabu* (Wednesday Market), because originally it only operated on that day. Now it is open every day, and all day until midnight, and stocks local produce and handicrafts. It is the best place to try some traditional Kedah fare, such as the *Dodol Durian*, a sweet cake made from the durian fruit.

SIGHTSEEING

Masjid Zahir

The mosque was officially opened in 1912, and is in the Moorish style of architecture. The state's Koran reading competition is held annually in the mosque.

Balai Besar

Facing Masjid Zahir, though with a large space in between, is Balai Besar, the audience hall. It was built in 1898 and embodies some aspects of Thai architecture. The Sultan holds audience in this building on his birthday and on other festive occasions.

Balai Seni Negeri

The State Art Gallery is near the Masjid Zahir and has a fine collection of paintings, antiques and historical relics. It is open daily 10am-6pm (closed Fri noon-2.30pm) and there is no admission fee, ph 733 1162.

Rumah Kelahiran Mahathir

Malaysia's Prime Minister, Dato' Seri Dr Mahathir Mohamad, was born in Alor Setar at 18 Lorong Kilang Ais, off Jalan Pegawi. The National Archives restored and gazetted the house as an historical building in 1992, and tours are now available.

The house contains much memorabilia from his youth. It is open daily 9am-6pm (closed Fri noon-3pm) and there is no admission fee, ph 733 4676.

Gunung Jerai

Formerly known as Kedah Peak, Gunung Jerai is a limestone outcrop that rises 1200m above sea level, and is south of Alor Setar. Myths and legends abound about this peak. According to one, a king who had fangs and lived on blood, used to live in the Bujang Valley on the foothills of this mountain. The Gunung Jerai Resort is popular with the locals because the cool, fresh mountain air is a change from the heat and humidity of the lowlands.

Lembah Bujang (Bujang Valley)

Lying between Gunung Jerai in the north and Sungai Muda in the south, this is regarded as Malaysia's richest archaeological area.

The Bujang Valley Archaeological Museum in Pengkalan Bujang, Merbok, houses numerous stone caskets, gem stones, beads, etc, that have been excavated from the 50 temples that have been discovered. Eight temples have been restored, using original materials, and are open to the public.

Kota Kuala Kedah

Located at the mouth of the Kedah River, this village is also known as Kota Kuala Bahang. *Kota* means "fort", and there was one here to ward off enemies who came from the sea. It was reported to have been built by stone masons specially brought in from India. Today it is a fishing village, known for its seafood restaurants among the historic sites.

SPORT AND RECREATION

The golf mania that exists in the rest of Malaysia is also alive and well in Kedah. The following clubs welcome visitors.

Royal Kedah Club, Pumpong, Alor Setar, ph 733 0467 - 9 holes.

Sungai Petani Golf Club, Jalan Sungei Layar, Sungei Petani, ph 420 960 - 9 holes.

Dublin Estate Golf Club, c/- Ladang Sungei Dingin, Karangan, ph 458 1026 - 9 holes.

Cinta Sayang Golf & Country Club, Persiaran Cinta Sayang, Sungai Petani, ph 441 4666 - 18 holes.

Harvard Golf Club, c/- Ladang Jelai, Bedong, ph 458 1026 - 9 holes.

LANGKAWI

Part of the state of Kedah, Pulau Langkawi is a group of 104 islands, most of them uninhabited, 27km off the coast of Kuala Perlis, and 112km north of Penang, at the point where the Indian Ocean melts into the Straits of Malacca.

The islands were once a haven for pirates, but now they are the ideal place for people who do not want crowds, and who want to get away from it all. The main industry was once fishing, but now it would have to be tourism.

Langkawi is steeped in legends of wronged maidens and lovelorn princes. Its white beaches are believed to have originated from the white blood that flowed from the body of a beautiful princess named Mahsuri. She was wrongly convicted of adultery, and executed, and as she died her white blood (proving her innocence) seeped into the ground. With her last words she cursed the island, saying that it would not prosper for seven generations. The period of the curse has passed, so Langkawi is free to reach its potential.

The island "capital" is Kuah, where the ferry from the mainland docks.

HOW TO GET THERE

By Air
Malaysia Airlines have several daily direct flights to Langkawi from Kuala Lumpur and from Penang.

By Ferry
High speed ferry shuttle services provide scheduled crossings from Kuala Kedah and Kuala Perlis to Langkawi.

TOURIST INFORMATION
Langkawi Tourist Information Centre is in Jalan Pesiaran Putra, Kuah, ph (04) 966 7789.

ACCOMMODATION
The following list of accommodation has prices for a double room per night, which should be used as a guide only. The telephone area code is 04.

International Standard
The Datai, Jalan Teluk Datai, ph 959 2500 - 108 rooms, 3 restaurants, cocktail lounge, coffee shop, swimming pool, sauna, fitness centre - RM478.
Pelangi Beach Resort, 07000 Pantai Lenang, ph 911 001 - 350 rooms, 3 restaurants, cocktail lounge, coffee shop, swimming pool, sauna, fitness centre - RM280.
Sheraton Langkawi Resort, 07000 Teluk Nibong, ph 955 1901 - 262 rooms, 1 restaurant, cocktail lounge, coffee shop, swimming pool, sauna, fitness centre - RM260.
Sri Legenda Garden Resort, Jalan Penarak, Kuah, ph 966 8919 - 123 rooms, 2 restaurants, cocktail lounge, coffee shop, swimming pool, sauna, fitness centre - RM213.
Holiday Villa Beach Resort, Lot 1698 Pantai Tengah, Mukim Kedarang, ph 911 701 - 258 rooms, 2 restaurants, cocktail lounge, coffee shop, swimming pool, fitness centre - RM210.
Berjaya Langkawi Beach Resort, 07000 Burau Bay, ph 959 1888 - 400 rooms, 3 restaurants, cocktail lounge, coffee shop, swimming pool - RM204.
Burau Bay Resort, 07000 Teluk Burau, ph 911 061 - 150 rooms, 1 restaurant, cocktail lounge, coffee shop, swimming pool - RM186.
The Gates Langkawi, Jalan Persiaran Putra, Kuah, ph 966 8466 - 177 rooms, 2 restaurants, cocktail lounge, coffee shop, swimming pool - RM130.

Budget
Asia Hotel, 1 Jalan Persiaran Putra, Kuah, ph 916 216 - RM50-70.
Captain Resort, 82 Jalan Penarak, Kuah, ph 917 100 - RM40-75.
Cindayu Resort, Jalan Ulu Merdeka, ph 911 749 - RM35-50.
AB Motel, Pantai Cenang, ph 911 300 - RM30-70.
Charlie Motel, Pantai Tengah, ph 911 200 - RM30-55.
Inapan Sri Inai, Panti Cenang, ph 911 986 - RM30+.
Beach View Motel, Pantai Cenang, ph 911 186 - RM25-50.
Sri Pulau Motel, Jalan Pejabat Pos, Kuah, ph 917 185 - RM20-30.

LOCAL TRANSPORT

The bus and taxi terminals are located near Kuah Jetty, and from there to the town is a 20 minute walk or a 5-minute taxi ride.

Bus

Buses run as follows:

From Kuah Town to Pantai Cenang - every hour 7am-6pm - RM1.40.

From Kuah Town to Pantai Kok and Burau Bay - every two hours 8am-4pm - RM1.70.

From Kuah Town to Padang Lalang and Teluk Ewa - every hour 7am-6pm - RM1.90.

Taxi

Taxi fares (as at time of publication) are as follows:

From Jetty to		From Airport to	
Kuah Town	RM4	Pantai Kok	RM12
Pokok Asam	RM6	Pantai Cenang	RM10
Pantai Cenang	RM12	Burau Bay	RM12
Pantai Kok	RM15	Jalan Penarak	RM15
Datai Bay	RM25	Tanjung Rhu	RM15
Tanjung Rhu	RM15	Pantai Tengah	RM12
Pantai Tengah	RM12	Telaga Tujuh	RM15
		Air Hangat Village	RM12
		Datai Bay	RM25.

ENTERTAINMENT

The entertainment offered here is the island itself. This is not the place for jet-set living, but rather more for the relaxed beachcombing type of holiday. Of course, the hotels and beach resorts offer exotic seafood, cooked as only the locals know how, but you won't find streets of restaurants offering dishes from different Asian countries as in other areas. **If you go to Langkawi looking for a place to relax, soak in the sun and turn a lovely golden-brown, you will not be disappointed. There are enough beaches here to provide you with your own private niche with nothing except the imprints of your own feet in the sand for miles around.** The islanders of course have their own favourite beaches, but don't limit yourself to just one or two.

Tanjung Rhu (Casuarina Beach) is lined by tall swaying casuarina trees, and is one of the best on the island. At low tide you can walk across the sandy stretch that joins Tanjung Rhu to a neighbouring island. However, when the tide swells, the sandy strip is covered. Tanjung Rhu is about 23km from Kuah Town.

At the southern tip of the island is a beautiful kilometre-long beach, Pantai Tengah (Central Beach). This is accessible by road from Kuah and is situated in a sheltered bay, with calm water suitable for water skiing.

Other popular beaches include Pantai Pasir Hitam (Beach of Black Sand) where the ground is literally covered with black sand, and Pebble Beach on Pulau Dayang Bunting, which is strewn with pebbles. Then there is Burau Bay on the west coast which has a white sandy shoreline and clear blue water.

The seas around the Langkawi group are clear in many spots, and excellent for snorkelling.

SIGHTSEEING

Kuah

Pulau Langkawi has been declared duty-free as long as visitors stay for a minimum of 72 hours, and the main street in Kuah Town has many shops selling duty-free goods.

The main attraction in the town is a picturesque mosque with Moorish arches, minarets and a golden dome, surrounded by palm trees.

Durian Perangin

This pretty waterfall is at the 9th milestone from Kuah, along a road lined with rubber plantations that turns off the main road. It is well sign-posted.

Mahsuri's Tomb

In a little village 12km from Kuah, this spot is recommended for lovers of folklore. It was here that the Malay princess Mahsuri was executed.

Padang Masirat (Field of Burnt Rice)

During an invasion after Mahsur's death, the islanders scorched their rice fields rather than abandon them to the invaders. Today, 19km from Kuah, the charred remains can still be seen at Padang Masirat. Occasionally traces of burnt rice are brought to the surface by heavy rains.

Telaga Tujuh (The Seven Wells)

A fresh water stream cascades 91m down through a series of seven pools. While it can be great fun sliding from one pool to another, the rock surfaces tend to be slippery, and it is not advisable to attempt sliding from the top-most pools. The lower pools are not hazardous, but still children should not be allowed to play without adult supervision.

Telaga Air Hangat (Hot Springs)

The legend that surrounds the hot springs is that there was a bitter quarrel between two of the island's leading families because of a rejected offer of marriage. The boy's family raided the girl's village and a violent battle ensued. All the pots, pans, plates and saucers in the village were shattered. A pot was flung at a place thereafter called *Belanga Pecah* (Broken Pot). Gravy was spilt at *Kuah* (gravy) and seeped into the soil at a place called *Kisap* (seep). Finally a jugful of hot water was spilt at the present site of Telaga Air Hangat (Hot Spring).

The Air Hangat Village is a new attraction and the complex covers 1.5ha. Attractions include a 3-tier hot spring fountain, 18m long hand-carved riverstone mural depicting the legends of Air Hangat, day-long outdoor entertainment program featuring Malaysian /ASEAN cultural dances and trad- itional games, live displays of Malaysian /ASEAN customs, tradit- ional crafts and participation in village activities such as padi planting.

There is a cafe, a lounge and a theatre restaurant, and duty-free shopping is avail- able at the pavilions. The village is 14km from Kuan Town, ph 959 1357.Open daily 10am-6pm, admission is RM4.

Tasek Dayang Bunting (Lake of the Pregnant Maiden)

This is a freshwater lake on the isle of the same name. According to local folklore, a married couple, childless for 19 years, drank from the lake and subsequently the wife gave birth to a baby girl. The lake has become a popular destination for childless couples from all over Malaysia.

Gua Langsir (Cave of the Banshee)

Near the Lake of the Pregnant Maiden, this cave is over 91m high and is home to thousands of bats, which perhaps explains its reputation for being haunted.

Taman Buaya Langkawi (Langkawi Crocodile Farm)

The 8ha farm is at Teluk Datai, about 32km from Kuah Town, and is open daily 9am-5pm. Calling it home are more than 1000 crocodiles, and the complex has been registered with the Convention on International Trade and Endangered Species (CITES). Attractions for visitors are: Feeding Pond; Species Pond; Breeding Pond; Show Pond, where man and crocodile "wrestle" with each other; and Bridge-Over-Pond, where you can get a closer look at these reptiles.

The farm has a fast-food shop and a souvenir shop, and admission is RM5 adult, Rm3 child, ph 959 2559.

Pulau Payar - Marine Park

The park consists of four islands set among coral gardens with schools of tropical fish. A trip is the ultimate for the dedicated diver, and the tourist information department has full information. Camping on these island is permitted, but prior approval must be obtained from the Fisheries Department at Alor Setar or Kuala Lumpur.

SPORT AND RECREATION

Apart from the beaches already mentioned, Langkawi has several lagoons that are excellent for water skiing, or you can rent a boat and tour around the whole island group.

If golf is your forte there are two gold clubs on the main island.

Datai Bay Golf & Country Club, Teluk Datai, ph 959 2620 - 18 holes.

Langkawi Golf Club, Jalan Bulut Malut, ph 966 7195 - 18 holes.

A beach in the Langkawi Group

PERAK

Perak has the world's richest tin deposits in its Kinta Valley. Covering an area of 21,000 sq km, it has a population of around 2 million people.

Perak is divided into nine districts and its major towns include Ipoh, Kuala Kangsar, Taiping, Teluk Intah and Lumut. Kuala Kangsar is the royal town of Perak, while Ipoh is the state capital and its administration centre.

HISTORY

The state of Perak Darul Ridzuan, the "Land of Grace", has been inhabited since prehistoric times. Remnants of the Stone Age period have been found in Kota Tampan in Lenggong.

In the early days the Malay Peninsula was well-known for its rich mineral resources, especially tin and gold. It is for this reason that the Peninsula was named "The Golden Chersonese" by the Greeks. One of the minerals, tin, was found in abundance in Perak. It is popularly believed that the state was so called because in the Malay language "perak" means silver colour.

The mineral wealth played an important role in determining the historical and economic growth of Perak. Its tin resources attracted such foreign powers as the Portuguese, Achinese, Bugis, Siamese, Dutch, and finally the British.

Perak is governed by a constitutional monarch or sultan. Under him is the State Council, comprising the state assemblymen headed by the Mentri Besar who is the Chief Executive of the state. The state's sultanate system is unique and rich and tradition. It does not practise the common hereditary system where the eldest son automatically becomes the ruler once the father dies. Traditionally six people have the right to succeed to the throne in sequence when the sultan dies. They are the Raja Muda, Raja di Hilir, Raja Kecil Besar, Raja Kecil Sulung, Raja Kecil Tengah and Raja Kecil Bongsu.

The men who fill all the above positions are descendants of Sultan Ahmaddin Shah, the 18th Sultan of Perak. The present and 34th Sultan of Perak is Sultan Azian Muhibbuddin Ghafarullahu-Lahu Shah.

HOW TO GET THERE

By Air
Malaysia Airlines has regular return flights to Ipoh from KL.

By Rail

The Ekonomi Malam Kuala Lumpur-Butterworth trains stop at Tapah, Kampar, Malim Nawar, Batu Gajah, Ipoh, Tanjung Rambutan, Chemor, Sungai Siput, Kuala Kangsar and Taiping.

Express trains only stop at Tapah, Ipoh and Taiping, although some include a stop at Kuala Kangsar.

By Bus

Several bus companies operate express services from both the south and the north that stop at Ipoh. It is also possible to pick up slower services that stop at more places in Perak.

By Taxi

Air-conditioned and non air-conditioned taxis ply major routes to Ipoh from Kota Bharu, Alor Setar, Penang, Taiping and Kuala Kangsar in the north; Cameron Highlands, Teluk Intan, Tanjung Malim and Kuala Lumpur in the south. Charges vary from RM6 to RM20 per person depending on the distance.

TOURIST INFORMATION

Information can be obtained from the following offices:

State Economic Planning Unit, Jalan Dato' Sagor, Ipoh, ph (05) 532 800.

Information Centre, c/- The Royal Casuarina, 18 Jalan Gopeng, Ipoh, ph (05) 532 008.

Lumut Tourist Information Centre, 32200 Lumut, ph (05) 934 057.

ACCOMMODATION

There is a wide variety of accommodation in the principal towns of Perak. Here is a selection, with prices for a double room per night, which should be used as a guide only.

The telephone area code is 05.

IPOH

The Royal Casuarina Hotel, 18 Jalan Gopeng, ph 505 555 - 217 rooms, 1 restaurant, cocktail lounge, coffee shop, swimming pool, fitness centre - RM218.

The Syuen, 88 Jalan Sultan Abdul Jalil, Greentown, ph 538 889 - 300 rooms, 1 restaurant, cocktail lounge, coffee shop, swimming pool, sauna, fitness centre - RM174.

Budget

Hollywood Hotel, 72-76 Jalan C.M. Yusuff, ph 515 322 - RM30-69.
City Hotel, 79 Chamberlain Road, ph 512 911 - RM22-55.

Embassy Hotel, 35-37 Jalan Chamberlain, ph 549 496 - RM21-30.
Diamond Hotel, 3-9 Jalan Ali Pitchay, ph 513 644 - RM17-35.
YMCA of Ipoh, 211 Jalan Raja Musa Aziz, ph 540 809 - rooms RM42-36 - dormitory RM7 per person.

KUALA KANGSAR
King Wah Hotel & Restaurant, 1 Jalan Dato' Sagor, ph 861 867 - RM16.
Tin Heong Hotel, 34 Jalan Raja Chulan, ph 862 066 - RM13-28.
Double Lion Hotel & Restaurant, 74 Jalan Kangsar, ph 862 020 - RM10-30.
Kuala Kangsar Rest House, Bukit Chandan, ph 863 872 - RM25-60.

LUMUT
Chalet Teluk Batek, ph 985 344 - RM57-80.
Dinding Hotel, 115 Jalan Titi Panjang, ph 935 494 - RM30.
Lumut Villa Inn, Bt. 1 Jalan Setiawan, ph 943 802 - RM25-45.
,ILumut Rest House, Jalan Iskandar Shah, ph 935 938 - from RM25.

PULAU PANGKOR
Beach Hut Hotel, Pantai Sri Bogak, ph 951 159 - RM50-250.
Sea View Hotel, Pasir Bogak, ph 951 605 - RM94-136.
Min Lian Hotel 1A, Jalan Besar, ph 951 294 - RM18-55.

TAIPING
Panorama Hotel, 61-79 Jalan Kota, ph 834 111 - RM70-140.
Meridien Hotel, 2 Jalan Simpang, ph 831 133 - RM47-60.
Mikado Hotel, 14 Jalan Boo Bee, ph 821 366 0 RM22-28.
Miramar Hotel, 30 Jalan Peng Loong, ph 821 078 - RM20-28.
Government Rest House, Jalan Sultan Mansor, Taman Tasik, ph 822 044 - RM35-45.
Baru Taiping Rest House, Chempaka Sari Satu, Jalan Mansor Shah, ph 822 571 - RM35-70.

EATING OUT
Perak has an astonishing variety of eating places, ranging from expensive restaurants to open-air food stalls that serve Eastern and Western dishes, including Malay, Chinese, Indian, Japanese, Thai, Korean and Continental.

Some establishments organise live music and floor shows. Certain restaurants in the cities hold Malaysian Cultural Shows, which make dining more interesting.

Whether it is early morning, lunchtime, snack time, evening or supper time, little roadside stalls with portable tables and chairs appear everywhere to quench the thirst and appease the appetite. Here dining is value for money with no service charge or tipping.

In Ipoh, typical open-air food stalls can be found along Jalan Osborne, at Ipoh Garden and opposite the old post office.

ENTERTAINMENT

When the sun goes down Ipoh becomes alive with its variety of entertainment as the nightclubs, discos and pubs open for business. There is an abundance of places to suit diverse tastes and different age groups. Among the better known discotheques in Ipoh are the Excelsior Club, the Blue Diamond and El-Amigo.

There are also cinemas and bowling alleys, and the local favourite sport - horse racing.

SHOPPING

Shopping in Perak is a unique experience. Ipoh offers many shopping areas, ranging from huge department stores to colourful bazaars with bargains. **Super Kinta, the Yik Foong Compleks and Perak Emporium are the main shopping centres in Ipoh,** and the main shopping streets are Jalan Sultan Idris Shah and Jalan Laxamana. Most of the shops are open daily 10am-10pm.

Tekat Benang Emas (Gold Embroidery)

This is a decorative embroidery that uses gold thread to satin-stitch elaborate swirls and abstract designs on a velvet base. The intricacy of the design depends on the person's creativity and skill. It is popularly used for bed-spreads, pillows and cushions that are a part of a traditional Malay bridal bedroom set, and also the bride's handbag. Tekat Benang Emas is available at Kampung Padang Changkat, Kuala Kangsar and at any of Perak's handicraft centres.

Bamboo Works of Art

Creating products from bamboo is a fascinating art. The long and rigid bamboo is first made pliable and then carved by skilled and patient craftsmen.

The heart of the industry is at Kampung Berala, Kati, where an exclusive bamboo-making centre is situated about 15km from Kuala Kangsar town. Examples of crafted bamboo products are coin-boxes, penholders and picture frames.

Sea Shell Designs

A wide range of handicrafts and antiques are peculiar to Perak, and among the most prized art forms are the sea shell and sea coral creations. **Lumut is popular for its corals and sea shells, which make attractive decorative pieces.**

The corals and shells are shaped into flowers, ships, birds and other forms. These sea shell and coral designs are favourite souvenirs, and are available in all Perak handicraft centres.

Traditional Handicraft

This is a prominent cottage industry in Perak. It is predominantly found in Kuala Kangsar and Taiping. There are a number of centres that sell local goods, and they are found at Enggor in Kuala Kangsar, the Ipoh Railway Station, and the Tourism Centre in Ipoh.

Labu Sayong (Earthenware)

Labu Sayong is a type of earthenware popular among the Malays in the kampung (village). It is a water pitcher, shaped like a pumpkin, to keep water cool. Water stored in these pitchers is also locally believed to have medicinal value.

The Labu Sayong is primarily produced at Kampung Kepala Bendang in Sayong, about 15km from Kuala Kangsar town. For those interested, there is a centre in Enggor, close to Kuala Kangsar which, besides offering a course in potters, also sells finished wares.

SIGHTSEEING

Ipoh

Geology Museum

This museum, in Jalan Harimau, was established under the Geological Survey Department in Ipoh in 1957. The main feature is its collection of more than 600 kinds of minerals, classified according to chemical content and structure. Open Mon-Fri 8am-4.15pm, Sat 8am-12.45pm, admission is free but visitors must first get an entry permission from the information counter.

Japanese Garden

Located near the Perak Turf Club, this public park recreates the aesthetics of a Japanese garden. It is open Mon-Fri 4-8pm, Sat-Sun 9am-8pm.

DBI Swimming Complex

The Dewan Bandaraya Ipon Swimming Complex is the largest and most modern complex of its king in South-East Asia, and has an Olympic-size pool, a diving pool, a beginners' pool, a children's pool, and the first wave pool in Malaysia. The complex is part of the Perak Sports Complex which also has a stadium with a velodrome and astroturf field. The complex is open daily 9am-9pm.

DR Seenivasagam Park

A good place to take a break if you are travelling with children, the park has a roller-skating rink, a playground and a mini-train course.

Darul Ridzuan Museum

This museum is located in Jalan Panglima, Bukit Gantang Wahab, and opened in August 1992. The building is more than one hundred years old, and was originally the residence of Malay dignitaries in the Kinta District. During the British Administration they built several fortresses as war shelters around the building.

The museum now contains exhibits relating to the history of Ipoh, and of the development of the mining industry and forestry in the state of Perak. It is open Mon, Tues, Wed, fri and Sat 9am-5pm, Thurs 9am-noon, and there is no admission fee.

Ipoh Railway Station

The station is reminiscent of that in Kuala Lumpur, and is affectionately known to the locals as the "Taj Mahal of Ipoh".

Tambun Hot Spring

A 15 minute drive from Ipoh town, at the foot of a limestone hill, is a natural hot spring. A complex has been erected that has saunas and restrooms and is open daily 3pm-12.30am. Entry is RM4.50.

Other hot springs in Perak are at Sungkai, Pengkalan Hulu, Kampung Ulu Slim in Slim River, Kampung Air Panas in Grik, and Manong in Kuala Kangsar.

Tambun's Pre-Historic Painting Cave

Visitors interested in archaeology will certainly like to visit this cave (in Malay Gua Lukisan Pra-Sejarah Tambun). It is located about 6km from Ipoh, on one of the limestone hills at Gunung Churam. There is a gallery of ancient paintings that were done about two thousand years ago, and are similar to the cave paintings found in Australia.

Perak Tong & Sam Poh Tong

There are huge limestone caves at Gunung Tasek, 6km north of Ipoh, and within them is the Perak Tong temple. It was built in 1926 by a Buddhist priest from China, and it has over 40 Buddha statues surrounding the main 12.8m sitting Buddha. From behind the main altar a passage leads into the cave's interior, from where 385 steps lead to a wonderful view of the surrounding countryside.

The Samp Poh Tong temple is in Gunung Rapat, 5km south of Ipoh. It has several statues of Buddha set among natural stalactites and stalagmites. There is also a wishing well, and a tortoise (symbol of longevity) pond where visitors can feed the creatures with stalks of vegetables. Outside the temple is a vegetarian restaurant.

Meh Prasit Temple

Also known as the Wat Thai, this temple houses the largest statue of the Lord Buddha in Malaysia - 24.38m long, 6.4m high and 4.5m wide. Inside the huge head of the reclining statue is a glass case containing a tiny fragment of a bone of the Lord Buddha. Glued to the body of the statue are thousands of gold leaves specially import- ed from Thailand.

Kellie's Castle

This is an interesting site to visit. It is located near Batu Gajah, about 30 minutes by car from Ipoh. The castle belong- ed to William Kellie Smith, an Englishman who was a rubber plan tation owner dur- ing the late 19th century. It is full of mystery. It is believed that the castle has more rooms than appar-

Kellie's Castle

ent, and a secret tunnel which no-one can find.

The construction of the castle was abruptly stopped after Kellie Smith left for England. He was reported missing and was later found dead at Lisbon in 1926.

Tempurong Cave

It is believed that this big limestone cave has existed since 8000BC. It is 24km from Ipoh City, and consists of five huge domes shaped like coconut shells. Each dome has stalactites and stalagmites with differing temperatures, water level, and content of limestone and marble. The cave was once used by communist terrorists from the Eighth Brigade as their High Command. Around 1930, Gurkha soldiers discovered the cave and declared it off-limits. It was only restored in 1990. **To reach the cave from Ipoh Bus Station, take the bus for Gopeng or Kampar. Stop at Kampung Gunung Mesah Hilir, and the path leading to the cave is about 5km from there.** Alternatively contact the Ketua Kampung of Gunung Mesah, ph (05) 391 380, for tourist services to the cave-cost is RM20 per person.

Kuala Woh Jungle Park

The park is about 13km from Tapah, on the way to the Cameron Highlands, and has a natural hot-water pool, waterfalls and picnic facilities. *Orang asli* (aborigines) live in this area according to their traditional way of life. They are friendly but very shy.

Kuala Kangsar

Masjid Ubudiah

This is one of the most beautiful mosques in Malaysia. Built during the reign of Sultan Idris Murshidul'adzam Shah I, the 28th Sultan of Perak, it stands beside the Royal Mausoleum at Bukit Chandan, Kuala Kangsar, 51km from Ipoh. Construction began in 1913 but was interrupted several times. Finally in 1917, the $200,000 mosque was opened by Sultan Abdul Jalil Karaa- matullah Shah. This imposing landmark, designed by a European engineer, has become a symbol of pride for Muslims in Perak.

Royal Mausoleum

The Royal Mausoleum is adjacent to Masjid Ubudiah. There are a total of seven mausoleums of the sultans of Perak, three of which are found inside the main mausoleum, while the rest are outside.

Besides the Royal Mausoleum there are other well-known mausoleums, such as the Daeng Sedili and Tok Janggut at Kota Lama Kiri, Kuala Kangsar. The tomb of J.W.W. Birch, the first British Resident of Perak, who was killed in Pasir Salak, is located at Pulau Besar, as is the mausoleum of his assassin, Si Puntum.

Istana Iskandariah

This palace, the official residence of the Sultan of Perak, is situated at Bukit Chandan, formerly called Changkat Negara. It was built in 1930 to replace the old palace, and is designed to have a few domes resembling a mosque. The front of the palace facing the sun gives the impression that the sun always shines upon Perak Darul Ridzuan, the "Land of Grace".

Royal Museum

Previously known as Istana Kenangan, Istana Tepas and Istana Lembah, the Perak Royal Museum is an amazing achievement in architecture. It was built without any architectural plans and without using a single nail. Situated near the Sultan of Perak's palace, the museum houses the Royal Regalia, photographs of the Royal Family, illustrations, and artifacts of the past and present monarchy in Perak. It is open daily 9am-6pm and there is no admission fee.

Tugu Keris

Tugu Keris, literally translated as Dagger Monument, is located at the Government Hill, near the Rest House in Kuala Kangsar. It was built in 1963 to commemorate the installation of the late Sultan Idris Shah, the 33 Sultan of Perak. The "Taming Sari" designed dagger, with its eyes pointing to the sky, is a symbol of power. Hang Tuah, the great Malay warrior, was the owner of the original Taming Sari.

Taiping

Perak Museum

This museum, the oldest in the country, was built in 1883 and houses an interesting collection of ancient weapons, ornaments, aboriginal implements and archaeological specimens from prehistoric times until the British era. Open daily 9am-5pm and there is no admission fee.

Taiping Lake Gardens

This 62ha park is one of the biggest and most beautiful parks in the country. It has lush greenery, a lake teeming with freshwater fish, a gazebo, a 9-hole golf course, and a profusion of colourful flowers. It is open daily 10am-6pm.

Taiping Zoo

One of the oldest in the country, this zoo is situated in the Lake Gardens and houses a variety of animals. One interesting feature is the presence of monkeys roaming about freely in the grounds. The zoo is also known as Taman Mergustua Idris Shah.

Teluk Intan

The Leaning Tower

The town of Teluk Intan is 90km from Ipoh and its main feature is the Leaning Tower of Malaysia. The tower slants to the left, reminiscent of the Pisa Tower in italy, and is situated in the centre of town. The pagoda-like structure was built in 1885 by a Chinese contractor, Leong Choon Choong. The dominating 25.5m tower appears to be made up of eight storeys instead of three. Initially the tower was used as a water storage tank for the town, but this stopped when the town commenced obtaining its water from Changkat Jong.

War Memorial

This memorial was constructed to commemorate Malaysian soldiers who died in the cause of peace and freedom.

Beach Resorts

Lumut

The town of Lumut is 84km south of Ipoh and can be reached by bus or taxi from Butterworth, Kuala Lumpur and other major towns. Lumut Country Resort is the place to stay if you are looking for a hotel of international repute, but there are also government rest houses and other smaller hotels in the town.

The annual Sea Festival (*Pesta Laut*) is held in October/November and attracts thousands of visitors. Contact the Perak Tourist Information Centre for the actual dates.

Teluk Batik

About 6.5km from Lumut lies Teluk Batik, a favourite spot for campers, picnickers, swimmers and sun-lovers. The stretches of white sandy beach are ideal for whatever activity you have in mind. You can rent rooms and chalets along the beach at bargain prices. Contact the Manager of Teluk Batik Chalets, ph 935 544, for reservations.

Pulau Pangkor

This beautiful island, still relatively unspoiled and underdeveloped, may be reached by ferry boat from Lumut in half an hour.

Pantai Puteri Dewi (Golden Sands)

A beautiful stretch of golden sandy beach on the north-west coast of Pangkor, Pantai Puteri Dewi means "Beach of the Lovely Princess". Legend says that a Sumatran princess came to the island in search of her warrior lover. Broken-hearted after learning of his death, she took her own life.

The ferry to this beach, and the Pan Pacific Resort, ph (03) 291 3757, leaves Lumut from 8am to 4pm daily and the journey takes about 45 minutes.

Pasir Bogak

They say the best parts of Pasir Bogak are the water and outdoor activities - scuba diving, fishing, camping, etc. The shallow crystal-clear water allows more than a glimpse of the vast coral reef that surrounds the island.

Accessible by ferry from Lumut, the journey only takes 30 minutes, and the ferry runs from 7am to 7pm. Accommodation ranges from hotels and government rest houses to budget "Atap Huts" at Mini Camps. The "Atap Hut" is triangular in shape and very quaint.

Pulau Pangkor Laut

There are other beach resorts that might stir interest and adventure... Pantai Rubiah in Lumut and Teluk Nipah in Pangkor.

Popularly known as "Fantasy Island" this is every tourist's dream. Maidens welcome you with garlands of flowers andsmiles to brighten up your holiday.

Pulau Pangkor Laut is an island resort of international standard offering excellent facilities, including 72 wooden atap chalets, swimming pools, fishing, sports hall, disco, restaurants, etc. It is situated to the west of the southern tip of Pulau Pangkor, and the ferry trip from Lumut takes 45 minutes.

Emerald Bay is a popular beach on this island, with translucent, emerald green water and snow white sandy shores.

You can also hire boats to discover the islands on the outskirts of Pulau Pangkor, such as Pulau Sembilan and Pulau Mentagor. A whole array of outdoor sights and activities are offered.

Hill Resort

Bukit Larut

Formerly known as Maxwell Hill, this is Malaysia's oldest hill resort. For further information see the chapter on Hill Resorts.

SPORT AND RECREATION

Golf

Royal Perak Golf Club, Jalan Sultan Azian Shah, Ipoh, ph (05) 573 266.

Green Fees (Visitors)
Weekdays   - RM150

Caddy Fee   - RM20(for all)

Green Fees (Guests)
Weekdays   - RM100
Weekends   - RM150

Bukit Jana Golf Club, Jalan Bukit Jana, Kamunting, Taiping, ph (05) 883 7500.

Green Fees (Visitors)
Weekdays   - RM50
Weekends   - RM80

Green Fees (Guests)
Weekdays   - RM30
Weekends   - RM50

Caddy Fee: Class A   RM14,
Class B   RM12,
Class C   RM8.

KELANTAN

Kelantan, which means "land of Lightning", is situated in the north-eastern corner of Peninsular Malaysia, and its rustic setting amidst padi fields and picturesque villages, will give you insights into a way of life that has endured the passing of time. Unspoiled beaches stretch along its 96km coast. It has an area of 13,931 sq km.

The capital of Kelantan is Kota Bharu.

HISTORY

The area's history dates back to between 8000 and 3000BC. Chinese historical documents chronicle the existence of a government with strong links to China. Kelantan was subsequently referred to as *Ho-lo-tan*, *Chih-Tu* and *Tan-Tan* in these records.

In the 18th century the provinces came under the rule of a powerful warrior, Long Yunus, whose descendants today make up the royal house of Kelantan.

Kelantan came under Thai and British influence before becoming part of the Federation of Malaya, and later Malaysia.

HOW TO GET THERE

By Air

Malaysia has daily direct flights to Kota Bharu from Kuala Lumpur and Penang.

By Rail

Express trains arrive daily from various destinations throughout Kelantan, and major towns in Peninsular Malaysia, including Singapore. For enquiries, ph (09) 796 989.

By Bus

Air-conditioned buses connect Kota Bharu with other towns in Peninsular Malaysia.

By Taxi

Taxis driving between Kota Bharu and Kuala Terengganu/Gua Musang charge between RM12 and RM15 per person.

Taxi services from Kuantan, Kuala Lumpur, Butterworth, Penang, Ipoh and Gua Musang charge between RM25 and RM40 per person, according to the distance travelled.

Airport transfers are RM10 per person.

TOURIST INFORMATION

The State Tourist Information Centre is in Jalan Sultan Ibrahim, Kota Bharu, ph (09) 748 5534.

ACCOMMODATION

Hotels in Kota Bharu are numerous, ranging from luxury class to the very modest no-frills establishments. Here is a selection, with prices for a double room per night, which should be used as a guide only. The telephone area code is 09.

Perdana Resort, Jalan Kuala Pa'amat, Pantai Cahaya Bulan, ph 773 3000 - 120 rooms, 1 restaurant, cocktail lounge, coffee shop, swimming pool - RM192.

Hotel Perdana, Jalan Mahmood, ph 785 0000 - 136 rooms, 1 restaurant, cocktail lounge, coffee shop, swimming pool - RM192.

Budget

Hotel Sentosa, Jalan Sultan Ibrahim, ph 743 292 - RM60-120.

Kencana Inn City Centre, Wisma Suaramuda Jalan, ph 740 944 - RM63-85.

Bharu Hotel, 1973A Jalan Dato Pati, ph 740 085 - RM20-70.

Hotel Sinaran Suria, Jalan Padang Garong, ph 743 310 - RM35-65.

Hotel Selesa, 2863C Jalan Sultanah Zainab, ph 748 129 - RM30-60.

Prince Hotel, 3953 Jalan Temenggong, ph 782 066 - RM25-55.

Milton Hotel, 5471A, B, C Jalan Pengkalan Chepa, ph 749 199 - RM20-45.

LOCAL TRANSPORT

Many points of interest in Kota Bharu are within walking distance of each other, while outlying attractions can be quite easily reached by bus, car or trishaw. In order to get the most out of your tour, we suggest that you use local tourist guides.

Bus

Local buses travel around town as well as to the outskirts and well-known tourist destinations. Visitors may board the bus at the Jalan Pendek Bus Station (for travel within Kota Bharu) or the Langgar Bus Station, Jalan Pasir Puteh and Jalan Hamzan Bus Station (for travel out of Kota Bharu).

Taxi

Kota Bharu has a good taxi service that enables visitors to get around town. Taxis may either be hired at the taxi stand at Jalan Pendek, or hailed from the roadside. Generally, however, taxis in Kota Bharu are used for long distance travel. For sightseeing, some taxis may be hired for the day.

Trishaws

These abound in Kota Bharu, and are a popular mode of transport. For the visitor it is ideal, since you may get a running commentary from the trishaw peddler, as you pass all the places of interest, and if you like, you may stop to take photos. Trishaws do not have meters so it is advisable to determine the price of the ride before stepping into one. You may most certainly bargain to get the best fare.

EATING OUT

Kota Bharu offers a variety of food for all tastes and temperament. While food stalls are scattered all around the town and many of the major hotels have their own restaurants, you may want to try the Night Food Stalls. These are found opposite the main bus terminal and are open from 6pm to midnight.

For Chinese food, try Kota Bharu's Chinatown at the junction of Jalan Padang Garong and Jalan Pengkalan Chepa.

SHOPPING

Kelantan is a good place to buy traditional handicrafts, including some from Thailand. Look for silk kaftans, batik scarves, silver trinkets, songkets, baskets and place mats.

Bazaar Buluh Kubu

This is a three-story shopping complex stocked with miniature souvenirs, knick-knacks and clothing.

New Central Market

Kelantan's Central Market is a food market, and most of the stall holders are women. Some think that this is a throwback to the time when the state was ruled by a princess, Cik Siti Wan Kembang, but whatever the reason, these women really know how to bargain.

Jalan Temenggong

This street is home to tastefully-decorated shops offering gold, jewellery, rich textiles and brassware.

SIGHTSEEING

KOTA BHARU

Gelanggang Seni

South of the information centre is the town's cultural centre, Gelanggang Seni, which is a must for the visitor. Kelantan is known as the cultural haven of Malaysia and at this centre it is possible to witness all the different aspects of that culture.

Giant kites chase each other in the sky, tops the size of dinner plates spin for hours, and there is the continual sound of the *rebana ubi* (drums).

In the evenings there are performances of shadow puppet plays and other aspects of Malay culture. Admission is free and show times are: Sat, Mon and Wed 3.30-5.30pm, Sat and Wed 9-10.30pm.

> Many of the attractions in Kota Bharu are located in what is known as the Cultural Zone, around Jalan Sultan and Jalan Hilir Kota. Opening hours are 10.30am-5.45pm Sat-Thurs.

Istana Batu (Royal Museum)

Built in 1939 during the reign of Sultan Ismail I, this building was used to house royal guests and as a venue for royal weddings. It has now been converted into the Royal Museum where regalia and palace items are on display. These include silverware, bedroom items and furniture. There is also a photographic exhibition on the life of the late Sultan o9f Kelantan. Admission is RM2 adult, Rm1 child.

Museum of Royal Traditions and Customs

Built in 1887 by Sultan Muhamad II for his grandson, Long Kundur, this former palace (*Istana Jahar*) now houses photographs, artifacts and exhibits on Kelantan's rich cultural heritage. The intricate wood carvings are testimony to superb craftsmanship. Admission is RM2.

State Mosque

Only a few paces from the Istana Jahar is the State Mosque. Completed in 1926 during the reign of Sultan Ismail, the Mosque took ten years to build. Visitors should be properly attired and should remove their shoes before entering. It may also be necessary to get permission from the caretaker.

Syura Hall (Islamic Museum)

Adjacent to the State Mosque is the Islamic Museum. Completed in 1914 during the reign of Sultan Muhamad, it contains records of the development and spread of Islam in the region. Kelantan is one of the centres of Islamic Learning. Admission is RM2.

War Museum

The War Museum occupies the oldest brick building in Kelantan, dating back to 1912. It houses Japanese memorabilia and documents relating to World War II. Admission if free.

Merdeka Square

In the centre of town is Merdeka Square. Built to commemorate the Malay warriors and patriots who died during the first world war, it is also the place where the Malay nationalist Tok Janggut, was hanged for opposing the British. It is also known as Padang Bank.

Handicraft Village and Craft Museum

This museum has a good display of Kelantan's range of handicrafts - silverware, songket, batik and woodcarvings - and visitors can buy as well as view.

Istana Balai Besar

A palace of old-world charm, the Istana Balai Besar was built in 1844, and replaced the Istana Kota Lama as the state's seat of administration. The name means "the palace with the large audience hall", and the building actually houses the Throne Room, the Hall of Audience and the State Legislative Assembly Hall. It has a beautifully carved interior and still serves as a venue for ceremonial functions and investiture ceremonies. Unfortunately, it is not open to the public at present.

BEACHES

Pantai Cinta Berahi

Situated about 10km north of Kota Bharu is what must be one of the most famous beaches in Malaysia, the Beach of Passionate Love. Fringed by swaying casuarinas and coconut palms, it is everyone's idea of a tropical paradise. To get there take SKMK Bus 10 from the Central Market.

Pantai Irama

The Beach of Melody is in the district of Bachok, about 25km south of Kota Bharu, and some say it is the most beautiful beach on the entire east coast. Take bus no 2A to Bachok.

Pantai Bisikan Bayu

The Beach of the Whispering Breeze is near Semerak in the district of pasir Puteh, about 50km from Kota Bharu. It is also known as Pantai Dalam Rhu, and is a great place for family picnics. From the main terminal in Kota Bharu, take bus no 3 to Pasir Puteh, then bus no 96 to Kuala Besut.

Pantai Seri Tujuh

The Beach of Seven Lagoons is the venue for the International Kite Festival and it lies on the border of Thailand and Kelantan at Kampung Tujuh in Tumpat, only 7km from Kota Bharu. Bus 43 from the main terminal will take you there via a very scenic route.

> **FISHING VILLAGE**
>
> It is becoming very popular to visit a fishing village, and two of the best known are *Sabak Beach*, 14km from Kota Bharu, and *Kuala Besar*, 15km from Kota Bharu. The best time to arrive at the villages is around 2.30pm when the fishing boats can be seen making their way to shore with the day's catch. When they come ashore the bargaining begins between the wholesalers and the fishermen, and although serious business, it looks like a lot of fun. Buses no 8 and 9 depart every half from the old market terminal to Sabak Beach, and bus no 28 leaves from the new central market to Kuala Besar every half hour.

WATERFALLS

There are many waterfalls in the Pasir Puteh district, about 35km from Kota Bharu. The most popular is **Jeram Pasu**, which is off the Kota Bharu-Pasir Puteh road at Kampung Pak Amat, and accessible by car. To get there by public transport, take bus no 3 from the main terminal to Padang Pak Amat, then a taxi to the waterfalls, about 8km away. Many people swim in the crystal clear water, but be warned, it is icy cold.

Another favourite is **Jeram Lenang**, although it is only 12m high. Take bus no 3 to Pasir Puteh, then a taxi.

The independent traveller with a car will be able to get to one of the highest waterfalls in the country, **Lata Beringin**. It falls 120m into a very scenic pool that provides a rejuvenating dip. The magnificent views and lush surroundings make this a popular camping spot. Lata Beringin is near the Sungai Pas Kesedar Land Scheme, and is accessible via a dirt track leading off from the Kuala Krai-Gua Musang highway.

WAT PHOTIVIHAN

The district of Tumpat on the Thai border offers scenic views of the countryside with traditional wooden houses built on stilts, buffaloes roaming free in the mud, and farmers toiling in green padi fields. To get there you cross the Sultan Yahya Bridge, the longest bridge on the East Coast.

In the vicinity there are several Buddhist temples, or wats, the most famous of which is the Wat Phothivihan, with its reclining Buddha. It is located at Kampung Jambu, about 12km north of Kota Bharu. To get there take bus no 29 to Kampong Jambu, where a sign-posted turning indicates the way to the temple.

Not far from the Sultan Yahya Bridge is the town of Pasir Mas, and 15km further on is Lake Toban, a freshwater lake popular with picnickers and fishing enthusiasts.

RIVER CRUISE AND JUNGLE TREKKING

Nature lovers will enjoy an upriver cruise of Sungai Kelantan into the rainforests of Kelantan. Take bus no 5 from the main terminal at 7.45am for Kuala Krai, then the 10am boat for Dabong. The boat ride takes about 2 hours, then you have about three hours to stroll around the village before the boat leaves at 3.15pm.

NOTES

TERENGGANU

The state of Terengganu, with a land area of 12,995 sq km, it between the states of Kelantan and Pahang. From the northern border with Kelantan, the coastline of Terengganu stretches down 225km to the border with Pahang. Within this stretch are blue waters, sparkling white sand and picturesque lagoons with fishing villages that rival any beach scene anywhere in the world.

Terengganu played a significant role in Malay history. The earliest evidence of Islamic presence in the Peninsula was found in Kuala Brang in the form of an inscribed stone (*batu bersurat*) dated circa 1303, which may be seen in the National Museum.

The average temperature throughout the year lies in the region of 26C, with perennial sunshine save for the monsoon season around November-January.

KUALA TERENGGANU

The capital of Terengganu, Kuala Terengganu, is on the coast half-way between Kota Bharu and Kuantan. It was basically a fishing town, but is becoming a busy petroleum centre. The town stands on the Terengganu River and has two main streets, an excellent market and a small esplanade.

HOW TO GET THERE

By Air
Malaysia Airlines operate daily direct services from Kuala Lumpur to Kuala Terengganu, with connecting services from other major cities and towns. The Sultan Mahmud Airport is only 18km from the town centre, ph (09) 626 4500.

By Bus
Express buses arrive and depart at the Central Bus Station at Jalan Sultan Zainal Abidin. Approximate fares are from:

Kuala Lumpur	RM	21.70
Kelantan		8.00
Ipoh		26.00
Penang		23.50
Kota Bharu		7.40
Johore Bahru		22.10

TOURIST INFORMATION

The State Tourist Information Centre is in Jalan Sultan Zainal Abidin, ph (09) 622 1553.

Outstation taxi fares to Kuala Terengganu are as follows from:	
Kuala Lumpur RM	140
Kelantan	60
Ipoh1	80
Penang	200
Kota Bharu	48

ACCOMMODATION

A range of accommodation facilities are available in town or by the beaches. International standard hotels provide first-class amenities and those by the beaches usually have tour programs for visits to surrounding attractions.

Here is a selection, with prices for a double room per night, which should be used as a guide only.

The telephone area code is 09.

Tanjong Jara Beach Hotel, 8th Mile, Off Dungun, ph 841 801 - 100 rooms, 1 restaurant, cocktail lounge, pool, sauna, fitness centre - RM236.

Primula Beach Resort, Jalan Persinggahan, ph 622 100 - 264 rooms, coffee shop, swimming pool, sauna, fitness centre - RM215.

Marang Resort & Safari, Lot 1 Jalan Dungun, ph 682 588 - 100 rooms, coffee shop, swimming pool - RM197.

Budget

Perhentian Island Resort, Pulau Perhentian Besar, ph 345 562 - RM40-90. *Taman Azimos Chalet*, 489 Pantai Peranginan air Tawar, ph 976 530 - RM35-70. *Flora Bay Chalet*, Telok Dalam Pulau Perhentian, ph 977 266 - RM30-50.

LOCAL TRANSPORT

Bus

Following are approximate bus fares for trips from Kuala Terengganu to interstate attractions to:

Marang	RM 1.00
Rantau Abang	3.00
Dungun/Tanjung Jara	4.00
Jertih	5.50
Besut	5.50

EATING OUT

There are many good restaurants in Kuala Terengganu, serving Malay, Chinese, Indian and Thai dishes. Western cuisine can be found at the hotels along with a local menu. Make sure you try Taman Selera in

Kuala Terengganu, as it serves a good variety of local food from 7pm to midnight nightly.

ENTERTAINMENT

Nightly activities need not end with the fabulous sunsets of Terengganu. There are places to go and things to do well into the small hours of the morning. **Not to be missed during the May-September period is the turtle-watching at the 18km stretch of sand at Rantau Abang. For further information see the Sightseeing section.** For an evening of more active involvement, try some of the international hotels that have discos and cabarets.

SHOPPING

Local handicrafts can be found in market squares, bazaars and little shops in Kuala Terengganu. The Central Market (*Pasar Payang*), near the Terengganu River, offers great scope for souvenir hunting, where wares such as batik, brocade, songket, brassware, mats and baskets are displayed alongside fresh produce.

Desa Craft formerly known as *Usaha Desa*, is an interesting handicraft centre that showcases songket, brassware, batik, souvenir items and also fashion wear of current batik designs. This centre was developed by the Terengganu State Economic Development Corporation as part of its effort to promote Kuala Terengganu as a popular tourist destination.

SIGHTSEEING

The Waterfront

This is a very interesting part of Kuala Terengganu. From this bustling district you can hire a boat for a small sum to ferry you to some of the idyllic islands, or take the passenger boat to Seberang Takir, well-known for its panoramic view of the South China Sea, and its dried fish and fish cracker industry.

Masjid Abidin

This stately mosque is located at Jalan Masjid, and was formerly known as *Masjid Besar* (Big Mosque) or *Masjid Putih* (White Mosque). An historical place, it was originally constructed of wood by the late Sultan Zainal Abidin II, but it was later rebuilt with bricks and concrete, and further improved, during the reign of Sultan Zainal Abidin III.

Terengganu State Museum Complex

Located at Jalan Cherong Lanjut, this museum has many interesting exhibits from the town's history and also includes an old bicycle used by the Japanese soldiers during their attack on the Malay Peninsula during World War II. The main museum is built on 16 stilts in accordance with the traditional architecture of Terengganu, and its four blocks are adjoined to represent a big family. There are ten galleries showcasing textiles, crafts, historical, royal, nature, art, petroleum, Islamic, new generation and contemporary arts.

Istana Maziah

Situated near Bukit Puteri, the palace is thought to have been built during the reign of Sultan Zainal Abidin III. It is the venue for royal birthdays and weddings, conferments of titles and welcoming of dignitaries. It was built to replace the Istana Hijau (Green Palace) that was destroyed by fire.

Marang Fishing Village

Only 15km from Kuala Terengganu, this fishing village is noted for its salted fish, fish and prawn crackers, and other delicacies. Several handicraft houses also make and sell traditional woven crafts from the pandanus or *mengkuang* leave.

Sekayu Waterfalls

A favourite with locals and visitors alike, this seven layered waterfall is tucked away in the rain forest, and is a great picnic spot. Only 56km, or a 45 minute drive from Kuala Terengganu, facilities include shelters, changing rooms, chalets and a rest house, ph (09) 681 2125.

Rantau Abang

The beach of Rantau Abang is 60km south of Kuala Terengganu, and this is where female Leatherback turtles make their lonely way from the high seas to lay their eggs in the unusually large brown-grained sand found here. The turtle inches her way ashore to lay the eggs in a large crater-like depression that she laboriously digs with her flippers.

Other beaches on the east coast where turtles may be seen are Kuala Abang, Ketapong Kubur and Jambu Bongkor. The laying season is from May to September.

The Leatherback turtle is extremely sensitive to noise or light, so if too many tourists gather, or if they make too much noise, the turtle will return to the sea without laying her eggs. The area is one of only six in the world visited by these turtles, and a turtle information centre in the vicinity gives further information on this rare species.

Pulau Duyung

The island is situated in the mouth of the Terengganu River, and is a centre of boat building. The art has been passed down from generation to generation, and the workers rely on memory and experience, not plans and blueprints. Pulau Duyung is also renowned for its dried and salted fish, and fish cracker industries. It is easily accessible by the Sultan Mahmud Bridge, or by boat from the Kuala Terengganu waterfront.

Pulau Kapas

From Marang Jetty, south of Kuala Terengganu, take a boat and head out about 6km to this island renowned for its clear emerald waters and beautiful coral. From the second world war until the late 80s the island was uninhabited. Construction of ten chalets, a small restaurant and three A-frame huts began in 1987, and now there are six resorts.

Pulau Kapas is a haven for swimming, snorkelling, wind surfing, kayaking, boating or just lazing around.

Pulau Perhentian

Off the north coast of Terengganu are the islands of Pulau Perhentian - Pulau Perhentian Besar and Pulau Perhentian Kecil. They are 21km off the coast of Terengganu, and accessible by boat from Kuala Besut.

A trip to these lush and exotic tropical islands offers scuba diving, snorkelling, deep sea fishing, swimming, wind surfing, sailing, boating and canoeing, virgin jungle, swaying palm trees, white sandy beaches, warm sapphire blue waters and a colourful coral garden. The islands are part of a national marine park so no fishing is allowed within 1 3.2km radius of the islands, and the collection of coral and aquatic life is prohibited. **There are several accommodation places on the islands, from huts to resorts.**

Pulau Redang

Pulau Redang is 50km off the coast of Kuala Terengganu and is one of the most beautiful islands in Malaysia. It offers the usual things found on tropical paradises - clear water, white sand, palm trees, coral gardens, etc - and has six resorts to enable visitors to enjoy their surroundings for longer periods.

The trip by boat from the village of Merang takes about two hours, and visitors should note that this island is also part of a national marine park so the same restrictions as above apply.

Bukit Keluang

This beach park in Besut, about 140km north of Kuala Terengganu, is accessible by road right up to the sea front. Three hillocks (*bukit*) with their contained beaches and the convergence of the Sungei Keluang Besar, the nearby Pulau ru and the sea into this area have created one of the most scenic sites in Malaysia.

There are toilets and change rooms, food and drink vendors, and a boardwalk along the seaward bluff of Bukit Keluang that provides access to numerous small coves and beaches at low tide.

PAHANG

Pahang is the largest state in Peninsular Malaysia. With an area of 35,960 sq km, it has vast tracts of rain forests and part of these form a National Park. The mountain range that runs from north to south and form a natural divider between east and west has the highest peak in Peninsular Malaysia, Gunung Tahan, the inspiration for many a mountaineer in this part of the world. Pahang's climate is tropical, ie hot and humid all year round with distinct wet and dry seasons.

On the coast the scenery and the way of life are similar to those in Kelantan and Terengganu. Fishing and village handicrafts are maintained, and Pahang's specialty is songket, the distinctive Malaysian brocade. The capital of Pahang is Kuantan.

KUANTAN

This is a colourful, bustling coastal town mid-way between Singapore and Kota Bharu. Kuantan has excellent hotels and restaurants, and a very colourful fish market with fresh catches of fish, prawns, squids and other varieties from the South China Sea.

HOW TO GET THERE

By Air
Malaysia Airlines fly direct to Kuantan from Singapore and KL.

By Bus
Express Bus Services run from major towns to Kuantan. Some approximate prices are from:

Kuala Lumpur	RM	12.20 (AC)
Kota Bharu	-	15.90 (AC)
Singapore	-	16.50 (AC)

TOURIST INFORMATION
The State Tourist Information Office is in Jalan Mahkota, Kuantan, ph (09) 513 3026.

ACCOMMODATION
There is a wide variety of accommodation in Kuantan itself, and of course, north of the town is Cherating Beach and the famous Club

Mediterranee, which combines activities with glamour and large doses of sophistication.

Here is a selection of accommodation with prices for a double room per night, which should be used as a guide only.

The telephone area code is 09.

The Legend Resort Cherating, Lot 1290 Mukim Sungai Karang, Cherating, ph 439 439 - 152 rooms, 2 restaurants, cocktail lounge, coffee shop, swimming pool, sauna, fitness centre - RM268.

Hyatt Kuantan, Telok Chempedak, Kuantan, ph 513 1234 - 340 rooms, 4 restaurants, cocktail lounge, coffee shop, swimming pool, sauna, fitness centre - RM226-252.

Coral Beach Resort, 152 Sungai Karang, Beserah Kuantan, ph 587 543 - 162 rooms, 1 restaurant, cocktail lounge, coffee shop, swimming pool, sauna, fitness centre - RM211.

Impiana Resort Cherating, Km32 Jalan Kuantan, Kemaman, ph 439 000 - 250 rooms, 1 restaurant, cocktail lounge, coffee shop, swimming pool - RM204.

Cherating Holiday Villa, Lot 1303 Mukim Sungai Karang, Cherating, ph 439 500 - 190 rooms, 1 restaurant, cocktail lounge, coffee shop, swimming pool, sauna, fitness centre - RM197.

Budget

Hotel Oriental Evergreen, Jalan Haji Abdul Rahman, Kuantan, ph 500 168 - RM77-105.

Champagne Emas Hotel, 3002 Jalan Haji Abbas, Kuantan, ph 508 820 - RM75-86.

Classic Hotel, Jalan Besar, Kuantan, ph 554 599 - RM65-110.

Simgita Hotel, 9th Mile, Kuantan Port, Kuantan, ph 587 254 - RM63-100.

Baru Raya Hotel, 134 Jalan Besar, Kuantan, ph 505 334 - RM63.

LBC Hotel, 59 Jalan Haji Abdul Aziz, ph 528 252 - RM33-53.

Gloria Maris Resort, 1/1402 Kampung Bahru Beserah, Cherating, ph 587 788 - from RM74.

Spag Holiday Villa, Kampung Cherating Lama, Cherating, ph 439 316 - RM40-60.

Cherating Bayview Resort, Kampung Cherating Lama, ph 939 248 - from RM50.

Cherating Inn Beach Resort, Kampung Cherating Lama, ph 439 343 - RM10-50.

Hotel Makmur, B14-16 Jalan Pasar Baru, Kuantan, ph 511 363 - RM22-44.

EATING OUT

Of course, if you are staying at one of the resorts, meals are provided, and the large hotels have international standard restaurants, but here are a few local restaurants you might try:

Tawakkai Restaurant, 13 Jalan Haji Abdul Aziz, ph 522 637.
Restoran Tiki, 9 Jalan Haji Abdul Aziz, ph 522 272.
Bilal Restaurant, 30 Jalan Tun Ismail, ph 523 217.
Honeycomb Coffee House, 2610-A Jalan Alor Akar, ph 523 434.

SIGHTSEEING

Teluk Chempedak
This is a fabulous stretch of beach that is only 5km from Kuantan. Visitors can take a short jungle trek through the Teluk Chempedak Forest Reserve to either Pelindung Beach or a mini-zoo.

The Handicraft Centre in Teluk Chempedak has a good range of handicrafts from all over the state, at reasonable prices.

Beserah
A small fishing village 10km from Kuantan, Beserah is unique in that the fishermen use water buffaloes to transport their catch from the boats to the processing area. Usually these animals are only seen in padi fields. The town also has a batik factory and many cottage industries.

Balok Beach
The beach is about 15km north of Kuantan and is a paradise for wind-surfers. It is home to the newest international standard hotel in Pahang, the Coral Beach Resort.

Cherating
Many think that all this town has to offer is Club Med, but in fact it is a village similar to many others in the state, except that it has great beaches. The locals are very hospitable and put on cultural shows, as well as offering their handicrafts for sale.

Chendor Beach
Chendor is just over a kilometre from Cherating, and is a good beach, but its claim to fame is that it is one of the sites chosen by the Leatherback turtles to lay their eggs.

Sungai Pandan Waterfalls
The park covers 11ha and is 25km west of Kuantan. It is easily accessible by a main road, then an 8km stretch of paved road. The area is a popular holiday spot, with many enjoying a swim in the pool at the bottom of the cascades.

Gua Charah
The Charah Cave is about 25km north-west of Kuantan at Panching. The cave is nature's work in limestone, but inside man has built a 9m

reclining statue of Buddha. The statue is flooded with sunlight at 11.59am daily from a hole in the cave's roof.

PEKAN

Kuantan is the administrative capital of Pahang, but the Royal capital is Pekan. The Sultan lives in a palace in Pekan, and if you are in Pahang on his official birthday on October 24, a visit would be a very memorable occasion.

Lake Chini

The lake is about 100km from Kuantan, and is the subject of many well-known myths. Legend says that an ancient Khmer city once existed near the lake, and interest in this legend has resulted in several expeditions being mounted by archaeologists, both local and foreign. It is also believed that monsters live in the deep waters of the lake and guard it. Mind you, I'm not sure what you would guard a lake against, but then I'm not an expert on legends.

The lake can be reached two ways: by road to Kampung Belimbing, then by boat on the winding Chini River; or by road via Segamat Highway, through the new town of Chini, and a 15 minute trip on palm oil estate roads.

State Museum

This museum has a very good collection of historical items such as the recently recovered treasures from a wrecked Chinese junk in the South China Sea. It also has a large quantity of glassware and ceramics from ancient China, and a well-documented exhibit of Pahang's ancient royalty.

PULAU TIOMAN

Tioman is the largest of a group of 64 volcanic islands, the smallest of which is a mere rock jutting up from the sea. The island is 38km long and 19km at its greatest width, and can be reached by boat from Mersing town, or by plane from either Kuala Lumpur, Singapore or Kuantan. Tioman is great for swimming and has good reefs for scuba diving. Accommodation ranges from a resort to chalets on the beach.

There are four other major attractions in the state of Pahang:

Taman Negara -	see the section on National Parks.
Genting Highlands -	see the section on Hill Resorts.
Cameron Highlands -	see the section on Hill Resorts.
Fraser's Hill -	see the section on Hill Resorts.

JOHOR

Johor is the southernmost state in Peninsular Malaysia. Because of its location it was known as *Hujung Tanah* (Land's End) in the old days. Its present name is said to come from an Arabic word *Jauhar* (Precious Stones) given by Arab merchants who first traded in this state.

Johor is the only state on Peninsular Malaysia to have both an east coast and a west coast. Consequently it has both the economic development associated with the west coast, and beautiful beaches and off-shore islands characteristic of the east coast.

Covering an area of about 18,985 sq km, Johor is bounded by Pahang (north), Negeri Sembilan and Melaka (west), South China Sea (east) and the Straits of Johor (south). It is linked to Singapore by the Johor Bahru Causeway, which is about 1km long. The population of approximately 2 million people comprises 54.8% Malay, 38.4% Chinese, 6.3% Indian and 0.5% others.

The capital is Johor Bahru.

JOHOR BAHRU

The Gateway to Malaysia from the south, Johor Bahru, or JB as it is referred to, is one of the fastest developing capitals in the country. Having been a municipality since April 1, 1980, the town has a population of more than 750,000 people. Way back in 1855, it was named Tanjung Putr, but Sultan Abu Bakar gave it its present name in 1866.

HOW TO GET THERE

By Air
Malaysia Airlines have several daily flights to Johor Bahru, and they connect with flights from other cities and towns in Malaysia. The airport is less than 25km from JB, and air-conditioned coaches ply to and from the airport to the town, and to Orchard Road, Singapore.

By Bus
All express buses arrive and department from Bangunan Mara, JB, ph (07) 227 220. Buses arrive from all major cities and towns in Peninsular Malaysia. There are also two bus services daily from Singapore to Johor Bahru. For further information contact National Express Kuala Lumpur, (03) 238 6990, or Johor Bahru, (07) 227 220.

By Rail

Malayan Railway operates both day and night services to Johor Bahru. For information on prices and timetables, ph (07) 224 727.

By Taxi

Outstation taxis travel from Kuala Lumpur, Malacca, Kuantan and even from Kota Bharu to Johor Bahru. Taxi Station, ph (07) 234 494.

TOURIST INFORMATION

Tourist information offices are found at:

1, 4th floor, Tun Abdul Razak Complex, Jalan Wong Ah Fook, ph (07) 222 3591.

Tanjung Puteri Tour Bus Complex, Johor Causeway, ph (07) 224 9485.

ACCOMMODATION

You can choose to stay at the Holiday Inn, an international standard hotel in the heart of JB itself, or at any of the 3- or 4-star hotels scattered around the town. Merlin Inn has a magnificent view of the Straits of Johor, while the 104 room Merlin Tower along Jalan Meldrum has a panoramic view of the town. The smaller hotels are popular with travellers on a budget. The Straits View Hotel, built in the 1930s, maintains an old world charm of the colonial period.

Following is a lost of some of the choices, with prices for a double room per night, which should be used as a guide only. The telephone area code is 07.

Holiday Inn Crowne Plaza, Jalan Dato Sulaiman, Taman Century Kb 779, ph 332 3800 - 350 rooms, 4 restaurants, cocktail lounge, coffee shop, swimming pool, sauna, fitness centre - RM312.

Putri Pan Pacific, "The Kotaraya", ph 223 3333 - 500 rooms, 8 restaurants, cocktail lounge, coffee shop, swimming pool, sauna, fitness centre - RM302.

Crystal Crown, 117 Jalan Tebrau, ph 333 4422 - 298 rooms, 1 restaurant, cocktail lounge, coffee shop, swimming pool, sauna, fitness centre - RM233.

Budget

Hotel Le Tien, 2 Jalan Siew Nam, ph 248 151 - RM51-66.

Fortuna Hotel, Jalan Meldrum, ph 233 210 - RM47-70.

First Hotel, 8th-10th Floor, Overseas Plaza,
    Jalan Station, ph 222 888 - RM40-60.

Hong Kong Hotel, 31A Jalan Meldrum, ph 246 407 - RM35-50.

Golden Court Hotel, 147 Jalan Sri Pelangi, ph 326 722 - RM32-55.

Hill Court Hotel, 26ABC Jalan Haya, Taman Maju Jaya, ph 324 254 - RM29-35.

LOCAL TRANSPORT

Taxis are the main form of transport in Johor Bahru, and for sightseeing to other places of interest such as Kota Tinggi and Desaru. Decide on the fare before the ride as most taxis do not have meters.

Trishaws are also available in KB.

EATING OUT AND ENTERTAINMENT

Johor Bahru has a busy nightlife from 7pm onward. The hawkers centre new Kompleks Tun Razak is usually packed during dinner time. The *Laska Johor* is a must for every first-timer down south. A variety of herbs and spices are used to make the gravy which is brownish in colour and spicy to taste. *Santan* (coconut milk), *kerisik* (fried coconut), onions, cucumber, *daun selasih* and other ingredients add to the taste, not forgetting the dash of chili and half-lime for that truly Malaysian flavour. The dish is also available during the day at the hawkers centre opposite the railway station.

Along the roads there are stalls selling *ayam percik*. This is barbecued chicken served with a special satay sauce. Johor is famous for its *longtong* which is glutinous rice made into compact cubes and served in curry. Other scrumptious foods are *satay, mee goreng, rojak, nasi tomato, mee bandung,* etc.

The Taman Sri Tebrau hawker centre offers mainly Chinese food, and there are quite a few stalls selling claypot rice and barbecued seafood, wrapped in banana leaves.

Jaw's 5 Seafood Restaurant, situated along Jalan Scudai, is very popular with the locals, Singaporeans and international tourists. There are attap-roofed huts designed in ancient Malay style, as well as a modern air-conditioned building to dine in comfort. The menu incorporates the best of Sze Chuan, Cantonese, Hainanese and Shanghai cuisines, and the prices are reasonable.

At Kukup, a little Chinese fishing village on the southernmost west coast of Johor, there are lots of restaurants built on stilts that specialise in seafood. From here you get a good view of the Straits of Malacca and the Indonesian shores. **Kong Kong fishing village on the east side of Johor is also renowned for its seafood.**

SHOPPING

Clay Industries Sdn Bhd, is one of the oldest and largest manufacturers of ceramic products and has a large range of tableware and decorative sculptures. For those interested to see how the ceramic items are produced, enquiries can be made through the administration office in Air Hitam, Johor, ph 784 201, to arrange for a tour of the factory.

JB Crafttown Handicrafts Centre, 36 Jalan Scudai, ph 367 346, is one handicraft shop you can't afford to miss. There is a wide variety of hand-drawn batik materials and paintings, Malaysian oil and water-colour paintings, straw mats, songket and hand-drawn T-shirts to choose from, not to mention the many souvenirs and trinkets. The centre is open daily 8.30am-5.30pm, and they will also arrange free tours of JB town and the centre itself to promote tourism in Johor.

SIGHTSEEING

Istana Besar
This palace, in Jalan Scudai, was built by Sultan Abu Bakar in 1866, and is the venue for royal ceremonies, investitures, state banquets and receptions. Since 1992 the palace has also been a museum.

Istana Serene
Also in Jalan Scudai, this is the residence of His Highness the Sultan of Johor. The Royal Mausoleum is close by, and ti has been the burial place for the Johor royal family since the change of the capital from Johor Lama. The mausoleum is not open to the public, but some fine examples of Muslim tombs can be found in the grounds.

Abu Bakar Mosque
Set on a hill, this is considered to be one of the finest mosques in Malaysia. The intricate architecture was designed by Tuan Haji Mohammad Arif, and it took eight years to build. It was finished in 1900 at a cost of RM400,000.

Sultan Ibrahim Building
Situated on Bukit Timbalan, this building houses the State Council Chamber, the State Secretariat and Government offices. The Saracenic character of the Grand Hall is certainly very interesting.

AIR HITAM
A favourite stopover for travellers, this busy little town, 88km north of JB is well-known for its pottery and clay products. There are also many coffee shops and roadside stalls, that are open 24 hours a day and provide really good food. Air Hitam has been aptly nicknamed "the town that never sleeps".

JOHOR LAMA
Of considerable historical interest, Johor Lama is a small village on the Johor River, 30km from Johor Bahru. Archaeological excavations have uncovered interesting relics and the fort has been restored.

Until 1587, Johor Lama was the royal seat of the Johor kingdom and a thriving port. In that year, however, the three-year quarrel between the Johor kingdom and the Portuguese culminated in a Portuguese raid on Johor Lama. With three galleons, a number of smaller ships and 500 men, the Portuguese attacked the Johor fort from July 20 to August 15, 1587. When the fort fell the city was sacked and a large booty of precious metals and other treasures was carried away by the Portuguese. The city never recovered after that. Today Johor Lama is easier reached by launch than by road.

GUNUNG LEDANG

Johor's highest peak soars to 1395m above sea level and is also known as Mount Ophir.

MERSING

Mersing, 136km from Johor Bahru, the take-off point to many islands, has its own appeal. In the town there is a wide bay with a rocky beach and a mangrove forest in front of the rest house. At low tide one can walk across to an opposite islet. In past years a rumour of sunken treasure being found off the Mersing coast near Pulau Batu Gajah turned Mersing from a quiet town into a tourist mecca. **The Merlin Inn located on Endau Road offers comfortable accommodation from RM85.**

DESARU

A resort approximately 98km north-east of Johor Bahru. Desaru has more than 25km of unspoiled beaches. All kinds of sports, from snorkelling, swimming and canoeing to jungle-trekking can be enjoyed here. For those who enjoy golf, there is an 18-hole course.

ISLANDS

Pulau Rawa

Rawa, about 16km from Mersing, is one of the many splendid islands of Johor. The lovely beaches are formed of white coral sand virtually covered with tall palms. There are coves to explore, and an off-shore coral reef teeming with marine life. *Rawa Island Resort* also has a restaurant that serves a wide variety of local, Western and Chinese food. **Rawa Safaris in Mersing operate return boat trips to Rawa and bookings should be made at least one week in advance.**

Pulau Sibu

This is another of Malaysia's picturesque islands. There are several resorts offering accommodation, and it is a good idea to arrange transport to the island through them. A fishing village is within walking distance of **Sibu Island Cabanas.** Fishing and snorkelling seem to be the only activities. An ideal place to get away from it all.

SABAH

Sabah is situated on the north coast of the island of Borneo. It has 1440km of coastline, with the South China Sea on the west and the Culu and Celebes seas on the east. Known as "The Land below the Wind" because it lies below the typhoon belt, temperatures seldom reach 33C, usually varying during the day between 23C and 31C.

Sabah is mountainous with lush tropical rain forests, and has an area of 74,500 sq km. Kota Kinabalu, the capital, is the eastern gateway to Malaysia with direct air links to Brunei, Hong Kong, the Philippines, Singapore, South Korea, Indonesia and Taiwan.

The people of Sabah are from 32 various indigenous groups. Amongst them are Kadazans, Muruts, Bajaus, Kedayans, Sulu, Bisaya, Rumanau, Minokok and Rungus.

KOTA KINABALU

Kota Kinabalu is a relatively new town, as evidenced by the many high-rise buildings. The original town was razed during the second world war and so a new carefully planned town was built. With a population of around 300,000, the city takes particular pride in its gold-domed State Mosque which is centrally positioned and overlooks most of the town.

HOW TO GET THERE

By Air
Malaysia Airlines has direct flights to Kota Kinabalu from Kuala Lumpur, Johor Bahru, Kuching, Singapore, Hong Kong, Manila, Seoul and Taipei. Singapore Airlines has direct flights from Singapore to Kota Kinabalu.

TOURIST INFORMATION
The Sabah office of Tourism Malaysia is on the ground floor of Wisma Wing Onn Life, no 1 Jalan Sagunting, Kota Kinabalu, ph (088) 248 698. The Sabah Tourist Promotion Corporation is at 51 Jalan Gaya, Kota Kinabalu, ph (088) 218 620.

ACCOMMODATION

There is a wide choice of accommodation in Kota Kinabalu, ranging from international standard to small budget hotels. Here is a selection with prices for a double room per night, which should be used as a guide only. The telephone area code is 088.

Shangri-La Tanjung Aru Resort, Locked Bag 174, ph 226 800 - 500 rooms, 1 restaurant, cocktail lounge, coffee shop, swimming pool, sauna, fitness centre - RM348-392.

Hyatt Kinabalu International, Jalan Datuk Salleh Sulong, ph 221 234 - 315 rooms, 3 restaurants, cocktail lounge, coffee shop, swimming pool, sauna, fitness centre - RM275.

Sabandar Bay Resort, Off Jalan Pantai Dalit, Jalan Sabandar, ph 787 722 - 139 rooms, 1 restaurant, cocktail lounge, coffee shop, swimming pool - RM198.

Budget

Hotel Holiday, Lot 1&2, Block F, Segama Compleks, ph 213 116 - RM66-99

Diamond Inn, 37 Jalan Haji Yakub, ph 213 222 - RM58-85.

Hotel Holiday Park, Mile 3 1/2 Jalan Penampang, ph 712 311 - RM58-85.

Ang's Hotel, 28 Jalan Pantai, ph 234 999 - RM57-74.

Pantai Inn, 57 Jalan Pantai, ph 219 221 - RM59-69.

City Inn, 41 Jalan Pantai, ph 218 933 - RM48-70.

Federal Hotel, 10 Jalan Haji Yakub, ph 221 906 - RM40-55.

Asia Hotel, 68 & 69 Bandaran Berjaya, ph 234 999 - RM37-52.

Travellers Rest Hostel, 3rd Floor, Bangunan Pelancongan, Sinsuran Complex, ph 240 625 - RM16-42.

LOCAL TRANSPORT

There are buses and mini-buses, but really the only way to travel is by taxi, which is not an expensive option, but do remember to settle on a price before the journey begins. Malaysia Airlines operate daily flights to Labuan, Lahad Datu, Sandakan and Tawau.

The other option for travelling to places on the west coast is rail, and this is a very scenic way to go. Trains leave from Tanjung Aru, a suburb of Kota Kinabalu, and travel south to Tenom, with a small north off-shoot from there to Melalap.

SHOPPING

Kota Kinabalu is not really the place to shop. If you want souvenirs the best place to pick them up is probably the shops in the larger hotels. There is a night market in the centre of town, but it is nothing to get excited about.

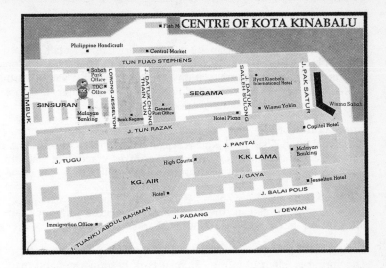

CENTRE OF KOTA KINABALU

SIGHTSEEING

Tanjung Aru

Situated 6km from Kota Kinabalu is the seaside resort of Tanjung Aru. It is a very popular spot and has more than enough accommodation for the hordes of holiday-makers who come to soak up the sun, sea and sand.

Tunku Abdul Rahman Park

The park consists of five islands that are only ten to 25 minutes away from Kota Kinabalu by speedboat. They are Pulau Gaya, Pulau Sapi, Pulau Mamutik, Pulau Manukan and Pulau Sulug, and they offer stretches of white sandy beaches, crystal clear waters, and some of the most diverse coral reefs and marine life in the world. They are ideal places to go for a picnic, particularly Sapi and Manukan, which have picnic facilities, and Mamutik and Manukan where there are rental cabins.

For more information see the section on National Parks.

Penampang

This is a Kadazan village, 13km from Kota Kinabalu. The Kadazans, whose girls are particularly beautiful with long, black hair, are the rice growers of the region. Each year they have harvest festivals lasting for several days. The rejoicing and merry-making is supposed to be good for the harvest. They make their own potent rice wine called *tapai* for this occasion.

Tuaran

A pleasant little place, Tuaran is a half-hour drive from Kota Kinabalu. The road to the town runs through farms, valleys, rubber plantations and forests. The agricultural station here is also worth a visit. Nearby is Mengkabong, a Bajau village built on stilts over the water. Transport around the village is by sampan or canoe.

Kota Belud

This small town 77km from Kota Kinabalu is galvanised into life every Sunday when the *Tamu* or open market takes place. Not only are goods exchanged here, but news and gossip as well.

Mount Kinabalu

Mt Kinabalu is set in the Kinabalu National Park. For more information see the section on National Parks.

Poring Hot Spring

The spring is 43km from the National Park headquarters and many find a swim in the pool very refreshing.

Kota Kinabalu

Kudat

The town is the home of the Rungus, members of the Kadazan race. It lies 238km north of Kota Kinabalu and may be reached by sea or road. Nearby is a beach with surf crashing on the shore, more for photographing than for swimming. Another beach, 8km away at Bak-Bak is reached by a road lined with coconut palms.

Sandakan

Lying on a bay on the north-eastern coast of Sabah and facing the Sulu Seas, Sandakan is 386km from Kota Kinabalu. It is a busy port, with ships loading timber, rattan, copra and birds' nests (for soup). Behind the port lies the town and beyond that are tall mountains. Three roads lead out of Sandakan, the Labuk road, the Leila road and the Sim-Sim road. The Labuk road leads back to Kota Kinabalu through palm oil, cocoa and fruit plantations, padi fields, farmlands and tropical forests.

Leila road goes along the coast, offering magnificent seascapes. Off shore are islands inhabited solely by seabirds, and turtles when they come into lay their eggs. **One of the islands off Sandakan is Berhala Island, ideal for picnicking and swimming, and within easy reach by motor launch. A lighthouse on the highest point offers interesting views for photographers.** The Sim-Sim road leads to prawn canneries, sawmills and shipyards.

Sepilok Orang-Utan Sanctuary

The Orang-Utan Sanctuary at Sepilok is about 24km from Sandakan, and should not be missed. Visitors can see the orang-utans being fed from a platform in the middle of the forest about 20 minutes' walk from the centre. Nicknamed the "wild man of Borneo" (arboreal anthropoid ape), the orang-utans are brought here for rehabilitation, and returned to the forest when they are able to fend for themselves.

Gomantong Caves

These caves can be reached by boat across the bay from Sandakan, then a 16km landrover ride through jungles and plains. At the caves, swifts build their nests high on the cave walls and roof. These nests are considered delicacies and are collected by men climbing on tall bamboo poles. The stalactite and stalagmite features of the caves are also interesting to study. A visit to the cave takes a full day and arrangements can either be made through a travel agency, or the Forestry Department in Sandakan.

SARAWAK

Sarawak lies on the north-west coast of the island of Borneo. It covers an area of approximately 124,450 sq km, making it the largest state in Malaysia. Kuching, the capital, is situated on the banks of the Sarawak River and is the gateway to a country of rain forests, unexplored ravines, plateaux and mountain ranges, rivers and exciting rapids. This is the land where fearsome head-hunters once roamed until the English adventurer, James Brooke set up his private kingdom in the beginning of the 19th century. James Brooke arrived in Sarawak in 1839 when the people were rebelling under the Brunei Sultanate. As a reward for the role he played in quelling the rebellion, the Pengiran Mahkota of Brunei made Brooke the Rajah of Sarawak in 1841. James was succeeded by his nephew Charles Brooke in 1868, who in turn was succeeded by his eldest son in 1917.

During the second world war Sarawak was occupied by the Japanese forces, but after the war it became a British Crown Colony. In 1963 Sarawak joined Malaysia. Now a land of lush tropical greenery, it has a population of 1.5 million made up of several indigenous groups, including Iban, Chinese, Malays, Bidayuh, Melanaus, Orang Ulu.

KUCHING

Kuching is located on the banks of the Sarawak River, approximately 32km from the sea. The town has beautifully landscaped parks and gardens, historic buildings, colourful markets, and an interesting waterfront.

HOW TO GET THERE

By Air

Kuching has an international airport, and Malaysia Airlines has direct services from Hong Kong, Johor Bahru, Kuala Lumpur, Kota Kinabalu, Manila, Sibu, Singapore and Tokyo.

TOURIST INFORMATION

The office of Tourism Malaysia is on the Ground Floor of Aurora Chambers in Jalan Tun Abang Haji Openg, ph (082) 246 575.

ACCOMMODATION

Following is a selection of available accommodation, with prices for a double room per night, which should be used as a guide only.

The telephone area code is 082.

Holiday Inn Damai Beach Resort, PO Box 2870, Kuching, ph 411 777 - 302 rooms, 1 restaurant, cocktail lounge, coffee shop, swimming pool, sauna, fitness centre - RM240.

Damai Lagoon Resort, Jalan Tunku Abdul Rahman, ph 234 900 - 250 rooms, 1 restaurant, cocktail lounge, coffee shop, swimming pool, sauna, fitness centre - RM236.

Riverside Majestic Hotel, Jalan Tunku Abdul Rahman, ph 247 777 - 250 rooms, 1 restaurant, cocktail lounge, coffee shop, swimming pool, sauna, fitness centre - RM220.

Kuching Hilton, Jalan Tunku Abdul Rahman, ph 248 200 - 322 rooms, 3 restaurants, cocktail lounge, coffee shop, swimming pool, sauna, fitness centre - RM200.

Holiday Inn Kuching, Jalan Tunku Abdul Rahman, ph 423 111 - 305 rooms, 2 restaurants, cocktail lounge, coffee shop, swimming pool, sauna, fitness centre - RM183.

Budget

Long House Hotel, 101 Jalan Abell, Pandungan, ph 249 333 - RM65-90.

City Inn, Lot 275-276 Abel Road, ph 414 866 - RM49-66.

Borneo Hotel, 30C-F Jalan Tabuan, ph 244 121 - RM48-73.

Country View Hotel, Jalan Tan Sri Ong Kee Hui, ph 247 111 - RM40-85.

Fata Hotel, Jalan Tabuan, ph 248 111 - RM40-85.

Arif Hotel, Jalan Haji Taha, ph 241 211 - RM31-50.

Palm Hotel, 29 Jalan Palm, ph 241 231.

SHOPPING

Kuching is excellent for buying tribal artifacts, and the best selection is to be found in the antique shops along Main Bazaar, Lebuh Wayang and Jalan Temple. Prices are high, but bargaining is expected. Jewellery is expensive too. It is also recommended that you spend a few hours at the Sunday Open Market at Jalan Satok near the suspension bridge. Here antiques could be found on sale alongside jungle produce.

SIGHTSEEING

Sarawak Museum

This is one of the finest museums in Asia, with an excellent collection of Borneon ethnological and archaeological items. Situated in Jalan

Tun Abang Haji Openg, it is open Tues-Sun 9am-6pm and there is no admission charge.

Sarawak Islamic Museum
Near the Sarawak Museum is this recently opened Islamic Museum, with eight galleries devoted to exhibits of Islamic past, architecture, coinage, weaponry, textiles, pottery and porcelain.

Sarawak State Mosque
Situated in the heart of the town, this is a magnificent gilt-domed building. The first mosque on this site was wooden, but this one is known as "the million dollar mosque". It was completed in 1968.

The Astana
The palace was built in 1874 by Rajah Charles Brooke. It is set among rolling lawns on the northern bank of the Sungei Sarawak, and is now the official residence of the head of state. The best view of the palace is from Pangkalan Batu on the opposite side of the river.

Kuching waterfront

Fort Margherita

Close by the Astana is the old Fort Margherita, which was built in 1879 and named after the second Rajah's wife Margaret. The fort was built to defend the town against pirates. It is now a Police Museum housing weapons, among which is the only cannon to be cast in Sarawak.

The Court House

The imposing facade of the Court House, built in 1874, has imaginative local art forms incorporated in the roof panels and the door and window grills. The Court House was the seat of the government during the rule of the White Rajahs. The clock tower was added to the building in 1883, and the obelisk to Charles Brooke was commissioned in 1924.

Tua Pek Kong Temple

The oldest Chinese temple in Kuching is located at the junction of Jalan Tunku Abdul Rahman and the Main Bazaar. It was built in 1876, and its most famous celebration is the Wang Wang which commemorates the spirits of the dead.

Hong San Temple

This temple was built in 1895 in honour of the god Kuek Seng. Legend has it that Kuek, a native of Hokkien province, became a god over a thousand years ago. He is believed to grant all requests from his faithful followers.

Skrang River Safari

This safari has to be undertaken with an organised tour. It begins with a four hour drive to the banks of the Skrang River, then continues down the shallow river by boat, occasionally shooting the rapids. The journey along this scenic river leads to a series of Iban longhouses. These community dwellings are made of ironwood and roofed with palm leaves or ironwood shingles. All the rooms in the longhouses are side by side, facing a long communal hall used for leisure activities like wood-carving and basket weaving. Guests are invited to attend nightly ceremonies, and partake of the rice wine that the Ibans make. Visitors are accommodated in a guest house belonging to the tour operators. These have basic amenities. For further information contact the Tourist Information Centre.

Pepper Plantations

Sarawak is the largest exporter of pepper in the country, and the plantations may be seen along the Kuching-Serian Road.

Sarawak Cultural Village

The village is built on 6ha at the foot of Mt Santubong, 35km from Kuching City, and close to the Damai Holiday Inn. A central man-made lake is surrounded by seven authentic replicas of ethnic houses - the Bidayuh centre house and longhouse, the Iban longhouse, the Penan hut, the Orang Ulu longhouse, the Melanau Rumah Tinggi, the Malay house and the Chinese farmhouse. In each house there are displays of artifacts made by the individual dwellers.

Demonstrations of arts and crafts are held continuously, and there is a one-hour cultural show held in the village's air-conditioned theatrette each day at 2pm.

The village is open daily 9am-5pm and admission is RM45 adult, RM22.50 child (6-12).

Santubong Fishing Village

The picturesque village of Santubong has good beaches and is the site of several archaeological discoveries. Hindu and Buddhist-influenced rock carvings have been found around the Santubong River delta. During the 7th and 13th centuries, Santubong was an important trading centre.

The village is 32km from Kuching and can be reached by express launch. Accommodation in government chalets is available, but bookings in advance are advisable through the District Office in Kuching.

Semenggoh Wildlife Rehabilitation Centre

The centre, 32km south of Kuching, is a 740ha forest reserve where orang-utan are free to wander and adapt themselves to life in the jungle.

A 30 minute walk on specially built boardwalks from the entrance to the centre takes visitors to view the rainforest and some tropical fruit trees. The centre is open daily 8.30am-3.45pm, and the best time to arrive is just before feeding time - 8.30-9am, 11.45am-noon and 3-3.15pm.

Information on the other attractions in Sarawak - Bako National Park, Gunung Mulu National Park and Niah National Park - are contained in the section on National Parks.

HILL RESORTS OF MALAYSIA

The Hill Resorts of Malaysia offer the visitor the opportunity to commune with nature and relax in the cool, fresh, invigorating climate. With the jungle literally at your doorstep, you may saunter along cool, peaceful jungle vales, admire the exotic flora and fauna, or simply sit and dream in front of a roaring log fire at night. For the more energetic there is golf, tennis, swimming, bowling and, of course, climbing on mountain peaks that rise to well over 1830m.

CAMERON HIGHLANDS

The Cameron Highlands, 1524m above sea-level, lie in the north-west corner of the state of Pahang in the centre of Peninsular Malaysia. The highlands are actually three districts in one. Less than 45km from Tapah, in the state of Perak, is **Ringlet**, one of the main agricultural centres of the Cameron Highlands. The soil is rich and the climate conducive to the growing of giant spring cabbages, lettuce, tomatoes and other temperate and sub-temperate vegetables and fruits.

Tanah Rata, the principal township, lies less than 13km away and another thousand feet up. There, the scenery seems to suddenly shift into high gear. The air is cool and clean, and there are jungle streams, lakes and waterfalls, and magnificent views.

Tanah Rata's natural assets have been cleverly and wisely exploited. There are chalets, cottages and good hotels, steak houses and all the solitude you could wish. There is a bank, a post office and a busy shopping centre. There is also a bus service and taxis are available. About 3km further up from Tanah Rata is the township of **Brinchang**. There in front of a beautiful 18-hole golf course is the modern international-standard Merlin Inn Resort.

HISTORY

In 1885 a government surveyor on a mapping expedition reported finding "a fine plateau with gentle slopes shut in by lofty mountains". The surveyor was William Cameron after whom these hills are named.

Tea planters, quickly realising the suitability of these hills for their crops, hastily claimed the plateau. Chinese vegetable growers settled in the valleys and later built a road to carry their produce to market. A wealthy planter came looking for the perfect hideaway, discovered the route and built a house there fore weekend retreats. Cameron Highlands, the mountain resort, has never stopped growing since.

HOW TO GET THERE

The Cameron Highlands are easily accessible. From Kuala Lumpur or Penang proceed by car or rail to the town of Tapah. From there make the ascent by bus or taxi along a two-way traffic road that winds through jungle and hill scenery, a distance of 60km. The climb from Tapah is gradual and hardly noticeable except for the fall in temperature. *The Ekspress Nasional* operates a daily bus service to Cameron Highlands from the Pudu Raya Bus Terminal in KL at 8.30am. Fares are RM30 adult, RM15 child (return).

ACCOMMODATION

Like most holiday resorts in Malaysia, the Cameron Highlands have off and peak seasons. The latter is in April, August and December, and in these months it is advisable to book accommodation well in advance. Following is a selection of available accommodation, with prices for a double room per night, which should be used as a guide only. Telephone area code is 05.

Garden Hotel, Tanah Rata, ph 941 911 - 46 rooms, restaurant, cinema, tennis courts, snooker - RM46-138.

Highland Hotel, Brincang, ph 901 588 - 244 rooms, restaurant, cocktail lounge - RM37-63.

Budget

Orient Hotel, 38 Jalan Besar, Tanah Rata, ph 901 633 - RM18-80
Town House Hotel, 41 Main Road, Tanah Rata, ph 902 868 - RM28-78
Tanah Rata Rest House, ph 901 254 - RM60-100.

AGRICULTURE

The Cameron Highlands are famous for their large brilliantly coloured flowers. With average day temperatures hovering around 21C and night temperatures around 10C the Cameron Highlands have become an important flower-producing centre. The much sought-after blooms find their way to all the main towns in Malaysia, and even reach as far as Singapore. Among the many varieties grown are roses, chrysanthemums, carnations, dahlias, geraniums, fuchsias, gladioli, and "everlasting flowers". Also market gardening has become an important economic activity in the district, particularly in the Ringlet and Brinchang areas.

FRUITS & TEA

Strawberries, passion fruit, tangerine oranges, grapefruit - these are some of the many varieties of fruit available in the Highlands. The tea planters who were among the first to "invade' the Cameron Highlands have now established vast acreages of high quality tea bush in various parts of the district. You can either take a drive or a walk and see the colourfully dressed women tea pickers among the buses, or if you like, visit a factory and see the whole process of production.

JUNGLE TRACKS AND MOUNTAIN CLIMBING/SPORTS

There are numerous jungle paths leading to such well-known hilltops as Gunung Beremban (1840m), Gunung Jasar (1695m) and Gunung Brinchang (2032m). On clear days a panoramic view of Ipoh, the Straits of Malacca and other towns can be seen from most peaks. Along most jungle paths and especially at the waterfalls - Robinson Falls and Parit Falls - brilliantly coloured butterflies flit among the trees, and butterfly nets can be purchased from the shops in Tanah Rata. If you don't have time to catch your own there are mounted displays in all of the three towns which you can purchase at reasonable prices.

For the sports-minded there is an 18-hole golf course with undulating fairways, a meandering stream and tricky greens. Visiting membership fees are reasonable and are graded according to the length of your stay. A modern clubhouse beside the first tee offers adequate facilities. There are also tennis and badminton course, and swimming is available in the natural jungle pool under the Parit Falls.

FRASER'S HILL

Like Rome, Fraser's Hill is built on seven hills. At 1524m above sea level, cool air is guaranteed. It is the closest hill station to Kuala Lumpur and is popular with visitors and residents alike.

Carving a road up through the hills was an engineering feat. In the early days bullock carts were used for the journey, but nowadays it is possible to go in perfect comfort by car or air-conditioned bus. There are several bungalows and a large hotel.

HISTORY

Fraser's Hill is named after a solitary adventurer, Louis James Fraser, who built a shack, operated a primitive mule train and traded in tin ore in the last decade of the 19th and the first decade of the 20th century.

In 1910, Bishop Ferguson-Davie of Singapore climbed the mountain in search of Fraser who had apparently disappeared. The search was not quite fruitless for he discovered what has become one of Malaysia's most popular resorts. It was surveyed in 1919 and development of what is now Fraser's Hill commenced soon after.

HOW TO GET THERE

By Bus
There is a regular bus service from Kuala Lumpur to Kuala Kubu Bahru, and from Kuala Kubu Bahru to Fraser's Hill.

Kuala Kubu Bahru to Fraser's Hill departs 8am and noon
Fraser's Hill to Kuala Kubu Bahru departs 10am and 2pm.
Kuala Lumpur - Kuala Kubu Bahru - RM2.50
Kuala Kubu Bahru - Fraser's Hill - RM2.10.

By Taxi
Kuala Lumpur - Fraser's Hill - RM60 per taxi, RM15 per person
Subang Airport - Fraser's Hill - RM90 per taxi (air-con), RM70 per taxi (non air-don).

By Car
The last 8km from the gap to the top of Fraser's Hill is along a narrow winding road that carried only one-way traffic from 6.30am-7pm.

Opening Times for Control Gates

Up-Going Traffic (At the Gap)	Down-Going Traffic (At Fraser's Hill)
7.00am - 7.30am	8.00am - 8.30am
9.00am - 9.30am	10.00am - 10.30am
11.00am - 11.30am	12.00pm - 12.30pm
1.00pm - 1.30pm	2.00pm - 2.30pm
3.00pm - 3.30pm	4.00pm - 4.30pm
5.00pm - 5.30pm	6.00pm - 6.30pm
7.00pm - 7.30pm.	

There is no control after 7.30pm and the gates remain open on both sides.

ACCOMMODATION

The Fraser's Hill Development Corporation runs bungalows and chalets with full catering facilities. There is also a government run rest house (Sri Berkat) and an international standard hotel (Hotel Merlin) right in the centre of Fraser's Hill. Peak season at this resort is in the months of April, August and December. For accommodation during peak season and on weekends, it is advisable to book well in advance. Fraser's Hill Development Corporation Bungalows range from

Ye Old Smokehouse, Cameron Highlands

RM35-65, ph (09) 382 044, and the Hotel Merlin, ph (09) 382 300, offers accommodation from RM100-350. For enquiries about the Seri Berkat Rest House, ph (09) 382 219.

SPORT AND RECREATION

Golf

Fraser's Hill has one of the few public golf courses in Malaysia. Contrary to popular belief, the site of the 9-hole course is not the remains of a tin mine! It was in actual fact constructed by sluicing down the hill-side into the valley of the Sungei Tras and to the dismay of the contractor, not a speck of tin was found in the process.

Playing hours: 7am until dusk daily.

Green fees:	weekdays -RM15 per day.
weekend and public holidays -	RM25 per day.
Caddy fees:	RM5 per round of 9 holes.

Golf sets are available for hire.

Tennis

Two hard courts are available for the use of visitors. The fee is RM5 an hour for daytime sessions, RM7 an hour for night sessions.

Sports Complex

The complex is situated in the town centre and provides a range of facilities - changing rooms for golfers, saunas, two squash courts, a heated swimming pool, conference facilities and a coffee shop and restaurant.Opening times: Mon-Fri and Sun - 9am-noon, 2-5pm. Sat and public holidays - 9am-noon, 2--5pm, 6-9pm.

Swimming

The Jeriau Waterfalls are a must when visiting Fraser's Hill. The cascading falls have been cleverly cupped into a swimming pool.

Less than 5km from the town centre, the falls are easily accessible by car. A full paved footpath (800m) leads to the pool.

Jungle Walks

The well-kept jungle paths and unusual flora are ideal for hikers. These paths lead to the peaks of the hills from which there are panoramic views of the main range of mountains.

Mini Zoo and Park

The mini zoo and park occupy 4ha close to the children's playground. Attractions include a fish pond, aviary, a rose garden, chrysanthemum garden, facilities for horse-riding and camping. Entrance fee is RM1.

PENANG HILL

Penang Hill is the name given collectively to a group of hills in the centre of Penang Island. A ride up the 692m Hill is a fascinating experience. The funicular railway that motors up the Hill is rare in the Far East, the only other being in Hong Kong.

The railway was built in 1923 and the old wooden carriages have since been replaced by modern coaches. One thing still hasn't changed though, you still need to change trains at the half-way point. In just 24 minutes you can feel the temperature dropping to a cool 18C, offering a change from the tropical warmth of the lowlands.

A bus serves the Summit Station to Strawberry Hill or Tiger Hill, but most visitors prefer to walk down the Summit Road. You can follow paths branching off this main road and stroll past picturesque bungalows and beautiful gardens.

HOW TO GET THERE

You can fly from Kuala Lumpur or travel by car or rail. The bottom station of the Hill Railway can be reached by taxi or by regular scheduled bus services.

The funicular rail service begins at 6.30am and ends at 9.30pm and fares are RM3 adult, RM1.50 children.

ACCOMMODATION

Many people plan to spend only a day here, but there is some good accommodation for those who wish to stay longer.

The twelve-room *Bellevue Penang Hill Hotel*, ph (04) 699 500, has modern facilities and room rates range from RM88 to RM110.

There are also several Government Bungalows that can be rented, although preference is given to government employees. Contact the State Secretariat in Georgetown, or MTPB, 10 Jalan Tun Syed Shah Barakbah, 10200 Pulau Pinang, ph (04) 261 9067.

FOOD AND DRINKS

At the summit of the Hill there are a number of restaurants, a tea kiosk and a hawker centre offering western and local meals.

FACILITIES

The population of the hill community is about 900 people, mainly vegetable farmers, so the peak has a post office, a police station, a mosque and a children's playground.

GENTING HIGHLANDS

One hour's drive from Kuala Lumpur, in the mountains of Gunung Ulu Kali is Malaysia's modern hill resort of Genting Highlands. It nestles 2000m above sea-level, and attracts a steady stream of visitors, especially at the weekends.

The climate is spring-like and the cool refreshing mountain air provides a most relaxing holiday in the clouds.

HOW TO GET THERE

By Coach

Genting Highlands operates its own air-conditioned coach service from Pudu Raya Bus Terminal in KL. There are eight scheduled trips per day.

By Bus

From Pudu Raya Bus Terminal the one way fares to Genting Highlands are RM5 adult, RM3 child, which includes the cable car ride. For more information, ph (03) 232 6863.

By Taxi

Taxi fares from Kuala Lumpur are RM5 per person, or RM20 per taxi.

ACCOMMODATION

The following prices are for a double room per night, which should be used as a guide only. The telephone area code is 03.

Genting Hotel, Genting Highlands Resort, ph 262 3555 - 600 rooms, 5 restaurants, cocktail lounge, coffee shop, swimming pool, sauna, fitness centre - RM265.

Awana Golf and Country Club, 8th Mile Genting Highlands Resort, ph 211 3015 - 529 rooms, 2 restaurants, cocktail lounge, coffee shop, swimming pool, sauna - RM265.

Theme Park Hotel, Genting Highlands Resort, ph 262 3555 - 377 rooms, 2 restaurants, cocktail lounge, coffee shop - RM215.

For reservations and enquiries contact Resorts World Berhad, 9th floor, Wisma Genting, Jalan Sultan Ismail, 50250 Kuala Lumpur, ph 262 2666, fax 261 6611.

ATTRACTIONS

Casino
Malaysia's first and only casino is a very glamorous place to try your luck. Games include Blackjack, Baccarat, Roulette, Keno, French Bull and Tai Sai, and Slot Machines.

Theatre Restaurant
With a capacity for 1200 diners, the theatre restaurant serves up gourmet Chinese cuisine and internationally renowned performers.

Artificial Lake
The 4ha lake provides boating facilities. The two islands within the lake contain a tea house and an aviary. A mini railway circles the shores of the lake.

Horse Ranch
The Awana horse ranch offers endless hours of equestrian sport. There are also carnival rides for children and beginners.

Cable Car
The cable car travel from 914m to 1768m and operates 8am-7.30pm Mon-Fri, 7am-8.30pm Sat Sun. Fares are RM3 adult, RM1.50 child (one-way).

Cave Temple
The Chin Swee temple is set within the slope of a hill 1460m above sea-level and it provides a panoramic view of the countryside.

Genting Theme Park
The park has games, high-tech rides and great shows with plenty of action, both indoors and out in the open. There

Sports
An indoor stadium has facilities for basketball, table tennis, badminton and squash.

A 160lane bowling alley and a heated indoor swimming pool are other sporting facilities.

But, of course, one must not forget about golf. The Awana Golf and Country Club, on top of a ridge 950m above sea-level, is an international class 18-hole golf course. It gets its name from the word *awan*, which means "cloud". The best weather for playing is March to October.

Green fees (for general public) -	Mon-Fri - RM80
	Sat-Sun - RM150
Caddy fee: Class A -	RM16 (per 18 holes).

MAXWELL HILL (BUKIT LARUT)

"The surrounding country with its groves of evergreens is very much like Switzerland in summer except perhaps the country is a little greener and more thickly wooded." This is how a visitor has described Bukit Larut (Maxwell Hill), Malaysia's oldest hill resort about 9km from Taiping in Perak State. **Access to the resort, at 1035m above sea-level, is by 4WD along a metalled one-way road** that has several hair-pin bends and a swift-flowing mountain stream visible at various points along its winding course.

There is a mid-way stop at the Tea Garden House, the area around which was once an extensive tea estate. From this point there is a panoramic view of the surrounding countryside - Taiping town, a bird's eye-view of the Taiping Lake Gardens, the green suburbs of Aulong and Simpang, and the 19km ruler-straight road from Taiping to Port Weld.

Most visitors go on an invigorating climb to the Cottage, the only accessible summit of Bukit Larut. From here, on a clear day, you can see the coastline from Pangkor Island to Penang.

HOW TO GET THERE

Taiping is accessible by road and rail from Kuala Lumpur.

The Government Land-Rover service up and down Bukit Larut operates at hourly intervals from 8am-6pm daily. It leaves from the foot of the hill, and fares for adults are:

to Tea Gardens -	RM1.00
Hut, Treachee and Speedy Rest House -	RM2.50
To the Cottage -	RM3.00

For bookings, ph (05) 827 243. **Note** that no self-drive cars/taxis/buses are allowed to travel up the hill.

ACCOMMODATION

There are a number of rest houses and bungalows on Bukit Larut.

Rumah Rehat Bukit Larut (Maxwell Rest House) - 1036m.
Rumah Beringin (Watson Bungalow) - 1036m.
Rumah Cendana (The Hut) - 1097m.
Rumah Rehat Gunung Hijau (Speedy Rest House) - 1113m.
Rumah Tempinis (Treachee Bungalow) - 1143m.

For reservations and current room rates, contact the Superintendent, Bukit Larut, Taiping, ph (05) 827 241.

Malaysian and European food are available at the Rest House. At the bungalows the caretaker can arrange for meals, or visitors can do their own cooking.

GUNUNG JERAI

Gunung Jerai is a massive limestone outcrop that rises 1200m above sea-level, south of Alor Setar in the state of Kedah.

Ruins of Hindu and Buddhist temples at the foot of the hills have proven that the area was an ancient centre of Hindu civilization. Legends abound about the famous *Raja Bersiong* (the king with fangs) who once ruled an ancient kingdom in the Bujang Valley at the foot of the mountains. Archaeological digs have uncovered a Temple on the Ninth Water pool (*Chandi Telaga Sembilan*), and many believe that this was the private pool of Raja Bersiong.

HOW TO GET THERE

Alor Setar is accessible by air from Kuala Lumpur, Penang and Kota Bharu.

Express buses, outstation taxis and trains have regular services from Butterworth to Alor Setar.

Approximately 33km south of Alor Setar is the town of Gurun, and jeeps make the 30 minute journey from there up to the peak. Fares are RM5 adult, RM3.50 child one-way.

ACCOMMODATION

The *Gunung Jerai Resort* is located at 1082m and offers 30 units and seven 2-bedroom units. Enquiries and reservations can be made to Kedah Resort, ph (04) 433 345, fax (04) 729 788.

In Gurun, the Gunung Jerai Rest House is at 427 Jalan Kolam Ayer, ph (04) 729 788, and rooms range from RM50.

ATTRACTIONS

The Sungai Teroi Forest Recreation Park has an enormous variety of herbs, ferns, flowering plants and climbers. Orchids, rhododendrons and pitcher plants also grown in profusion.

Picnic sites are scattered all over the park, usually with great views of the surrounding countryside.

Between the picnic areas there are **hiking trails** through the most scenic routes, and all the trees along the way are labelled for easy identification.

Dams have been built in the mountain stream to provide **swimming** holes, and **overnight shelters** have been provided for the adventurous who would like to spend the night in the mountains.

At the peak is the **Museum of Forestry** which has a wealth of information about, naturally enough, forests.

KINABALU PARK

Situated 72km north of Kota Kinabalu in the state of Sabah is the ultimate adventure region, Kinabalu Park, home to Mt Kinabalu, one of the tallest mountains in South-East Asia at 4101m.

Poring Hot Springs are 43km from Park Headquarters, and well worth the trip

HOW TO GET THERE

By Bus
Mini buses depart daily at 2pm from Kota Kinabalu to Ranau, stopping enroute at Kinabalu Park. The one way fare is RM13 per person.

By Taxi
Taxis can be chartered from Kota Kinabalu and the fare is approximately RM120. Remember to negotiate the fare before starting the journey.

ACCOMMODATION

Kinabalu Park
Kinabalu Lodge, c/- Sabah Park, PO Box 10626, 88806 Kota Kinabalu, ph (088) 211652, have a wide range of accommodation from hostels with dormitory rooms to double storey cabins and the lodge. Prices range from RM10 to RM360 per night, so contact the above postal address for full advice.

Electricity, piped water and firewood are provided. Meals are available at the club house and Steak House. Basic cooking facilities are also provided.

Poring Hot Springs
Here is found the *Poring Old Cabin* with 3 rooms and the *Poring Hostel* with a dormitory room for 24 persons.

No canteen facilities are available, so visitors are advised to bring their own food. Enquiries can be made at the telephone number above.

On the Mountain
There are four huts on the mountain:
Laban Rata Rest House - 55 bunks
Gunting Lagadan - 44 bunks
Panar Laban Hut - 12 bunks
Sayat Sayat Hut - 8 bunks.

Basic cooking facilities are provided at the mountain huts. Visitors are advised to bring their own food for cooking.

CLIMBING ARRANGEMENTS

Climbers must be accompanied by a registered guide, and porter services are available if required.

Guide fees are:	1-3 persons -	RM25 per day
	4-6 persons -	RM28 per day
	7-8 persons -	RM30 per day.
Climbers Permit Fee is:	RM10 (over 18 years old)	
	RM 2 (under 18 years old)	
Porter fees are:	RM25 per day (maximum 11kg.	

All these fees must be paid at Kinabalu Park.

WHAT TO TAKE

The following items are considered to be essential for visiting the Park.

Comfortable shoes - tennis shoes or hiking boots are ideal.

Warm clothing - night-time temperatures can drop below freezing point. Gloves and head covering are necessary. Pack all clothing in a plastic bag. **Rain gear. High energy trail food** - chocolates, nuts, raisins and high glucose foods. **Water bottles. Torches/flashlights.**

Headache tablets, paper tissues, plastic bags and band-aids.

ATTRACTIONS

There are many nature trails meandering through the Park Reserve, and guided walks are available.

The two-day ascent up the summit trail begins at 1829m above sea-level, and the trail passes through forests of oak; moss, ferns, orchids and bamboo at the lower levels to stunted scrub-like vegetation at higher altitudes.

Panar Laban at 3353m has basic accommodation for climbers to spend the night before the second phase of the climb starts early the next day. It should be noted, however, that although the climb usually takes two days, some hikers prefer to stretch it to three so that they have time to appreciate the beautiful flowers and birds.

Poring Hot Springs are 43km from the Park Headquarters. The word *poring* is Kadazan for bamboo, which is prolific in the surrounding forests. The Japanese style baths are in restful garden settings on the fringe of lush tropical rain forest. Nearby trails lead to waterfalls, bat caves and an orchid centre. There is also a 30m high canopy boardwalk that lets visitors observe the exotic flora and fauna. A visit to the springs is well worthwhile, especially after a long hard climb.

NATIONAL PARKS OF MALAYSIA

While the Ice Ages were causing far-reaching climatic changes across the northern hemisphere and afflicting the flora and fauna of the rest of the world, the Malaysian jungles remained untouched by nature or man for an estimated 100 million years. They are believed to be older than the jungles of the Congo or the Amazon.

Amongst the many splendid gorges, rivers and towering hills, Malaysia's National Parks provide an adventure tour with a full quota of thrills - boating through swirling rapids, stalking big game with a camera, fly-fishing for giant carp, bird-watching, mountain-climbing, exploring limestone caves, swimming in placid river waters, and camping amidst the majesty of giant tropical trees.

TAMAN NEGARA

Taman Negara comprises 4343 sq km, and is situated partly in Pahang, partly in Kelantan and partly in Trengganu. The National Park, accessible to visitors, is contained in the state of Pahang, bounded on the south-east by the Tembeling River. The headquarters of the Park is at Kuala Tahan, and it is invariably the first point of call for all visitors to the park.

HOW TO GET THERE

By Car

Travel to Jerantut by way of Mentakab or Raub (3-4 hours from Kuala Lumpur). From Jerantut, Kuala Tembeling is a further 16km to the north along a narrow, steep road. Follow the signs from Kuala Tembeling.

By Bus

Services leave from the bus station at Jalan Tun Razak in Kuala Lumpur to Temerioh. The journey is then continued by another bus, or by taxi.

There is also a bus service operating between Kuantan and Jerantut, from where you can pick up a bus or taxi.

By Train

A night train leaves Singapore at 10pm and arrives at Tembeling Halt at 7.57am next morning. From Tembeling Halt it is a half-hour walk to the jetty.

From Kota Bahru, a south bound train leaves from Tumpat at 10am and reaches Jerantut by 7.30pm.

By Taxi

Taxis from Kuala Lumpur leave for Temerloh and Jerantut from Puduraya Bus Terminal on Jalan Pudu.

By Boat

The journey by boat from Kuala Tembeling to Kuala Tahan takes from 2 to 2 1/2 hours, depending on the condition of the river.

By Air

Pelangi Air offer packages from Kuala Lumpur and Kerteh that include return air fare, full board and lodging and tours. For further details contact Pelangi Air, ph (03) 746 3000

ACCOMMODATION

Taman Negara Resort has 15 chalets that comprise 11 units of superior class, 2 units of deluxe, and 2 one-bedroom suites, all with private facilities. Future additions will take the total to 51 units, 7 deluxe units, two 2-bedroom suites and a 12-room rest house.

There are visitor lodges at Kuala Terenggan and Kuala Kenyam, and fishing lodges at Lata Berkoh and Kuala Perkai. The lodges have beds and bedding, a kerosene stove, lanterns, eating utensils and water. The fishing lodges have beds and mattresses, but visitors have to supply their own bedding and cooking equipment.

Tents are available for hire, and there are plenty of campsites.

For further information contact:

Wildlife and National Parks Department

Km10, Jalan Cheras

56100 Kuala Lumpur - ph (03) 905 2872.

For reservations contact:

Taman Negara Resort

Kuala Lumpur Office

2nd floor, Istana Hotel

Jalan Raja Chulan

50250 Kuala Lumpur - ph (03) 245 5585.

TRAVEL WITHIN THE PARK

This is mainly by river, but there are numerous jungle paths for the more energetic to follow. Between Kuala Tahan and Kuala Terenggan there is a series of seven rapids which, if there is sufficient water, may be negotiated non-stop by outboard, but when the water is low, passengers are required to get out and walk along the river bank until the boatmen push the boat into deeper water. Visitors are requested not to attempt to assist in any way with the handling of the boat, since the stones of the river bed are slippery and inexperienced help is generally more of a hindrance to men who are used to the work.

On the downward trip through the rapids, it is normal to ship a certain quantity of water, as the boat negotiates rough water at speed. It should also be remembered that early morning travel in a fast boat can be rather chilly.

CLOTHING

For everyday trips in the Park the ubiquitous jungle green or khaki drill is excellent, and that together with jungle boots, or short rubber-soled boots and puttees should be sufficient. One or two changes, of course, are essential for comfort.

For normal wear around camp ordinary shirts and slacks suffice. A jacket, cardigan or pullover is handy if early morning travel by boat is envisaged, as the air at that time of the day is very cold. Each visitor should have a good torch (flashlight).

For jungle travel on foot, especially in the wetter months, it is best to be dressed in as leech-proof a manner as possible. The most practical is the normal jungle green or khaki slacks and shirt with jungle boots closely laced up, the socks inside and underneath the trouser leg. For the most part, however, leeches are seldom troublesome enough to give rise to concern, and can be dealt with quite easily.

STORES

It is not necessary for visitors to bring their own food to Taman Negara as there are full catering facilities at the Resort. Provisions for journeys further afield may be purchased from the mini market at Kuala Tahan, at reasonable prices.

No catering facilities are provided at the outlying lodges, so visitors must do all their own cooking there.

All payments for boat trips, accommodation, etc, are made at the office at the end of your stay, ie on the morning of departure.

PHOTOGRAPHY

Photography of river scenery and wildlife in salt licks is the most popular attraction. For still cameras two types of film should be brought - a fast panchromatic film for use in poor light, and a much slower one for out-door photography in the sun. A telephoto lens is essential if good pictures of wildlife are required, as is flash equipment.

Colour film may be used, but it is generally difficult to obtain enough light for animal photography at salt licks.

SALT LICKS

There are six salt-licks within easy reach of Kuala Tahan and Kuala Terenggan. A large variety of wildlife come to these salt licks to drink the water and eat the chemically impregnated soil. At Jenut Belau, sambar, barding deer, wild pigs and tapir are visitors, and the same animals may be seen at Jenut Tabing salt lick. These two licks are within easy reach of the park headquarters at Kuala Tahan. Observation hides have been built at the hides so that the visitor can watch unseen.

ANGLING

The rivers in Taman Negara are well-stocked with fish, those most frequently encountered being members of the Carp family, which includes the well-known Mahseer of India known locally as Kelah. The Kelah can be found in the swifter reaches and a line of about 12lb breaking strain will give the best results since they run up to about 20lbs.

The Kelasa (Sceleropages formosus) will put on a wonderful fighting display, leaping high out of the water and moving at amazing speed. They are to be found in the fast flowing rivers at points where the water is deep and relatively quiet. To add to the angler's difficulties, they particularly enjoy those small dents along river banks where old driftwood collects.

All these fish can be taken on artificial bait, the most successful being 1" to 1.5W silver and silver/copper spoons. The ordinary treble hooks, however, should be changed for special mahseer hooks as the crushing power of the jaws of these fish is enormous. The line should be at least 91m in length, although 137m is a safer length particularly when progress along the river bank is impossible due to boulders and high steel shores.

Fishing can be undertaken from a slowly paddled boat or from the bank, which also includes wading as long stretches of boulders do not permit progress along the water's edge.

Fishing Areas

Probably the most spectacular river in the park is the Sungei Tahan, which falls some 152m from Kuala Teku at the foot of the Gunung Tahan massif, to its mouth at Kuala Tahan. The lower reaches, up to the barrier of Lata Berkoh, are reasonably placed and there are many large pools containing plenty of fish. Above Lata Berkoh cataract, there is a seemingly endless succession of pools and rapids, all excellent fishing water but seldom fished. A week camping holiday up here at the right time should be a worthwhile experience.

Sungei Kenyam so far as been the most patronised fishing river, and some very good catches have been made. The further one goes beyond Kuala Kenyam Kechil, the better the water seems to be. To reach the best fishing water you normally need a two-day trip. Thus the visitor who wishes to avail himself of a week of good fishing in the Kenyam requires no less than a 10-day stay.

The most suitable times of the year for fishing are the months of February-March and July-August. During the other months, sport is liable to be spasmodic owing to local rainfall.

SWIMMING
About a ten minute walk from Kuala Tanah, at Lubok Simpon, there is a fine swimming pool. The short trip may also be made by boat.

GUNUNG TAHAN
Many people have climbed this mountain (2187m), which is the highest in Peninsular Malaysia. The main obstacle is time. From Kuala Tahan to Kuala Teku (at the base of the mountain) it takes two-and-a-half days on foot. From Kuala Teku to the summit, the journey must be done in two stages owing to the scarcity of water. Thus to reach the top, travelling time is five days. The return journey takes roughly one day less. Guides must be hired. The ascent of Gunung Tahan is nevertheless a memorable experience and well worthwhile to anyone who is really interested.

OTHER INTERESTING POINTS
Within the area of the park there are many limestone hills and outcrops. Anyone interested in speleology will be well rewarded by a visit to the limestone caves that were used by aborigines and elephants; some have crude drawings on the walls, and in addition there is the challenge of rock climbing. It takes about 2 1/2 days of travel by boat and on foot.

Not so far afield is the solitary peak of Guling Gendang which gives a fine view of the park from its summit. It is 590m in height, and the return trip from Kuala Tahan can be made in a full day. Camping in the vicinity can also be arranged.

TUNKU ABDUL RAHMAN NATIONAL PARK

The park, comprising the five islands of Pulau Gaya, Pulau Sapi, Pulau Mamutik, Pulau Manukan and Pulau Sulug, and the surrounding seas, covers a total area of approximately 4931ha.

Being so close to Kota Kinabalu, the park is a great tourist attraction for visitors from overseas as well as local people. It also offers snorkellers and scuba-divers an opportunity to view the underwater world of coral life. For non-swimmers going to the park, the excellent nature trail system provides many happy hours of hiking and studying the flora and fauna typical of tropical islands.

HOW TO GET THERE

A number of tour companies run ferry services to the island in addition to sunset cruises, day excursions, island hopping, etc. Special diving trips are also on offer.

Boats for ferry services to the islands usually depart at hourly intervals on the hour from 8am-4pm daily. Departure points are the jetty in front of Hyatt Kinabalu and Tanjung Aru Beach Marina. Passengers are advised to be at the departure points about 15 minutes before departure time.

PULAU GAYA

The largest of the island, 1483ha, Pulau Gaya is an attractive island for swimming, snorkelling, picnicking and camping. It also has interesting beach flora. The forest is typical of the lowland rain forest. It has a good beach at Bulijong Bay - called Police Beach because the police had target practice there before the park was gazetted. The water in the bay is crystal clear and calm, except during the monsoon periods. Casuarina trees provide excellent shade for picnickers. Day-use facilities include a large public shelter, toilets and changing rooms. Fresh water is available.

The island has some 21km of graded nature trails with gentle slopes for visitors who are interested in exploring.

PULAU SAPI

This island (10ha) is the most popular and best developed in the Tunku Abdul Rahman National Park.

It has a clean sandy beach and crystal clear waters. Day-use facilities provided on the island include a jetty with a shelter and diving board, public toilets, barbecue stands, beach shelters and picnic tables. Camping is permitted, but visitors must bring their own food and camping equipment.

PULAU MAMUTIK

Mamutik (4ha) is quite rich in corals especially on the eastern reef on the north-eastern tip of the island. Interesting sights are the delicate white colonies of Distichopora and clusters of red Dendrophyllia corals - both are fairly rare.

Mamutik Island is the nearest to Kota Kinabalu, and has a rest house and a bungalow with cooking facilities that accommodated eight to the people. There are also camping facilities for those who like to rough it.

PULAU MANUKAN

About 21ha in size, this island resembles a big whale basking in the sun. It has a long beach on the eastern side.

The park headquarters are on this island, and it is the only other island that has accommodation facilities. There are 20 chalets that can accommodate 4 people, but they have no cooking facilities. There is a restaurant, though, as well as public shelters and picnic tables. Enquiries and reservations may be directed to the National Park Headquarters in Kota Kinabalu, ph (088) 211 652.

PULAU SULUG

The furthest island from Kota Kinabalu, Pulau Sulug has some of the best coral reefs in the park. There are beautiful shallow coral beds and several large coral heads along the reef rim. Fish are plentiful. The reef here is extensive, varied and densely packed with Acropora, Montipora, Seriatopora, Pocillorpora and Echinopora corals. **The island, however, has never been developed and has no facilities.**

Mengkabong, Sabah.

GUNUNG MULU NATIONAL PARK

All the major inland vegetation types of Borneo can be found within the 52,866ha Gunung Mulu National Park. It also has Sarawak's second highest peak, and the most extensive and spectacular cave system in the world.

Between 1976 and 1984, expeditions surveyed over 26 caves with 159km of passages, and it is thought that this is actually only about 30% of the total cave system.

Mulu's Sarawak Chamber is 600m long, 450m wide and 100m high, and is the largest natural chamber in the world. Deer Cave is the largest cave passage known to man at 100m wide and 120m high. Most of it is illuminated, and after a rain storm, it is possible to see 190m waterfalls pouring from the roof. Clearwater Cave is the longest cave system in South-East Asia, at 51.5km.

Gunung Mulu, Sarawak's second highest peak at 2376m is alongside Gunung Api (1750m), and both are over 5 million years old. The pinnacles are on the side of Gunung Api, about 900m up. They have been sculpted and grooved by rain for all these years, and now rise above tree tops to a height of 45m.

HOW TO GET THERE

Malaysia Airlines have several flights daily from Miri to Marudi, or travel by road to Kuala Baram then take an express boat to Marudi.

From Marudi to Mulu, the cheapest way is to take a commercial express boat to Kuala Apoh or Long Panai on the Tutoh River, a 3-hour journey. The express departs Marudi at noon and returns the next day in the morning.

Fares are as follows:

Express boat fare Kuala Baram to Marudi	- RM12
Express boat fare Marudi to Kuala Apoh	- RM10
Marudi to Long Panai (high tide only)	- RM12

Longboat from Kuala Apoh or Long Panai to Mulu National Park RM35 per person, subject to a minimum charge of RM150 for less than 4 passengers.

Short longboat trips	- Kuala Apoh to Long Terawan	RM7
	- Long Panai to Long Terawan	RM5.

On arrival at the park visitors are advised to report to the Park Ranger at the Park Headquarters.

ACCOMMODATION

It is necessary for visitors to book their accommodation in advance and to obtain permits from the National Parks and Wildlife Office, Forest Department in Miri. The booking fee is RM20 per party, and the maximum party size is 10 persons. Bookings must be confirmed 5 days in advance, or the fee will be forfeited.

A large rest house at the park headquarters has three suites and eight ordinary rooms. There are also hostels down the river at Long Pala. Each hostel has two bedrooms with double bunks for four to six persons, a kitchen and bathroom. Cutlery, crockery and bed-linen are included.

Guesthouses at Long Pala provide simple accommodation and restaurant facilities.

GUIDES

Experienced guides are available at RM20 per day, plus RM10 per night away from home. Minimum rate for the Mulu summit trip is RM110 (4 days, 3 nights) and for the pinnacles RM80 (3 days, 2 nights). Larger parties will require more than one guide. Bookings can be made through the National Parks and Wildlife Office in Miri, or the Park Ranger in Mulu. No visitor will be allowed to enter the park without an authorised guide.

For further information please contact:
National Parks and Wildlife Office
1st Floor, Wisma Sumber Alam
93050 Kuching
Sarawak - ph (082) 442 180.

BAKO NATIONAL PARK

Situated on a peninsula to the east of the Bako River near Kuching, this park has an area of 2742ha. Millions of years of erosion have created a coastline of steep cliffs, rocky headlands and stretches of white sandy bays.

HOW TO GET THERE

The park is accessible from Kuching along a 37km road and a short ferry ride across Sungai Santubong. The Bako Road is flanked by coconut plantations before reaching Kampung Bako near the mouth of the Bako River. Visitors then board a longboat for a 25 minute river trip. The return fare is RM50 per boat-load.

A regular bus service operates from Kuching to Kampung Bako.

ACCOMMODATION

For enquiries and reservations contact Bako National Park Rest House and Bungalow, National Park & Wildlife Office, 93000 Kuching, ph (084) 246 477. Room rates are from RM22.

VEGETATION

The land is moderately hilly, rising from sea-level to about 244m. The coastline of the park is indented by many sandy bays, often backed by steep cliffs beyond which a gentle plateau spreads into the wooded interior.

Within this relatively small area at least seven major types of vegetation typical of Sarawak are found. They are mangrove forest, sandy beach forest, sandstone cliff vegetation, alluvial forest, peat swamp forest, lowland dipterocarp forest and kerangas (heath) forest. The sandstone cliff vegetation and kerangas scrub on the plateau are characteristic of the park.

Visitors will be interested in the ant plants and carnivorous plants whose peculiar characteristics give an insight into some fascinating aspect of nature at work. The carnivorous pitcher plant (Nepenthes), sundew (Drosera) and bladderwort (Utricularia) are abundant on the kerangas scrub. The ant plants or Mrymecophytes live in association with colonies of ants. They include baboon's head (Hydnophytum formicarium), samboko (Myrmecodia tuberosa), Pitis-pitis kecil (Dischidia) and the fern Phymatodes sinuosa which frequently drapes stunted bonsai-like trees on the padang vegetation.

The various vegetation types offer an excellent opportunity for scientific studies in tropical rain forest, particularly on the adaptations of the many plant species under different ecological conditions.

FAUNA

Long-tailed macaques, monitor lizards, pigs and sambar deer are common. The long-nosed monkey or arang blanda (hasalis larvatus) can sometimes be spotted along the coast. It is endemic to Borneo and is protected in Sarawak. Reptiles and amphibians appear in and out of the water in the interior.

BEACHES

Beaches at Telok Assam (hostel area), Telok Paku and Telok Pandan Kechil provide good safe swimming at mid and high tides. Telok Paku and Telok Pandan Kechil are about 45 and 90 minutes walk respectively from Telok Assam.

JUNGLE PATHS

There is a well -demarcated system of paths within the park that may be followed without difficulty or fear of getting lost. Maps in the Interpretation Centre and rest houses show the layout of trails through various vegetation types. The main paths are Lintang, Tanjong Sapi, Telok Paku, Telok Pandan Kechil, Telok Tajor, Bukit Kerning Gondol and Ulu Serait.

WEATHER

As the sea can be rough from October to March, it may not be possible to visit the park during this period. A park warden will advise whether visits are possible.

NIAH NATIONAL PARK

Niah National Park protects 3102ha of forest and limestone, situated in the Miri District of Sarawak. Dominating the landscape is Guning Subis at 394m.

Here it is possible to explore the great number of limestone caves, observe the collection of edible birds' nests, and view prehistoric wall paintings, as well as the preserved remains of the artists themselves. This is also the site of archaeological excavations carried out by the Sarawak Museum in the late fifties.

HOW TO GET THERE

By Taxi

The Niah National Park can be reached from Miri or Bintulu, by first going to Batu Niah. The taxi fare from Bintulu to Batu Niah is RM30 per person, while from Miri to Batu Niah it costs RM15 per person.

By Bus

There are bus services between Bintulu and Batu Niah, and the fare is RM8.50 one way.

By Boat

From Batu Niah you can use a longboat to go to the Park Ranger's office and the fare is RM5 for a return trip per boat load. Alternatively you can follow the footpath from Batu Niah down the Niah River to the Bungalow, which takes 45 minutes. Otherwise, if you have your own transport, you can drive along the Sim Kheng Hong Road right to the Park Headquarters.

ACCOMMODATION

The park has four rest houses, one large hostel and a campfly. Rates are:

Rent of Rest House	RM60 per night per room
Rent of Room	RM30 per night
	(each room has 4 single beds)
Rent of Hostel	RM3 adult, per night
	RM1 student, per night
Campfly -	RM2 per night.

The rest house and hostel have electricity, showers, refrigerator and cooking facilities. Accommodation has to be booked in advance at the park's office in Miri.

WILDLIFE

Three species of swiftlets and 12 species of bats are found in the caves. The thing to watch for is the bats rushing out of the entrance to the Great Cave in their millions, yet never colliding with each other. Other wildlife found in the Cave include earwigs, naked bats, lizards, centipedes, scorpions and snakes. In the surrounding forests you can find long-tailed macaques, hornbills, squirrels, flying lizards and many species of butterflies.

THE CAVES

The hostel and the rest houses are on opposite sides of the Niah River at Pangkalan Batu. To get to the caves if you are staying at the hostel you will have to cross the river by boat, which costs RM0.50 per person. A 3km boardwalk trail then leads to the Great Cave. The Painted Caves are another 30 minute walk away.

The Great Cave is an historical monument within the Niah National Park. As such, visitors to the caves are required to observe certain regulations prohibiting the digging, collecting or removing of any object, natural or man-made, from the caves. Similar regulations are also enforced within the park.

Also please note that it is dangerous to walk inside the caves on your own, as you can easily get lost or fall into deep gullies, some measuring hundreds of metres deep. Only with an experienced local guide and a good torch (flashlight) will you be able to move about safely in the darkness.

INDEX OF MAPS

INDEX